Masonic Secret Signs
and Passwords

This edition is dedicated to Mansour Hatefi,
Past Grand Master and Grand Secretary of
the Grand Lodge of the District of Columbia.

Masonic Secret Signs and Passwords

The 1856 Edition of Jeremy L. Cross' *The True Masonic Chart*

Edited and introduced by
Guillermo De Los Reyes

WESTPHALIA PRESS
An imprint of Policy Studies Organization

Masonic Secret Signs and Passwords
The 1856 Edition of Jeremy L. Cross'
The True Masonic Chart

For information:
Westphalia Press
1527 New Hampshire Ave., N.W.
Washington, D.C. 20036

ISBN-13: 978-0944285961
ISBN-10: 0944285961

Updated material and comments on this edition can be found at the Policy Studies Organization website:
http://www.ipsonet.org/

INTRODUCTION TO THE NEW EDITION

———

Jeremy Cross (1783-1861) made his living as a teacher of Masonic ritual. He became a Mason in 1808, and became the friend of Thomas Smith Webb, who was himself deeply influenced by the English Masonic scholar William Preston.

In 1819 Cross published *The True Masonic Chart or Hieroglyphic Monitor*, much of which he owed to Webb.

The *Monitor* of Webb had first appeared in 1797. Webb had borrowed much from Preston. On the other hand, the engravings were a new feature and became popular with those learning the ritual. Cross was appointed Grand Lecturer by many Grand Lodges, and traveled throughout the United States, teaching Lodges, Chapters, Councils, and Encampments.

He was neither scholar nor original thinker. There are unsettled arguments over those few

E

innovations in his work that he might have produced on his own. But his influence on Freemasonry was enormous since his book and his travels shaped the ritual deemed official in countless lodges. This twelfth edition includes a number of supplements not found in other editions and hence has a utility that the others do not have.

Guillermo De Los Reyes

F

OFFICERS

OF THE

GENERAL GRAND CHAPTER

OF THE

UNITED STATES OF AMERICA,

ELECTED AT BOSTON (MASS.), SEPTEMBER, 1850

AND YEAR OF R. A. M., 2380.

~~~~~~~~~~~~~~~~~~~~~

M. E. C. ROBERT P. DUNLAP,
Of Maine, Gen. G. H. P

M. E. C. JOS. K. STAPLETON,
Of Maryland, Dep. G. G. H. P

M. E. C. WILLIS STEWART,
Of Kentucky, Gen. G. K.

M. E. C. THOS. W. LEWIS,
Of Louisiana, Gen. G. S

M. E. C. REV. PAUL DEAN,
Of Massachusetts, Gen. Grand Chaplain.

M. E. C. BENJ. B. FRENCH,
Of District of Columbia, Gen. Grand Sec'y.

M. E. C. EDWARD A. RAYMOND,
Of Massachusetts, Gen. G. Treasurer.

M. E. C. NATHAN B. HASWELL,
Of Vermont, Gen. G. Marshall

TO THE

OFFICERS

OF THE

GENERAL GRAND CHAPTER

OF THE

UNITED STATES OF AMERICA

THIS

LITTLE VOLUME

IS

RESPECTFULLY DEDICATED

BY

THE AUTHOR.

INTRODUCTION TO THE FIFTH EDITION

THE rapid sale and extensive circulation of former editions of the TRUE MASONIC CHART, have furnished the best proofs of its merits, while a constant and increasing demand for the Work would alone justify its republication. The present edition is intended, not only to supply that demand, but also to fulfil, in part, an intention put forth by the Author on the publication of the fourth edition—to give a brief History of Free Masonry, from its commencement up to the establishment of the same in the United States. This History is comprised in the present edition. It is from the pen of an able writer and accomplished Mason, and will be a valuable acquisition to the Fraternity. The reader will perceive, that special attention has been given to the due arrangement of the various Masonic Emblems and Hieroglyphics, so as to maintain inviolable the *ancient landmarks* of the order. The importance of this need not be urged upon the real craftsman; but some late attempts at innovation (*happily rebuked by the skilful and experienced*) demand, at this time, renewed vigilance in the faithful. The Author has faithfully endeavored to render this volume, now respectfully submitted, worthy the patronage and attention of his Brethren, as an interesting, useful, and correct guide: that it may prove such to all of the Fraternity who may consult its pages, is the earnest wish of

THE AUTHOR.

PREFACE TO THE FIRST EDITION.

HAVING been honored by the approbation of the Officers of the General Grand Chapter of the United States, and of most of the Grand Lodges, and Officers of Grand Lodges in the individual States, as a Grand Lecturer; and having, by virtue of their sanction and authority, officiated in that capacity for several years; the Author of this volume has had an opportunity of witnessing the mode of lecturing and working, in many different Lodges. It is not surprising, therefore, if, in the course of his experience, some errors in the practice of these branches should have fallen within his observation. These have undoubtedly originated from a want of uniformity; and although they may not be considered as radical evils, in relation to the hidden mysteries of the Fraternity, yet they would certainly be regarded as defects in that system, the perfect preservation of which is at once the pride and glory of every enlightened mason.

Among these errors may be mentioned—the improper classification of masonic emblems; and a difference in the mode of working.

To obviate these inaccuracies is the object of this work. It contains a classification of the emblems, together with illustrations, which have been approved and adopted by a majority of the Lodges of the United States. So far, therefore, as they are connected with the mode of working, and of lecturing, the evils which have been suggested, will be obviated by an attention to this treatise: and so far only does the Author claim any merit in having contributed towards establishing a standard, which he flatters himself may serve as a safe and sure guide to his Brethren, in some parts of their labors.

The illustrations, &c., are selected from the compilations of Preston, Webb, and other established authorities, accompanied by such alterations and amendments as were deemed necessary to a strict conformity with the *Ancient System.*

With a hope that his exertions to benefit them may not prove fruitless, the Author respectfully submits his work TO THE FRATERNITY OF FREE AND ACCEPTED MASONS THROUGHOUT THE UNITED STATES.

PREFACE TO THE THIRD EDITION.

Since the publication of the first edition of the Masonic Chart, it has been adopted as a Text-Book by most of the Lodges and Chapters in this country.

The highest expectations of the Author have been more than realized in the reception of the first and second editions by his Masonic Brethren. Its beneficial effects in promoting a uniformity in our mode of working and lecturing, have induced him to present to the Fraternity the third edition, with some additions and emendations. If his labors shall in any degree contribute to the advancement of a Society in which he feels a lively interest, he will be abundantly compensated. It has been his constant aim to place the Masonic Institution upon its proper basis. The correct Mason will ever be more esteemed than the over-zealous or coldly indifferent members of the Society. A Mason who is thoroughly acquainted with the tenets and nature of this Institution, ranks it among the first of human origin, and as inculcating the purest of moral principles, and as having a powerful tendency, where strict discipline is judiciously administered agreeably to the tenets of the Institution, to improve the morals of its members, and to open and expand their hearts to acts of charity and pure benevolence. Those who elevate masonry to a level with revealed religion, and those who rank it below the standard of pure morality, are equally unacquainted with its true object.

That every Brother and Companion may possess a correct knowledge of the nature and principles of our excellent Institution, and that their conduct may be such through life as to convince all with whom they may have intercourse, that our great aim is to inculcate FRIENDSHIP, MORALITY, BROTHERLY LOVE, and CHARITY, is the earnest and sincere wish of

THE AUTHOR.

ADVERTISEMENT.

In presenting to the Sir Knights and the Masonic fraternity his third edition of the Templars' Chart, the Author would here state that he has introduced an entire new set of emblems, which are much improved from the former editions, without any alteration in the order, or of their application as approved at first by the General Grand Encampment of the United States. He has also added a supplement to the volume, containing the Thirty Ineffable degrees with their illustrations, which he hopes will meet the approval of the fraternity. The Author here regrets to state that he has much cause of complaint, from the unwarrantable freedom that several of the fraternity have made with the emblems and illustrations both of the "*Masonic*" and "*Templars*" Chart, and appropriating them to their own use—especially those of the latter—as they were nearly all new designs of his own, and were never before published. All those emblems, with their classification, he considers as his property, and those who have taken them and have appropriated them to their own use, have committed so many infringements upon his copy-right.

We have been favored by two notices of the last edition of the Masonic Chart, by two distinguished Masons and Sir Knights, which are so appropriate to elucidate his views of the subject, that he would here introduce extracts from them, in order that the Sir Knights may judge whether the Author has not had cause for his remarks.

THE MASONIC CHART.

[BY JEREMY L. CROSS.]

To the Editors of the New York Express :

A WRITER in the Masonic Mirror, of Philadelphia, of the date of May 5, 1852, in reply to some. commendatory remarks of Mr. Mitchell, of the "Signet," upon the "Masonic Chart,'" has indulged in strictures upon this work extremely unjust, to which I would respectfully call the attention of the Masonic Fraternity. In a reply to a very just remark of the Editor of the Signet, to the effect that it was obviously unjust and at variance with every principle of Masonic equity, that the labors of Brother Cross should be appropriated to the pecuniary benefit of others. The Philadelphia writer undertakes to justify such appropriations, and most strongly puts forth the assertion, that the Masonic Chart contains nothing which is properly the fruit of Cross's labors. Alluding to Cross and Webb and other Masonic authors, he says, in reference to the emblems contained in this book, that "the ownership of these beautiful emblems belonged to the order long before any of the present writers ever joined the institution." Upon this assumption he therefore very naturally undertakes to justify those persons who, long since the publication of Cross's Chart, have put forth publications so nearly similar to Cross's Chart, that an cr-dinary observer would pronounce them almost exact copies. Now as to the "beautiful. emblems" of which this writer speaks, it is true, so far as any of them had been designated on the Masters' Carpet relating to the first three degrees alone, and embracing only a part of

1*

the emblems of these degrees, contained in the Chart,
may, perhaps, without impropriety be said to belong
to the order, looking at them as simple emblems, without any reference to their relations to other things;
but every intelligent mason knows that a considerable
and most essential part of the emblems of the three
first degrees contained in the Masonic Chart were never
designated on the Masters' Carpet, nor were many of
them ever seen or known until designed and published
in that book by Cross in 1819; much more so is this
true as respects the emblems of the R. Arch Chapter
and Council Degrees. Let the man who questions
Cross's authorship of the great body of these emblems
tell us when and where he ever saw them before the
first publication of the chart. When the Philadelphia
writer says they belonged to the order, let him tell
where the order obtained them, and point out the member of the order who ever put forth any such claim, or set
up any pretence that any such emblems were in existence
until after the publication by Cross of his book. But it
should be remembered that it is not the emblems simply
that enter into the consideration of Cross's right as an
author. It may be, and undoubtedly is true, that many
of these emblems were in use and belonged to the order
before Cross published, and it is equally true that
many others of them were by him first presented to the
craft.

The emblems may have all been in existence and yet
of little practical use. It was the arrangement and classification of these emblems and their adaptation to the
work in the several degrees in such form as to secure
uniformity, which constituted the chief value and excellency of Cross's publication. It was not in the designing, or in the engraving, or in the publication of the
emblems merely that Bro. Cross was regarded as ren
dering a great service to the fraternity, but it was in the
exhibition of them in such form as to give value to the
lectures, and to enable the intelligent and well informed
mason to practice skilfully in the work of the order,

and especially it was in adopting such an arrangement that intelligent masons everywhere might, by means of it, adopt the same system of work. It is now thirty-three years since Bro. Cross first published the Masonic Chart. For years previous the population of our country had increased, masonic lodges and chapters had been multiplied, and members had been added to the fraternity, and in proportion to this increase there was a want of uniformity in the work, and such irregularities had crept in many Lodges as to have almost effaced the ancient landmarks of the order. During this period the attention of some of the most enlightened and distinguished men of the order were directed to disseminate light and to improve the craft in the knowledge of the true mode of work, by means of Masonic lectures.

Several brethren distinguished for their zeal and knowledge of the work and mysteries of the craft, were commissioned by the highest authority of the order in the United States as Lecturers; and visited the lodges in many of the States of the Union as they had opportunity, and introduced and gave instruction in the work which had been established in various Grand Lodges, and sanctioned by the highest authority in the country; at this period, about forty years ago, Bro. Cross was commissioned by several Grand Lodges and Chapters as Grand Lecturer, and was recommended by His Excellency De Witt Clinton, Governor of New York, Gen. Thos. H. Cushing, an officer in the United States Army, Hon. Lyman Law, a member of the U. S. Congress, with many other distinguished masons and officers of the United States General Grand Chapter, and several State Grand Chapters. Under such sanction, he devoted several years to the services of the Masonic fraternity, and in connection with other brethren, visited many of the States, and introduced and perfected in numerous Lodges, the established work. While engaged in these duties, Brother Cross was impressed with the importance of a standard work upon the plan of the Chart, and in consultation with distinguished Masons in different places, and by their advice, he undertook the task, and as the result, the Masonic Chart was prepared and published. It was received with general favor, and was immediately adopted as the standard text book of the Order by a large number of the Grand Lodges and Grand Chapters of the country, and was specially sanctioned, approved, and recommended to general use, by the officers of the General Grand Chapter, with Gov. Clinton at the head.

The writer of this article was then on the stage of life, and an active member of the Fraternity, and acquainted with the leading Masons in different sections of the country, and he well remembers that the work of Brother Cross was received with great favor, and its publication was regarded as of great service to the Order—with the exception of some few persons in Philadelphia, where there has always prevailed to some extent a spirit not exactly in harmony with the brethren of the other States, especially as it regards the Chapter Degrees.

There was never heard at the time of this publication, nor for many years after, a question raised as to the value of the work, or as to the importance of the services rendered the order by Bro. Cross; and even in Philadelphia, the great body of the brethren afterwards concurred in the general sentiment of the country, and the work was pruned from some extraneous matter with which it had been affected, and they came up in most of their Lodges near to the standard adopted in other States. Those persons who have in effect copied Cross's book, and put it forth as their own, within the last few years, may satisfy their own consciences that they are doing right in thus appropriating to their own use another's; but they will never convince the great body of their brethren that they are not, so far as Brother Cross is concerned, committing a piratical wrong.

The writer of this article has no connection whatever with Bro. Cross, nor any interest in his book; but having had knowledge from the beginning of these matters, as an act of justice he has written this article.

BENJAMIN FRANKLIN.

W. L. Ormsby Sc

I am fraternally Yours

J. L. Cross

THE TRUE

MASONIC CHART,

OR

HIEROGLYPHIC MONITOR;

CONTAINING

ALL THE EMBLEMS EXPLAINED

IN THE DEGREES OF

ENTERED APPRENTICE, FELLOW CRAFT, MASTER MASON,
MARK MASTER, PAST MASTER, MOST EXCELLENT
MASTER, ROYAL ARCH, ROYAL MASTER
AND SELECT MASTER:

DESIGNED AND DULY ARRANGED AGREEABLY TO THE

LECTURES,

BY R. W. JEREMY L. CROSS, G. L.

TO WHICH ARE ADDED

𝔍llustrations, 𝕮harges, 𝔖ongs, &c.,

WITH ADDITIONS AND EMENDATIONS;

ALSO,

A HISTORY OF FREEMASONRY,

BY A BROTHER.

TWELFTH AND STEREOTYPE EDITION.

NEW YORK:

PUBLISHED BY A. S. BARNES & CO.,

51 JOHN STREET,

AND SOLD BY BOOKSELLERS GENERALLY THROUGHOUT THE
UNITED STATES

1856.

ADVERTISEMENT.

In presenting the fourth edition of THE MASONIC CHART to the Fraternity, the Author is happy to state that but few alterations in the last edition are necessary, except in the Emblems and Hieroglyphics, which are much improved by new designs, emendations, and additions. While he believes the work has been much improved in accordance with the principles of the Institution, he yet feels conscious that some defects may be discovered by the scrutinizing eye of his more experienced Brethren: he would therefore solicit their forbearance and candor. In taking a retrospective view of the Institution, it is truly gratifying to every upright and correct Mason, to notice the great improvement which has been made within a few years past. In an institution like ours, however, which is founded on the MORAL LAW OF GOD, and requires that all her members should walk in accordance thereto, we can easily discern that much remains to be done. Especially should it not be forgotten, that the very nature of the Institution forbids the admission of any to membership, except men sustaining the straitest moral character, and that no Lodge can be justified in receiving candidates solely for the purpose of increasing their members or their funds. Let them strictly adhere to the Masonic rule, and let the "internal and not the external qualifications of the man" be the standard for admission. As every man, on entering a Lodge, first puts his trust in GOD, and then takes the "HOLY SCRIPTURES to be the rule and guide of his faith and practice," so none should be suffered to remain members who deviate therefrom.

It is the intention of the Author of this little volume, by the leave of Divine Providence, to present to his Masonic Brethren, as soon as convenient, a new and improved edition of the "MASONIC BOOK OF CONSTITUTIONS," a work which is often alluded to, but seldom seen, except in a few Lodges. It is designed to give a brief History of Masonry from its commencement up to the present time comprising

also observations on the regulations of Lodges, duties of
Officers, admission of Candidates, duty of Discipline, forms
of Petitions, Warrants, Charters, &c. &c., with a complete
list of all the Encampments, Councils, Chapters and Lodges
in the United States. The Author is well aware, that in
many parts of our country, which have been highly favored
with Masonic light and knowledge, a work of this kind
would be of minor consequence; but there are many sections
which have not been thus highly favored, and where it
would tend to advance the true interests of the Institution.

   The Author would improve this favorable opportunity, in
calling upon all Christian Masons to lend their aid in ele-
vating the Institution to its proper level, by influencing every Mason, by example, exhortation and persuasion, to live
up to the moral precepts which are inculcated in it;—at the
same time to guard them against relying on any merit in
their own works as a title to that REST beyond the grave,
which is prepared for the children of God—and to point
them to HIM who is the WAY, the TRUTH and the LIFE, to
the LION of the tribe of Judah, to the great WATCHMAN of
Israel, to our DIVINE REDEEMER, whose name is the only
name which is given under Heaven whereby men can be
saved, who has made an atonement for sin by the shedding
of his own blood, and who has promised that whosoever be-
lieveth on Him shall not perish but have everlasting life.

   That all his Brethren may not only be found *Worthy, Free
and Accepted Masons,* but qualified by the SPIRIT of our GOD
for a seat in that House not made with hands, Eternal in the
Heavens, is the earnest prayer of

                                        THE AUTHOR

INTRODUCTION.

---

*Form of a PETITION to be signed by a Candidate
for Initiation.*

To the W. Master, Wardens, and Brethren of
——— Lodge No. ——, of Free and Accepted Masons.

The subscriber, residing in ———, of lawful age,
and by occupation a ———, begs leave to state,
that, unbiased by friends, and uninfluenced by mercenary motives, he freely and voluntarily offers himself as a candidate for the mysteries of masonry, and
that he is prompted to solicit this privilege by a
favorable opinion conceived of the Institution, a desire of knowledge, and a sincere wish of being serviceable to his fellow-creatures. Should his petition
be granted, he will cheerfully conform to all the
ancient established usages and customs of the Fraternity.　　　　(Signed)　　　　A. B.

The following recommendation is to be signed by
two members of the Lodge to which the application
is made :

This may certify, that we the subscribers are personally acquainted with Mr. A. B. ; and from a confidence in his integrity, and the uprightness of his
intention, do cheerfully recommend and propose him
as a proper candidate for the mysteries of Masonry.

Recommended by　　C. D.
Avouched for by　　E. F.

2.

ON OPENING AND CLOSING LODGES.

THE ceremony of opening and closing a Lodge with solemnity and decorum, is universally admitted among Masons ; and though the mode in some Lodges may vary, and in every degree must, in some particulars, still an uniformity prevails in every Lodge, and the variations, if any, are only occasioned by want of method, which a little application might easily remove. To conduct this ceremony with propriety, ought to be the study of every mason, but more especially those who are called to officiate as officers of the Lodge. To those of our brethren who are thus honored, every eye is naturally directed for propriety of conduct and behavior; and from them, our brethren who are less informed will expect an example worthy of imitation. From a share in this ceremony, no mason can be exempted : it is a general concern, in which all must assist ; the first notice of which is given by the W. M., with a request of the attention and assistance of his brethren. No sooner has it been signified, than every officer repairs to his station, and the brethren rank according to their degrees. The next object is to detect impostors among ourselves ; and for this purpose recourse is had to our peculiar rites as masons. This object being accomplished, our next care is directed to the external avenues of the Lodge, and the proper officers, whose province it is to discharge that duty, execute their trust with fidelity, and by certain mystic forms, of no recent date, intimate that we may safely proceed.

At opening the Lodge, two purposes are wisely effected : the master is reminded of the dignity of character which he is to maintain from the elevation of his office, and the brethren of the reverence and respect due from them in their sundry stations. These are not the only advantages resulting from a due observance of this ceremony; the mind is drawn with reverential awe to the Supreme Architect of the Universe, and the eye fixed on HIM who is the only author of life and immortality. Here we are taught to worship and adore the supreme JEHOVAH, and to supplicate his protection and assistance in all our well-meant endeavors. After the customary salutations, the master pronounces the Lodge to be opened in due and ancient form, and assumes the government, and under him his wardens; the brethren with one accord unite in duty and respect, and the business of the meeting is conducted with order and harmony.

At the closing of a Lodge, a similar ceremony takes place as at opening:—the avenues of the Lodge are guarded; a recapitulation of the duties of the officers is rehearsed; a proper tribute of gratitude is offered up to the Great Author of our existence, and his blessing invoked and extended to the whole fraternity.

If it should be deemed necessary that the Lodge be opened in the several degrees, for dispatch of business, when that in the first degree shall have been finished, the W. Master, after due inquiry of the wardens and brethren, will proclaim it to be his will and pleasure that the Entered Apprentices' degree be dispensed with for the purpose of opening on the Fellow Craft degree, and all who are not Fellow Crafts are requested to retire. When the necessary precautions are taken that none remain but those who are entitled to this privilege, the sentinel is again reminded of his duty, and the Fellow Craft's degree opened in due form. When the business in this degree shall have been finished, the Lodge is dispensed with, as in the first degree, and a Master's Lodge opened in due form. After the business in the Master's Degree is finished, the

Lodge is closed and the labors of the Fellow Crafts resumed: if nothing should offer in this degree, the Lodge is closed and the labors of the Entered Apprentices resumed. Should nothing further offer in this degree, the records of the evening having been read and approved, the Lodge is closed in due and ancient form.

These are but faint outlines of the ceremonies which prevail among masons, in every country, and distinguish all their meetings.

FORMS OF PRAYERS, CHARGES, &c.

A Prayer used on opening a Lodge.

Most holy and glorious Lord God, the great Architect of the universe, the Giver of all good gifts and graces: Thou hast promised, that "where two or three are gathered together in thy name, thou wilt be in the midst of them and bless them." In thy name we assemble, most humbly beseeching thee to bless us in all our undertakings, that we may know and serve thee aright, and that all our actions may tend to thy glory, and to our advancement in knowledge and virtue. And we beseech thee, O Lord God, to bless our present assembling, and to illuminate our minds, through the intercession of the Son of Righteousness, that we may walk in the light of thy countenance; and when the trials of our probationary state are over, be admitted into THE TEMPLE "not made with hands, eternal in the heavens." So mote it be. Amen.

A Prayer at Closing.

Supreme Architect of the universe, accept our humble praises for the many mercies and blessings which thy bounty has conferred on us, and especially for this friendly and social intercourse. Pardon, we beseech thee, whatever thou hast seen amiss in us since we have been together; and continue to us thy presence, protection, and blessing. Make us sensible of the renewed obligations we are under to love thee supremely, and to be friendly to each other. May all our irregular passions be subdued, and may we daily increase in *Faith*, *Hope*, and *Cha-rity;* but more especially in that *Charity*, which is the bond of peace, and the perfection of every virtue May we so practice thy precepts, that, through the merits of the Redeemer, we may finally obtain thy promises, and find an entrance through the gates into the temple and city of our God.

So mote it be. Amen.

Benediction at Closing.

May the blessing of Heaven rest upon us and all regular masons! May brotherly love prevail, and every moral and social virtue cement us!

So mote it be. Amen

Charge at Closing.

BRETHREN:—

We are now about to quit this sacred retreat of friendship and virtue, to mix again with the world. Amidst its concerns and employments, forget not the duties which you have heard so frequently inculcated, and so forcibly recommended in this Lodge. Be diligent, prudent, temperate, discreet. Remember, that around this altar, you have promised to befriend and relieve every brother, who shall need your assistance. You have promised, in the most friendly manner to remind him of his errors, and aid a reformation. These generous principles are to extend further. Every human being has a claim upon your kind offices. Do good unto all. Recommend it more " especially to the household of the faithful." Finally, brethren, be ye all of one mind; live in peace; and may the God of love and peace delight to dwell with and bless you.

RECOMMENDATIONS

[For the information of those of the Fraternity with whom
the Author of this little volume has not had the pleasure of
an acquaintance, he would submit the following, from a
large number of Certificates, in testimony of his masonic
qualifications.]

TO THE FRATERNITY OF FREE AND AC-
CEPTED MASONS THROUGHOUT THE
UNITED STATES OF NORTH-
AMERICA—GREETING.

KNOW YE, That we, the undersigned, having duly examined our worthy Companion, JEREMY L. CROSS, do find
him well *skilled* and correct in the Lectures and mode of
working in the three first Degrees of *Ancient Free Masonry*,
as received, sanctioned, and directed to be taught, by the several Grand Lodges of New Hampshire, Massachusetts,
Rhode Island, Connecticut, Vermont, New York, and New
Jersey; also, with the Lectures and mode of working in the
several Degrees of Mark Master, Past Master, Most Excellent Master, and Royal Arch Masonry, as sanctioned and
directed to be taught by the Officers of the General Grand
Royal Arch Chapter of the United States of North America.
We do therefore cheerfully recommend him as fully competent to teach the same.

Duly appreciating the utility that would arise from a
greater uniformity in our mode of working and Lecturing;
and as the good of the INSTITUTION demands it; we do
therefore earnestly recommend to the whole FRATERNITY, to
receive, sanction, and adopt the same.

Witness our Hands:

M. E. and Hon. DEWITT CLINTON, Gen. Grand High
Priest of the Gen. Grand Royal Arch Chapter of the U.
States of America· also Grand Master of the Grand
Lodge of New York.

M. E. HENRY FOWLE, Esq., D. G. G. H. Priest of the
G. G. R. A. C. of the U. S. A.; also Deputy Grand High
Priest of the Grand Chapter of Massachusetts.

M. E. THOMAS SMITH WEBB, Esq., P. D. G. G. H.
Priest of the G. G. R. A. C. of the U. S. A.; also Past
Grand Master of the Grand Lodge of Rhode Island.

M. E. JOHN SNOW, Esq. G. G. King of the G. G. R. A.
C. of the U. S. A.; also G. H. Priest of the Grand Chapter of Ohio.

M E. JOHN HART LYNDE, Esq., P. G. G. King of the G. G. R. A. C. of the U. S. A.; also Past Senior G. Warden of the Grand Lodge of Connecticut.

M. E. PHILIP P. ECKEL, Esq., G. G. Scribe of the G. G. R. A. C. of the U. S. A.; also Past G. High Priest of the Grand Chapter of Maryland and Dist. of Columbia.

M. E. PETER GRINNELL, Esq., G. G. Treasurer of the G. G. R. A. C. of the U. S. A.

M. E. OTIS AMIDON, P. G. G. Secretary of the G. G. R. A. C of the U. S. A.

M. W. JOHN HARRIS, Grand Master,
R. W. ALBE CADY, Senior G. Warden,
R. W. STEPHEN BLANCHARD, Junior G. Warden,
R. W. HORACE CHASE, G. Lecturer,
} of the Grand Lodge of New Hampshire.

M. W. FRANCIS J. OLIVER, G. Master,
R. W. JOHN DIXWELL, Deputy G. M.
R. W. AUGUSTUS PEABODY, Senior G. Warden,
} of the Grand Lodge of Massachusetts.

M. W. JOHN CARLILE, Grand Master of the Grand Lodge of Rhode Island.

R. W. LYMAN LAW, Deputy G. Master,
R. W. THOMAS H. CUSHING, Senior G. Warden,
} of the Grand Lodge of Connecticut.

M. W. LEMUEL WHITNEY, G. Master of the Grand Lodge of Vermont.

M. W. JAMES GILES, G. Master of the Grand Lodge of New Jersey

---

WE, the undersigned, Officers in the General Grand Royal Arch Chapter of the United States of America, DO APPROVE and RECOMMEND "The True Masonic Chart, or Hieroglyphic Monitor," designed and arranged by our worthy Companion, JEREMY L. CROSS, as entitled to the attention and use of the Craft; being a valuable assistant in elucidating the various Masonic Emblems, and enabling the diligent Craftsman to acquire the Lectures in the several degrees of *Ancient Free Masonry*.

M. E. DEWITT CLINTON, General Grand High Priest.

HENRY FOWLE, Deputy Gen. Grand High Priest.

JOHN SNOW, General Grand King.

PHILIP P. ECKEL, General Grand Scribe.

PETER GRINNELL, General Grand Treasurer.

JOHN ABBOT, General Grand Secretary.

DAVID G. COWAN, General Grand Marshal.

JOHN HARRIS, Past. Gen. Grand Marshal; also M W G. Master of the Grand Lodge of New Hampshire

WE, the Subscribers, Officers of the Grand Royal Arch Chapter of Connecticut, having examined "The Masonic Chart, or Hieroglyphic Monitor," designed by our Worthy Companion, R. W. JEREMY L. CROSS, for the use and instruction of the Craft, with pleasure recommend the same as a necessary and useful Manual for all Free Masons; containing an elegant and comprehensive view of all the Symbols used in Lecturing upon the several Degrees of *Ancient Masonry.*

> M. E. LYMAN LAW, G. H. Priest.
> M. E. LABAN SMITH, D. G. H. Priest.
> E. DAVID DEMING, G. King.
> E. THOMAS H. CUSHING, G. Scribe
> Comp. HENRY CHAMPION, G. Treasurer
> HORATIO G. HALE, G. Secretary.
> MENZIES RAYNER, G. Chaplain.
> SAMUEL GREEN, G. Marshal.

Extract from the Proceedings of the Most Worshipful Grand Lodge of Connecticut, May,. A. L. 5820.

RESOLVED, That this Grand Lodge approve of the Masonic Chart, published by Brother JEREMY L. CROSS, and recommend it to be used as a Masonic Text-Book in all the Lodges working under this jurisdiction.

> *A true copy from the minutes.*
> Attest—WM. H. JONES, G. Secretary.

Extract from the Proceedings of the Grand Royal Arch Chapter of Connecticut, year of R. A. M. 2350.

RESOLVED, That this Grand Chapter approve of the Masonic Chart, published by Companion JEREMY L. CROSS, and recommend it to be used as a Text-Book in the several Chapters under their jurisdiction.

> *A true copy from the minutes.*
> Attest— E. GOODRICH, Jun., Grand Secretary.

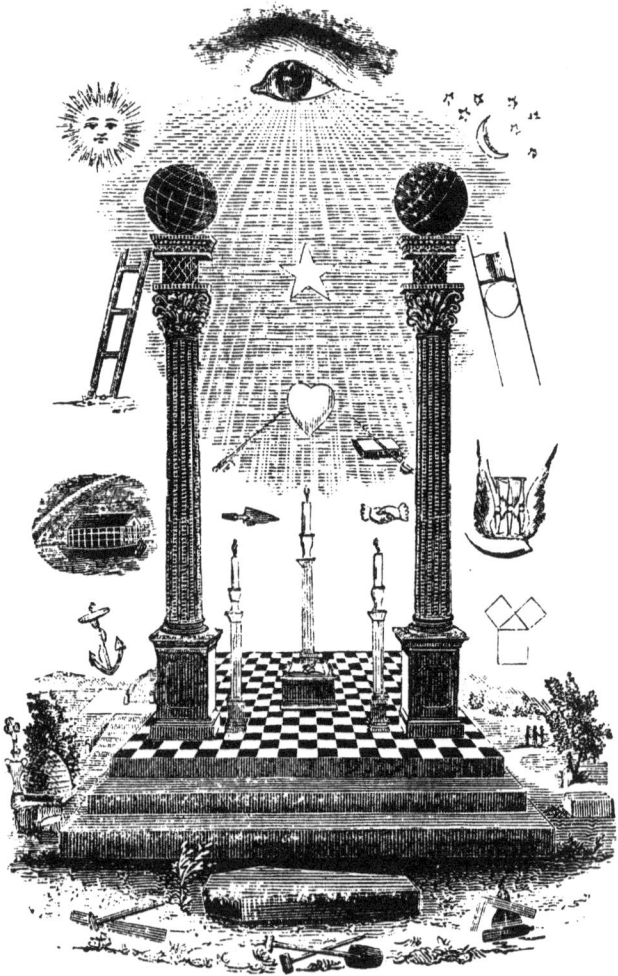

MASTERS CARPET

THE TRUE

MASONIC CHART,

OR

HIEROGLYPHIC MONITOR

BY

R. W. JEREMY L. CROSS G. L.

Improved

Stereotype Edition,

With the History of

FREE MASONRY

BY A

BROTHER.

NEW YORK

A. S. BARNES & CO.

51 JOHN-STREET.

ENTERED APPRENTICE DEGREE.

SECTION FIRST.

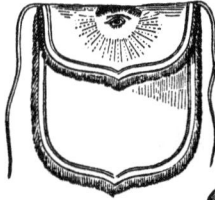

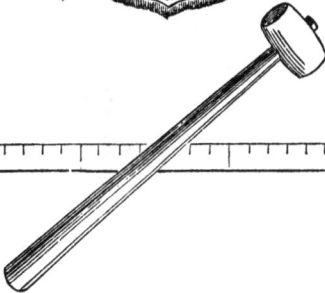

SECTION SECOND.

SECTION THIRD.

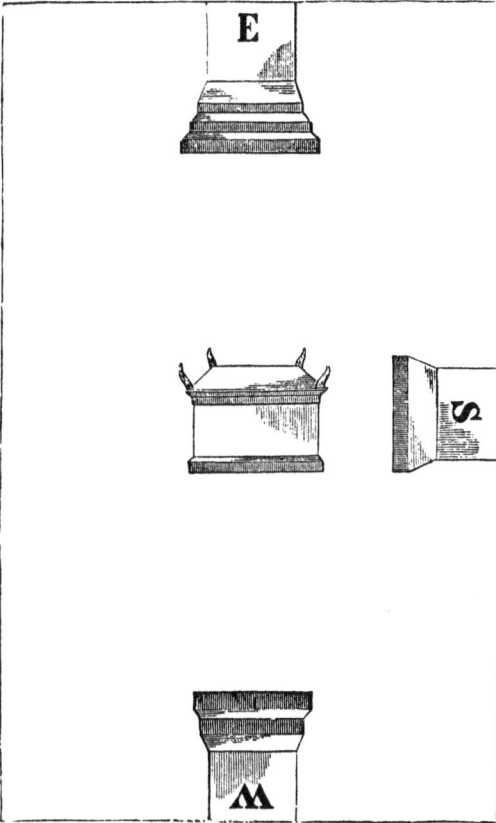

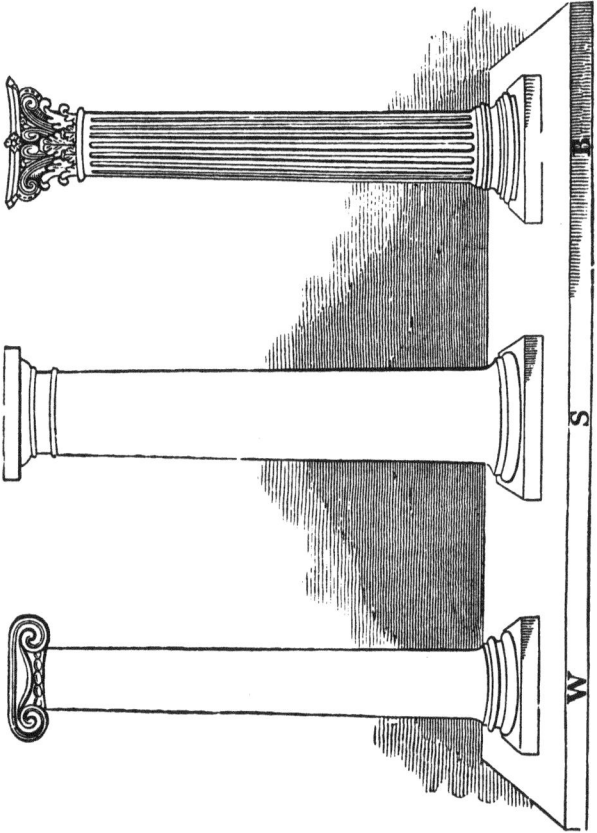

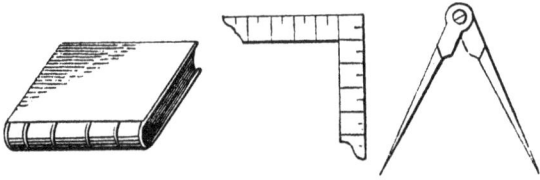

9

MOVABLE

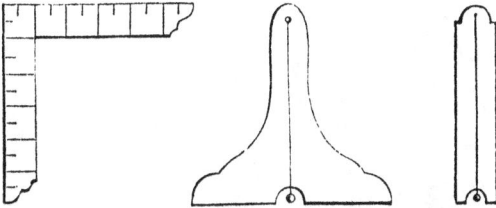

IMMOVABLE.

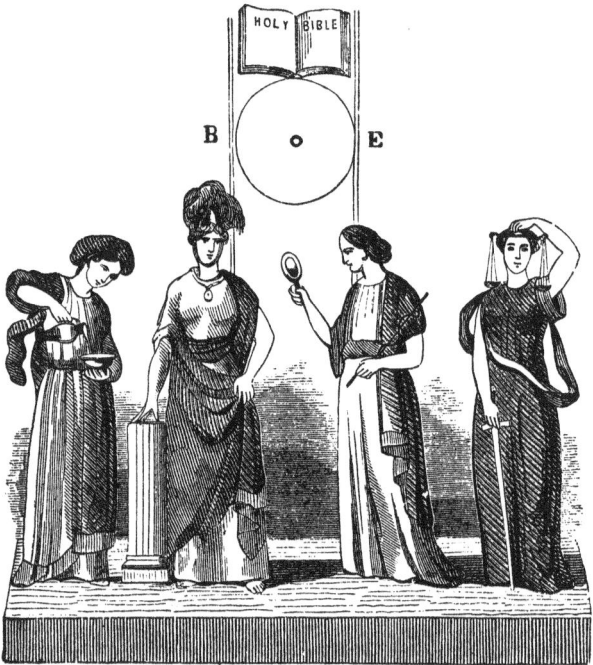

FELLOW CRAFT'S DEGREE

SECTION FIRST.

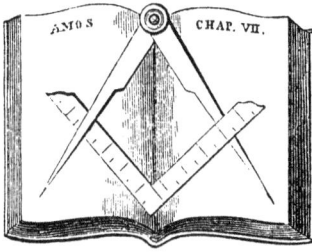

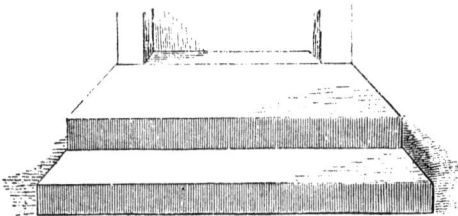

SECTION SECOND.

COMPOSITE

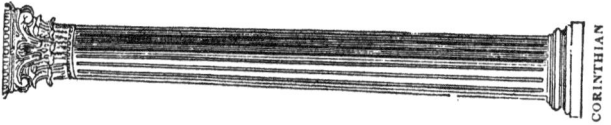

CORINTHIAN

IONIC

DORIC

TUSCAN

MASTER MASONS DEGREE.

SECTION FIRST

SECTION SECOND.

SECTION THIRD.

1,453. *Columns.*

2,906. *Pilasters.*

3. *Grand Masters.*

3,300. *Overseers.*

80,000. *Fellow Crafts.*

70,000. *Entered Apprentices.*

$7 \Big\} \dfrac{1}{6}$

$5 \Big\} \dfrac{2}{3}$

3

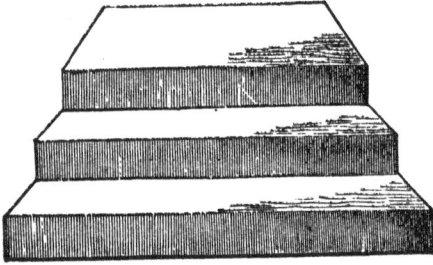

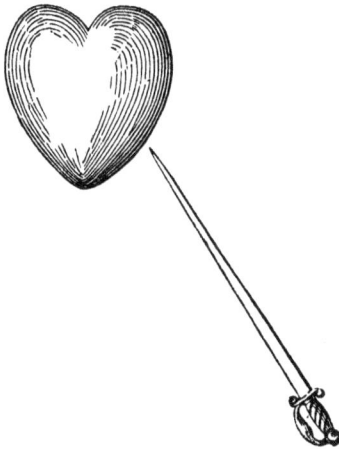

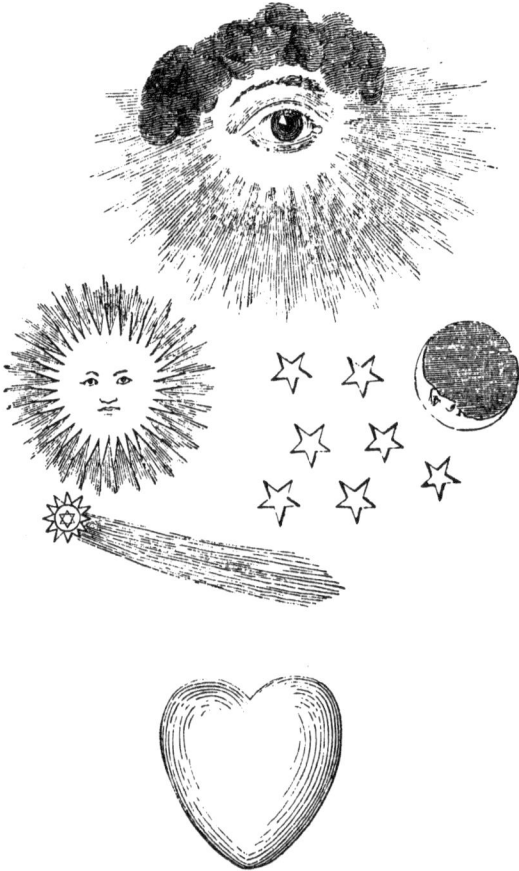

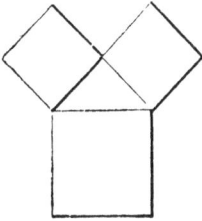

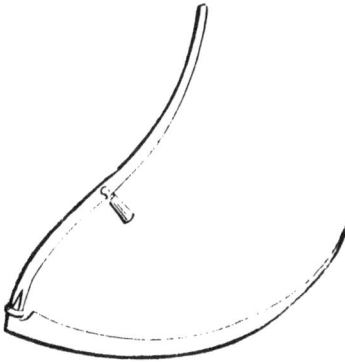

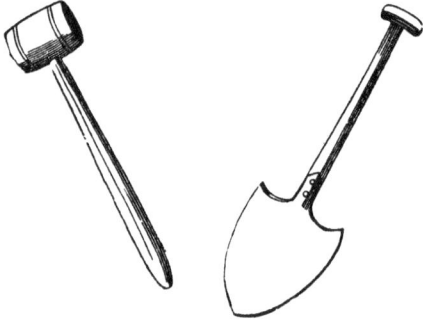

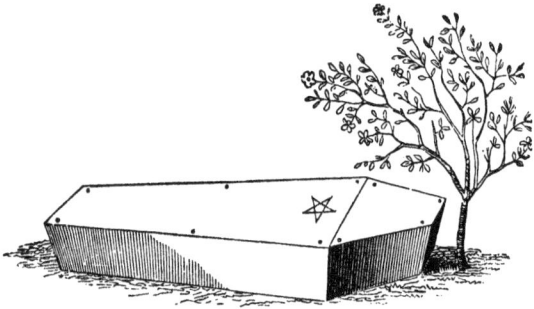

MARK MASTER'S DEGREE

SECTION FIRST.

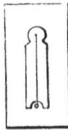

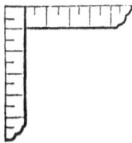

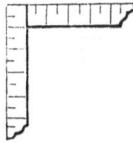

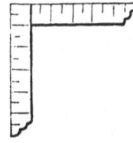

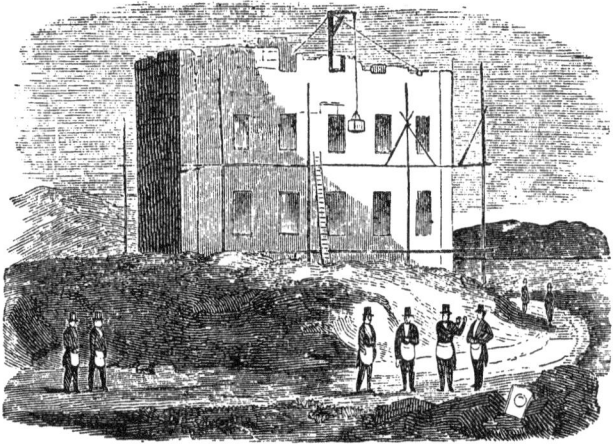

SECTION SECOND.

II. CHRONICLES, II.—XVI.

PAST MASTERS DEGREE.

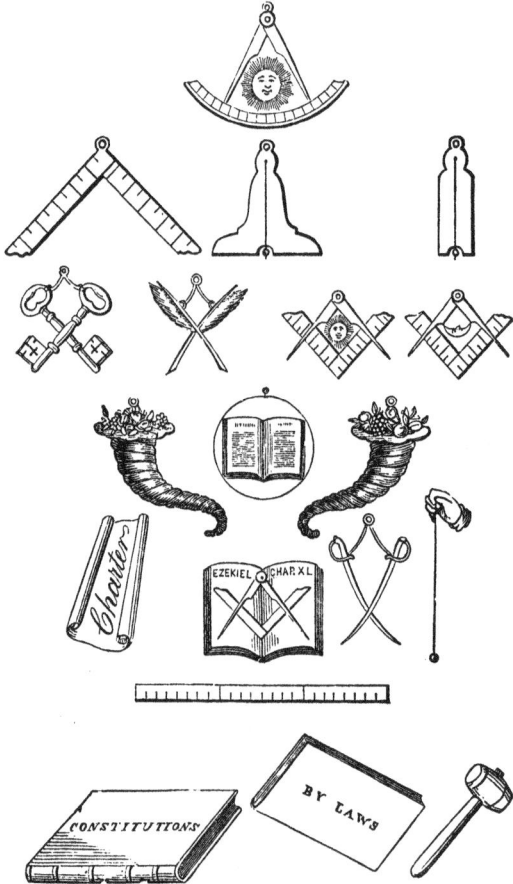

MOST EXCELLENT MASTER'S DEGREE.

ROYAL ARCH DEGREE.

SECTION FIRST.

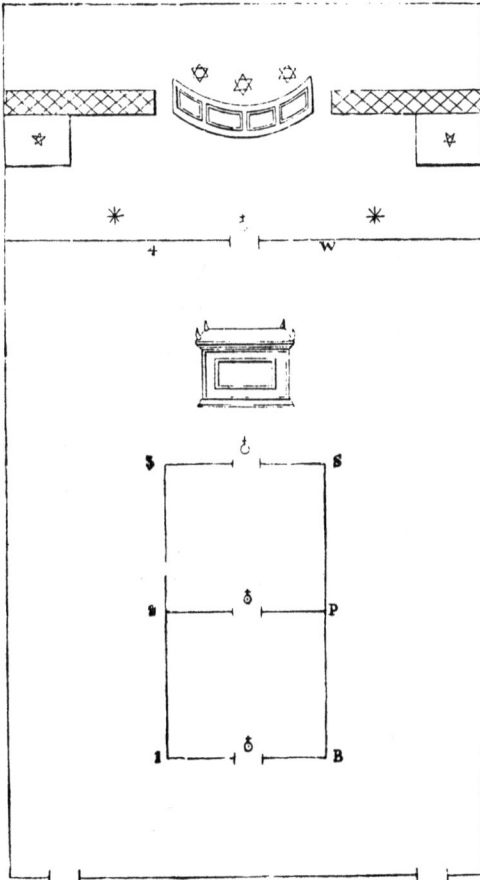

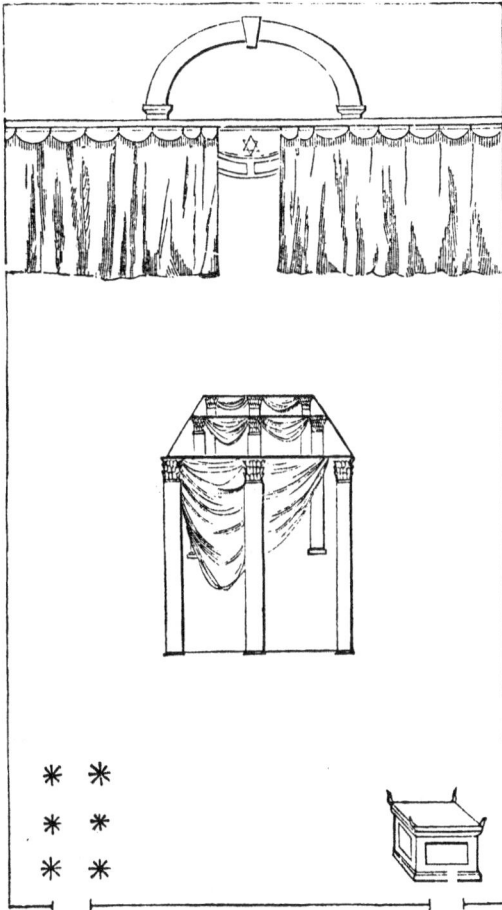

EXODUS, III, I.—II.

DESTRUCTION OF JERUSALEM BY NEBUCHADNEZZAR.

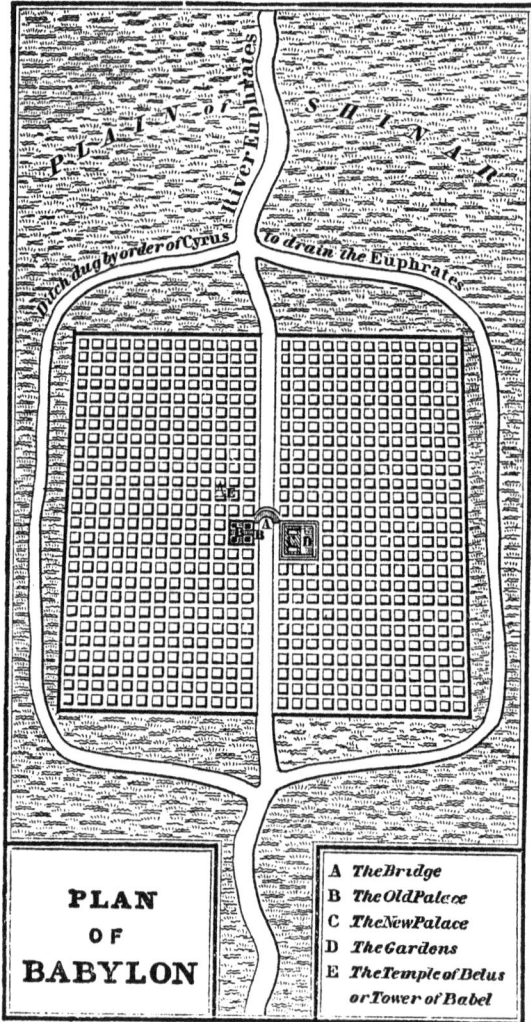

PLAN

OF

BABYLON

A The Bridge
B The Old Palace
C The New Palace
D The Gardens
E The Temple of Belus
   or Tower of Babel

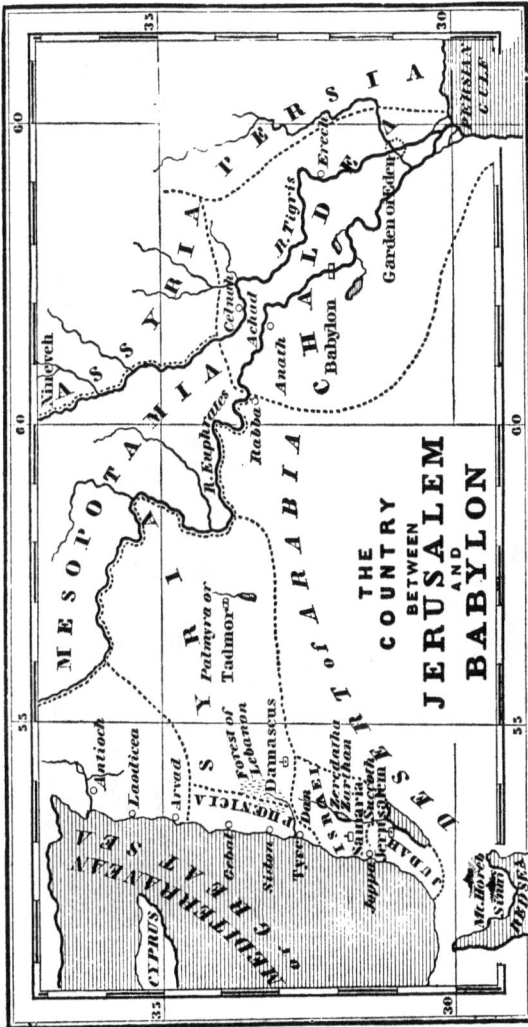

THE
COUNTRY
BETWEEN
JERUSALEM
AND
BABYLON

PALMYRA, OR TADMOR.

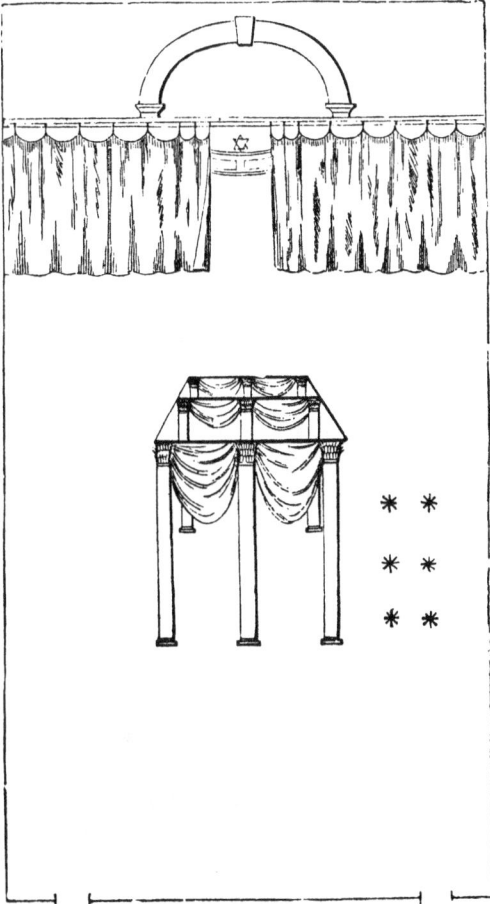

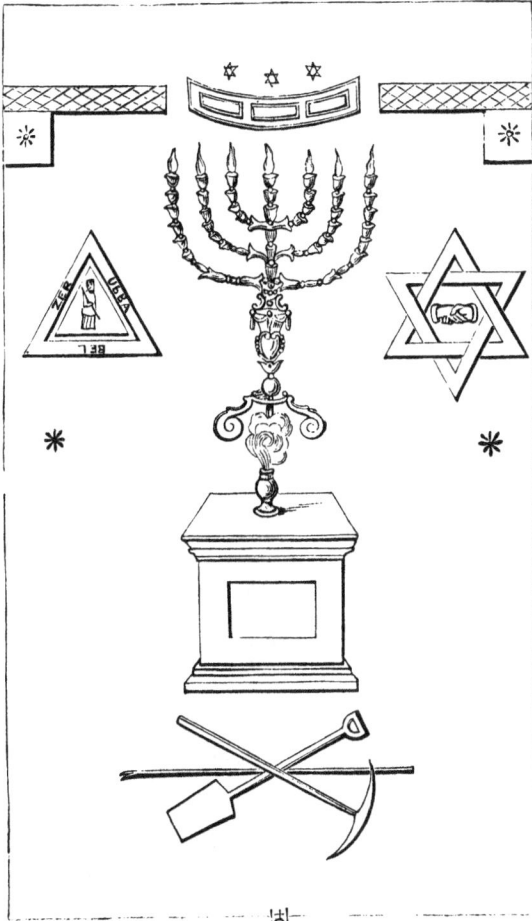

EZRA, v I –II.

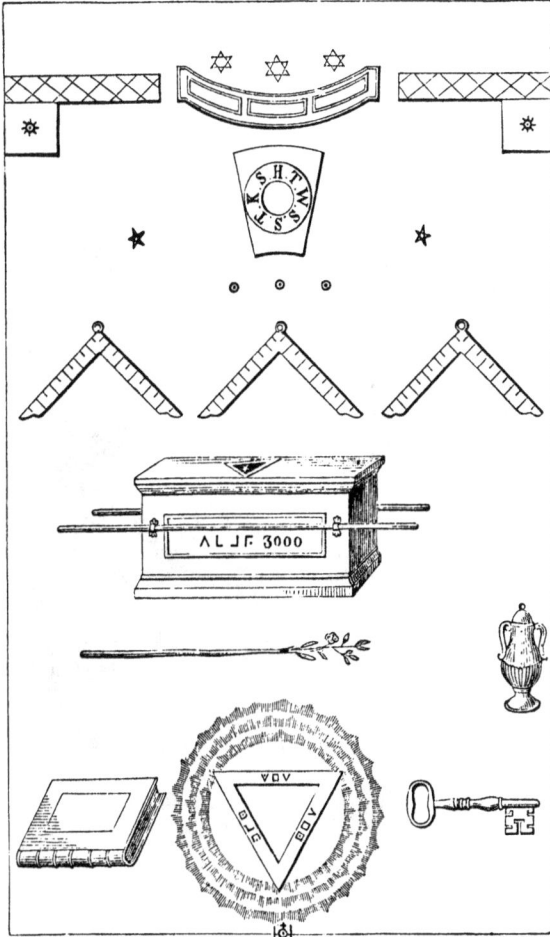

ROYAL ARCH MASONRY.

ROYAL MASTER'S DEGREE.

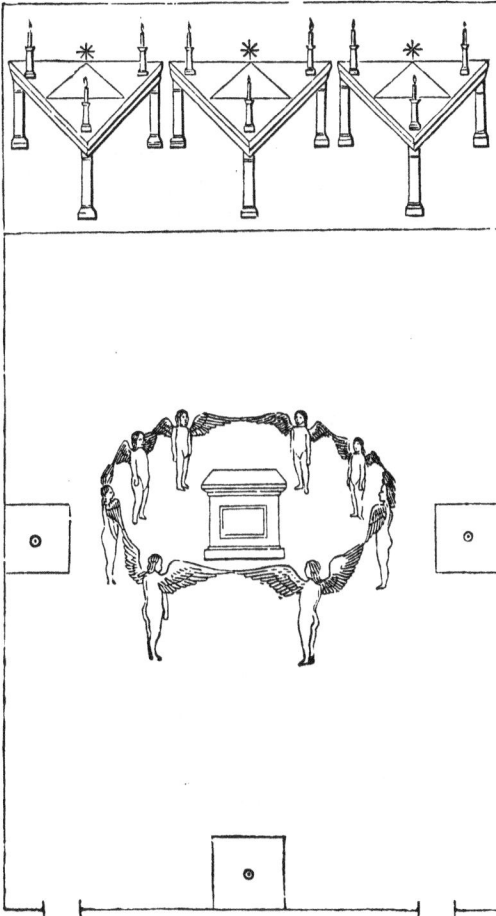

SELECT MASTER'S DEGREE.

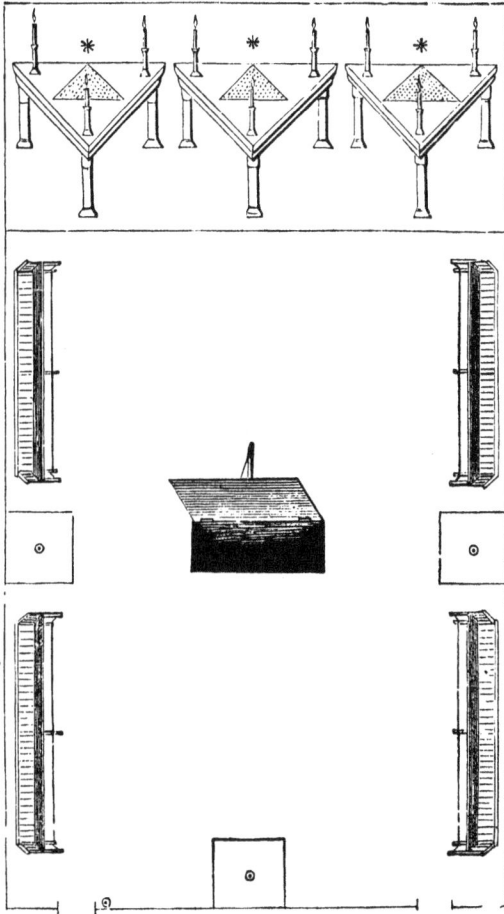

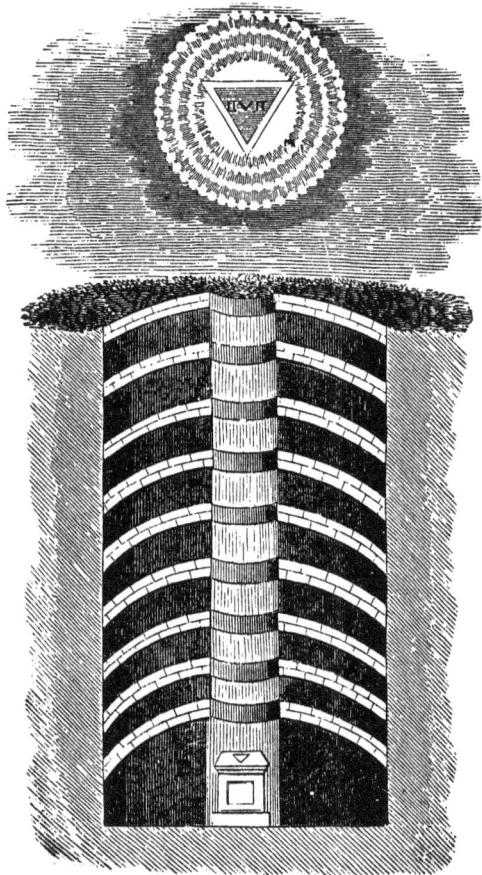

PROSTYLE TEMPLE.

Adam

HOLINESS TO THE LORD

Enoch

Noah

Hiram
Solomon
Hiram ab
Zerubbabel
Jeshua
Haggai

Shem
Ham
Japheth

Moses
Aholiab
Bezaleel

GENERAL
GRAND
CHAPTER
U. S. A.

ENTERED APPRENTICE'S DEGREE.

SECTION FIRST.

THE first section consists of general heads; which though short and simple, carry weight with them, and qualify us to try and examine the rights of others to our privileges, while they prove ourselves. It also accurately elucidates the mode of initiating a candidate into our ancient order.

A Prayer used at the Initiation of a Candidate.

Vouchsafe thine aid, Almighty Father of the universe, to this our present convention; and grant that this candidate for masonry may dedicate and devote his life to thy service, and become a true and faithful brother among us! Endue him with a competency of thy Divine Wisdom, that by the secrets of our art he may be better enabled to display the Beauties of Holiness, to the honor of thy holy name! So mote it be. Amen.

The following passage of scripture is rehearsed during the ceremony.

Behold! how good and how pleasant it is for brethren to dwell together in unity:

It is like the precious ointment upon the head. that ran down upon the beard, even

2

Aaron's beard, that went down to the skirts of his garment:

As the dew of Hermon, and as the dew that descended upon the mountains of Zion : for there the Lord commanded the blessing, even life for evermore.

Towards the close of the section is explained that peculiar ensign of masonry the *lamb-skin*, or *white leather apron*, which is an emblem of innocence, and the badge of a mason ; more ancient than the golden fleece or Roman Eagle ; more honorable than the star and garter, or any other order that could be conferred upon the condidate at that or any future period, by king, prince, potentate, or any other person, except he be a mason ; and which every one ought to wear with pleasure to himself, and honor to the fraternity.

This section closes with an explanation of the working tools, which are, the *twenty-four inch gauge* and the *common gavel*.

The *twenty-four inch guage* is an instrument used by operative masons to measure and lay out their work ; but we, as free and accepted masons, are taught to make use of it for the more noble and glorious purpose of dividing our time. It being divided into twenty-four equal parts, is emblematical of the twenty-four hours of the day, which we are taught to divide into three equal parts ; whereby are found eight hours for the service of God, and a distressed worthy brother ; eight for our usual vocations ; and eight for refreshment and sleep.

The *common gavel* is an instrument made use of by operative masons to break off the corners of rough stones, the better to fit them for the builder's use ; but we, as free and accepted masons, are taught to make use of it for the more noble and glorious purpose of divesting our hearts and consciences of all the vices and superfluities of life ; thereby fitting our minds as living stones for that spiritual building, that house not made with hands, eternal in the heavens.

SECTION SECOND.

The second section rationally accounts for the ceremony of initiating a candidate into our ancient institution

The Badge of a Mason.

Every candidate, at his initiation, is presented with a *lamb-skin* or *white leather apron*.

The *lamb* has in all ages been deemed an emblem of *innocence:* the lamb-skin is therefore to remind him of that purity of life and conduct, which is so essentially necessary to his gaining admission into the Celestial Lodge above, where the Supreme Architect of the universe presides.

SECTION THIRD.

The third section explains the nature and principles of our Constitution. Here also we receive instructions relative to the *form, supports, covering, furniture, ornaments, lights* and *jewels* of the Lodge, how it should be *situated*, and to whom *dedicated*.

From East to West, and between North and South, Free-Masonry extends ; and in every clime are masons to be found.

Our institution is said to be supported by *Wisdom, Strength* and *Beauty ;* because it is necessary that here should be wisdom to contrive, strength to support, and beauty to adorn, all great and important undertakings.

Its *covering* is no less than a clouded canopy, or a starry-decked Heaven, where all good masons hope at last to arrive, by the aid of the theological ladder, which Jacob, in his vision, saw ascending from earth to heaven ; the three *principal rounds* of which are denominated *Faith, Hope* and *Charity ;* and which admonish us to have faith in God, hope in immortality, and charity to all mankind.

The greatest of these is *Charity ;* for our Faith may be lost in sight ; Hope ends in fruition ; but

Charity extends beyond the grave, through the bound-less realms of eternity.

Every well-governed Lodge is furnished with the *Holy Bible*, the *Square*, and the *Compasses*.

The Holy Bible is dedicated to God; the Square, to the Master; and the Compasses, to the Craft.

The Bible is dedicated to God, because it is the in-estimable gift of God to man; * * * the square to the master, because it is the proper masonic emblem of his office; and the compasses to the craft, because, by a due attention to their use, they are taught to circumscribe their desires, and keep their passions within due bounds.

The *Ornaments* of a Lodge are the *Mosaic pavement*, the *indented tessel*, and the *blazing star*. The *Mosaic pavement* is a representation of the ground floor of King Solomon's temple; the *indented tessel*, that beautiful tesselated border, or skirting, which surrounded it; and the *blazing star* in the centre, is commemorative of the Star which appeared, to guide the wise men of the East to the place of our Saviour's nativity.

The *Mosaic pavement* is emblematical of human life, chequered with good and evil; the *beautiful border* which surrounds it, those manifold blessings and comforts which surround us, and which we hope to enjoy by a faithful reliance on Divine Providence, which is hieroglyphically represented by the *blazing star* in the centre.

The *moveable* and *immoveable* Jewels also claim our attention in this section.

The *rough ashler* is a stone as taken from the quarry in its rude and natural state.

The *perfect ashler* is a stone made ready by the hands of the workmen, to be adjusted by the working tools of the Fellow Craft. The *trestle-board* is for the master workman to draw his designs upon.

By the *rough ashler*, we are reminded of our rude and imperfect state by nature; by the *perfect ashler* that state of perfection at which we hope to arrive by a virtuous education, our own endeavors, and the blessing of God ; and by the *trestle-board*, we are also reminded, that as the operative workman erects his temporal building agreeably to the rules and designs laid down by the master, on his trestle-board, so should we, both operative and speculative, endeavor to erect our spiritual building agreeably to the rules and designs laid down by the Supreme Architect of the universe, in the great Books of nature and revelation, which is our spiritual, moral and masonic trestle-board.

Lodges were anciently dedicated to King Solomon, as it is said he was the first Most Excellent Grand Master : Yet masons professing Christianity dedicate theirs to St. John the Baptist, and St. John the Evangelist, who were two eminent Christian patrons of masonry ; and since their time, there is represented, in every regular and well-governed Lodge, a certain *point within the circle,** embordered by two perpendicular parallel *lines*, representing St. John the Baptist and St. John the Evangelist ; and upon the top rests the Holy Scriptures. In going round this circle, we necessarily touch upon these two lines, as well as the Holy Scriptures ; and while a mason keeps himself circumscribed within their precepts, it is impossible that he should materially err.

Of Brotherly Love.

By the exercise of brotherly love, we are taught to regard the whole human species as one family ; the high and low, the rich and poor ; who, as created by one Almighty Parent, and inhabitants of the same planet, are to aid, support, and protect each other. On this principle, masonry unites men of every country, sect and opinion, and conciliates true friendship

---

* The *point* represents an individual brother, the *circle* of the boundary line, beyond which he is never to suffer his prejudices or passions to betray him.

among those who might otherwise have remained at a perpetual distance.

Of Relief.

To relieve the distressed, is a duty incumbent on all men ; but particularly on masons, who are linked together by an indissoluble chain of sincere affection. To soothe the unhappy ; to sympathize with their misfortunes ; to compassionate their miseries, and to restore peace to their troubled minds, is the great aim we have in view.   On this basis, we form our friendships and establish our connections.

Of Truth.

Truth is a divine attribute, and the foundation of every virtue.   To be good and true, is the first lesson we are taught in masonry.   On this theme we contemplate, and by its dictates endeavor to regulate our conduct: hence, while influenced by this principle, nypocrisy and deceit are unknown among us ; sincerity and plain dealing distinguish us ; and the heart and tongue join in promoting each other's welfare, and rejoicing in each other's prosperity.

An Explanation of the four CARDINAL VIRTUES which are TEMPERANCE, FORTITUDE, PRUDENCF and JUSTICE.

Of Temperance.

Temperance is that due restraint upon our affections and passions, which renders the body tame and governable, and frees the mind from the allurements of vice.   This virtue should be the constant practice of every mason ; as he is thereby taught to avoid excess, or contracting any licentious or vicious habit, the indulgence of which might lead him to disclose some of those valuable secrets, which he has promised to conceal and never reveal, and which would consequently subject him to the contempt and detestation of all good masons. * * * *

Of Fortitude.

Fortitude is that noble and steady purpose of the mind, whereby we are enabled to undergo any pain, peril, or danger, when prudentially deemed expedient. This virtue is equally distant from rashness and cowardice; and, like the former, should be deeply impressed upon the mind of every mason, as a safe-guard or security against any illegal attack that may be made by force or otherwise, to extort from him any of those valuable secrets with which he has been so solemnly intrusted, and which were emblematically represented upon his first admission into the Lodge. * * * * *

Of Prudence.

Prudence teaches us to regulate our lives and actions agreeably to the dictates of reason, and is that habit by which we wisely judge, and prudentially determine, on all things relative to our present as well as to our future happiness. This virtue should be the peculiar characteristic of every mason, not only for the government of his conduct while in the Lodge, but also when abroad in the world. It should be particularly attended to, in all strange and mixed companies, never to let fall the least sign, token, or word, whereby the secrets of masonry might be unlawfully obtained. * * * * *

Of Justice.

Justice is that standard, or boundary of right, which enables us to render to every man has just due, without distinction. This virtue is not only consistent with divine and human laws, but is the very cement and support of civil society; and as justice in a great measure constitutes the real good man, so should it be the invariable practice of every mason, never to deviate from the minutest principles thereof. * * * * *

The illustration of these virtues is accompanied with some general observations peculiar to masons. Due veneration is also paid to our ancient patrons.

CHARGE at Initiation into the First Degree.

BROTHER,

As you are now introduced into the first principles of masonry, I congratulate you on being accepted into this ancient and honorable order :—ancient, as having subsisted from time immemorial, and honorable, as tending, in every particular, so to render all men who will be conformable to its precepts. No institution was ever raised on a better principle, or more solid foundation; nor were ever more excellent rules and useful maxims laid down, than are inculcated in the several masonic lectures. The greatest and best of men, in all ages, have been encouragers and promoters of the art; and have never deemed it derogatory to their dignity, to level themselves with the fraternity, extend their privileges, and patronize their assemblies. There are three great duties, which, as a mason, you are charged to inculcate—to God, your neighbor, and yourself. To God, in never mentioning his name, but with that reverential awe which is due from a creature to his Creator; to implore his aid in all your laudable undertakings, and to esteem him as the chief good :—to your neighbor, in acting upon the square, and doing unto him as you wish he should do unto you :—and to yourself, in avoiding all irregularity and intemperance, which may impair your faculties, or debase the dignity of your profession. A zealous attachment to these duties, will insure public and private esteem.

In the State, you are to be a quiet and peaceful subject, true to your government, and just to your country; you are not to countenance disloyalty or rebellion, but patiently submit to legal authority, and conform with cheerfulness to the government of the country in which you live. In your outward demeanor, be particularly careful to avoid censure and reproach.

Although your frequent appearance at our regular meetings is earnestly solicited, yet it is not meant that masonry should interfere with your necessary vocations; for these are on no account to be neglected; neither are you to suffer your zeal for the institution to lead you into argument with those who, through igno rance, may ridicule it.

At your leisure hours, that you may improve in masonic knowledge, you are to converse with well-informed brethren, who will be always as ready to give, as you will be ready to receive, instruction.

Finally, keep sacred and inviolable the mysteries of the order; as these are to distinguish you from the rest of the community, and mark your consequence among masons. If, in the circle of your acquaintance, you find a person desirous of being initiated into masonry, be particularly attentive not to recommend him, unless you are convinced he will conform to our rules; that the honor, glory and reputation of the institution, may be firmly established. and the world at large convinced of its good effects.

FELLOW-CRAFT'S DEGREE.

SECTION FIRST

THE first section recapitulates the ceremony of initiation into this class; and instructs the diligent craftsman how to proceed in the proper arrangement of the ceremonies used on the occasion. It should therefore be well understood by every officer and member of the Lodge.

Amos vii. 7, 8.

" Thus he shewed me; and behold the Lora stood upon a wall made by a plumb-line, with a plumb-line in his hand. And the Lord said unto me, Amos, what seest thou? And I said, A plumb-line. Then said the Lord, Behold, I will set a plumb-line in the midst of my people Israel: I will not again pass by them any more."

The working tools of a fellow craft are here introduced and explained; which are the *plumb, square* and *level.*

The *plumb* is an instrument made use of by operative masons, to raise perpendiculars; the *square*, to square the work; and the *level*, to lay horizontals; but we, as free and accepted masons, are taught to make use of them for more noble and glorious purposes : The *plumb* admonishes us to walk uprightly in our several stations before God and man, *squaring* our actions by the square of virtue, and remembering that we are travelling upon the *level* of time, to " that undiscovered country, from whose bourne no travel- ler returns."

SECTION SECOND.

The second section of this degree refers to the origin of the institution; and views masonry under two denominations, operative and speculative The period stipulated for rewarding merit, is here fixed , and the inimitable moral to which that circumstance alludes, is explained. The celestial and terrestrial globes are considered; and here the accomplished mason may display his talents to advantage, in eluci- dating the *Orders of Architecture*, the *Senses* of human nature, and the liberal *Arts* and *Sciences*, which are severally classed in a regular arrangement.

Masonry is considered under two denominations ; operative and speculative.

Operative Masonry.

By operative masonry, we allude to a proper ap- plication of the useful rules of architecture, whence a structure will derive figure, strength and beauty, and whence will result a due proportion and a just cor- respondence in all its parts. It furnishes us with dwellings, and convenient shelters from the vicissi- tudes and inclemencies of seasons : and while it dis- plays the effects of human wisdom, as well in the choice, as in the arrangement, of the sundry materials of which an edifice is composed, it demonstrates that a fund of science and industry is implanted in man, for the best, most salutary, and beneficent purposes.

Speculative Masonry.

By speculative masonry, we learn to subdue the passions, act upon the square, keep a tongue of good report, maintain secrecy, and practise charity. It is so far interwoven with religion, as to lay us under obligation to pay that rational homage to the Deity, which at once constitutes our duty and our happiness. It leads the contemplative to view, with reverence and admiration, the glorious works of creation, and inspires him with the most exalted ideas of the perfec- tions of his divine Creator.

In six days, God created the heavens and the earth, and rested upon the seventh day;—the seventh therefore, our ancient brethren consecrated as a day of rest from their labors ; thereby enjoying frequent opportunities to contemplate the glorious works of creation, and to adore their great Creator.

Peace, Unity and Plenty, are here introduced and explained.

The next is the doctrine of the Spheres in the sci ence of Astronomy, introduced and considered.

Of the Globes.

The Globes are two artificial and spherical bodies, on the convex surface of which are represented, the countries, seas, and various parts of the earth, the face of the heavens, the planetary revolutions, and other particulars.

The Use of the Globes.

Their principal use, beside serving as maps to dis- tinguish the outward parts of the earth, and the sit- uation of the fixed stars, is to illustrate and explain the phenomena arising from the annual revolution, and the diurnal rotation, of the earth round its own axis. They are the noblest instruments for improv- ing the mind, and giving it the most distinct idea of any problem or proposition, as well as enabling it to solve the same. Contemplating these bodies, we are inspired with a due reverence for the Deity and his works, and are induced to encourage the studies of astronomy, geography and navigation, and the arts dependent on them, by which society has been so much benefited.

As the five Orders of Architecture are considered in this section, a brief description of them may not be improper.

Of Order in Architecture.

By order in architecture, is meant a system of all the members, proportions and ornaments of columns and pilasters;—or, it is a regular arrangement of the projecting parts of a building, which, united with those of a column, form a beautiful, perfect and complete whole.

Of its Antiquity.

From the first formation of society, order in architecture may be traced. When the rigor of seasons obliged men to contrive shelter from the inclemency of the weather, we learn that they first planted trees on end, and then laid others across, to support a covering. The bands which connected those trees at top and bottom, are said to have given rise to the idea of the base and capital of pillars; and from this simple hint originally proceeded the more improved art of architecture.

The five orders are thus classed;—the *Tuscan Doric, Ionic, Corinthian*, and *Composite*.

The Tuscan

Is the most simple and solid of the five orders. It was invented in Tuscany, whence it derives its name. The simplicity of the construction of this column renders it eligible where ornament would be superfluous.

The Doric,

Which is plain and natural. is the most ancient, and was invented by the Greeks. Its column is eight diameters high, and has seldom any ornaments on base or capital, except mouldings; though the frieze is distinguished by triglyphs and metopes ; and triglyphs compose the ornaments of the frieze.

The Doric is the best proportioned of all the orders

3

The several parts of which it is composed, are founded on the natural position of solid bodies. In its first invention, it was more simple than in its present state. In after times, when it began to be adorned, it gained the name of Doric; for when it was constructed in its primitive and simple form, the name of Tuscan was conferred on it. Hence the Tuscan precedes the Doric in rank, on account of its resemblance to that pillar in its original state.

The Ionic

Bears a kind of mean proportion between the more solid and delicate orders. Its column is nine diameters high; its capital is adorned with volutes, and its cornice has dentals. There is both delicacy and ingenuity displayed in this pillar; the invention of which is attributed to the Ionians, as the famous temple of Diana at Ephesus was of this order. It is said to have been formed after the model of an agreeable young woman, of an elegant shape, dressed in her hair; as a contrast to the Doric order, which was formed after that of a strong, robust man.

The Corinthian,

The richest of the five orders, is deemed a masterpiece of art. Its column is ten diameters high, and its capital is adorned with two rows of leaves, and eight volutes, which sustain the abacus. The frieze is ornamented with curious devices, the cornice with dentals and modillions. This order is used in stately and superb structures.

Of the Invention of this Order.

It was invented at Corinth, by Callimachus, who is said to have taken the hint of the capital of this pillar from the following remarkable circumstance. Accidentally passing by the tomb of a young lady, he perceived a basket of toys covered with tile, placed over an acanthus root, having been left there by her nurse. As the branches grew up, they encompassed the bas-

ket, till, arriving at the tile, they met with an obstruc-
tion, and bent downwards. Callimachus, struck with
the object, set about imitating the figure : the vase of
the capital he made to represent the basket ; the abacus
the tile : and the volutes the bending leaves.

The Composite

Is compounded of the other orders, and was con-
trived by the Romans. Its capital has the two rows
of leaves of the Corinthian, and the volutes of the Ionic.
Its column has quarter-rounds, as the Tuscan and
Doric order ; is ten diameters high ; and its cornice
has dentals, or simple modillions. This pillar is gen-
erally found in buildings where strength, elegance
and beauty are displayed.

Of the Invention of Order in Architecture.

The ancient and original orders of architecture
revered by masons, are no more than three ; the Doric,
Ionic, and Corinthian, which were invented by the
Greeks. To these the Romans have added two ;
the Tuscan, which they made plainer than the Doric ;
and the Composite, which was more ornamental, if not
more beautiful, than the Corinthian. The first three
orders alone, however, show invention and particular
character, and essentially differ from each other : the
two others have nothing but what is borrowed, and
differ only accidentally ; the Tuscan is the Doric in
its earliest state ; and the Composite is the Corinthian
enriched with the Ionic. To the Greeks, therefore,
and not to the Romans, are we indebted for what is
great, judicious and distinct, in architecture.

Of the Five Senses of Human Nature, which are, HEARING, SEEING, FEELING, SMELLING, and TASTING.

Hearing

Is that sense by which we distinguish sounds, and
are capable of enjoying all the agreeable charms of

music. By it we are enabled to enjoy the pleasures of society, and reciprocally to communicate to each other our thoughts and intentions, our purposes and desires ; while thus our reason is capable of exerting its utmost power and energy.

The wise and beneficent Author of Nature intended, by the formation of this sense, that we should be social creatures, and receive the greatest and most important part of our knowledge by the information of others. For these purposes, we are endowed with hearing, that by a proper exertion of our rational powers, our happiness may be complete.

Seeing

Is that sense by which we distinguish objects, and in an instant of time, without change of place or situation, view armies in battle array, figures of the most stately structures, and all the agreeable variety displayed in the landscape of nature. By this sense, we find our way on the pathless ocean, traverse the globe of the earth, determine its figure and dimensions, and delineate any region or quarter of it. By it we measure the planetary orbs, and make new discoveries in the sphere of the fixed stars. Nay, more : by it we perceive the tempers and dispositions, the passions and affections, of our fellow creatures, when they wish most to conceal them ; so that though the tongue may be taught to lie and dissemble, the countenance would display the hypocrisy to the discerning eye. In fine, the rays of light, which administer to this sense, are the most astonishing part of the animated creation, and render the eye a peculiar object of admiration.

Of all the faculties, sight is the noblest. The structure of the eye, and its appurtenances, evince the admirable contrivance of nature for performing all its various external and internal motions ; while the variety displayed in the eyes of different animals, suited to their several ways of life, clearly demonstrates this organ to be the masterpiece of Nature's work.

Feeling

Is that sense by which we distinguish the different qualities of bodies : such as heat and cold, hardness, and softness, roughness, and smoothness, figure, solidity, motion, and extension.

These three senses, Hearing, Seeing, and Feeling, are most revered among masons.

Smelling

Is that sense, by which we distinguish odors, the various kinds of which convey different impressions to the mind.   Animal and vegetable bodies, and indeed most other bodies, while exposed to the air, continually send forth effluvia of vast subtilty, as well in the state of life and growth, as in the state of fermentation and putrefaction.   These effluvia being drawn into the nostrils along with the air, are the means by which all bodies are smelled.   Hence it is evident that there is a manifest appearance of design in the great Creator's having planted the organ of smell in the inside of that canal, through which the air continually passes in respiration.

Tasting

Enables us to make a proper distinction in the choice of our food.   The organ of this sense guards the entrance of the alimentary canal, as that of smelling guards the entrance of the canal for respiration.   From the situation of both these organs, it is plain that they were intended by nature to distinguish wholesome food from that which is nauseous.   Every thing that enters into the stomach, must undergo the scrutiny of tasting , and by it we are capable of discerning the changes which the same body undergoes in the different compositions of art, cookery, chemistry, pharmacy, &c.

Smelling and tasting are inseparably connected ; and it is by the unnatural kind of life men commonly lead in society, that these senses are rendered less fit to perform their natural offices.

3*

Of the Seven Liberal Arts and Sciences;—which are, GRAMMAR, RHETORIC, LOGIC, ARITHMETIC, GEOMETRY, MUSIC, and ASTRONOMY.

Grammar

Teaches the proper arrangement of words, according to the idiom or dialect of any particular people ; and that excellency of pronunciation, which enables us to speak or write a language with accuracy, agreeably to reason and correct usage.

Rhetoric

Teaches us to speak copiously and fluently on any subject, not merely with propriety alone, but with all the advantages of force and elegance, wisely contriving to captivate the hearer by strength of argument and beauty of expression, whether it be to entreat or exhort, to admonish or applaud.

Logic

Teaches us to guide our reason discretionally in the general knowledge of things, and directs our inquiries after truth. It consists of a regular train of argument, whence we infer, deduce and conclude, according to certain premises laid down, admitted, or granted ; and in it are employed the faculties of conceiving, judging, reasoning and disposing; all of which are naturally led on from one gradation to another, till the point in question is finally determined.

Arithmetic

Teaches the powers and properties of numbers, which is variously effected, by letters, tables, figures, and instruments. By this art, reasons and demonstrations are given, for finding out any certain number, whose relation or affinity to another is already known or discovered.

Geometry.

Geometry treats of the powers and properties of

magnitudes in general, where length, breadth, and thickness, are considered, from a point to a line, from a line to a superficies, and from a superficies to a solid.

A point is a dimensionless figure ; or an indivisible part of a space.

A line is a point continued, and a figure of one capacity, namely, length.

A superficies is a figure of two dimensions, namely length and breadth.

A solid is a figure of three dimensions, namely, length, breadth, and thickness.

Of the Advantages of Geometry.

By this science, the architect is enabled to construct his plans, and execute his designs ; the general to arrange his soldiers ; the geographer to give us the dimensions of the world, and all things therein contained ; to delineate the extent of seas, and specify the divisions of empires, kingdoms and provinces. By it, also, the astronomer is enabled to make his observations, and to fix the duration of time and seasons, years and cycles.

In fine, geometry is the foundation of architecture, and the root of the mathematics.

Music

Teaches the art of forming concords, so as to compose delightful harmony, by a mathematical and proportional arrangement of acute, grave, and mixed sounds. This art, by a series of experiments, is reduced to a demonstrative science, with respect to tones and the intervals of sound. It inquires into the nature of concords and discords, and enables us to find out the proportion between them by numbers.

Astronomy

Is that divine art, by which we are taught to read the wisdom, strength and beauty, of the Almighty Creator, in those sacred pages, the celestial hemisphere.

Assisted by astronomy, we can observe the magni-tudes, and calculate the periods and eclipses of the heavenly bodies. By it, we learn the use of the globes, the system of the world, and the preliminary law of nature. While we are employed in the study of this science, we must perceive unparalleled instances of wisdom and goodness ; and, through the whole cre-ation, trace the glorious Author by his works.

[Here an emblem of Plenty is introduced and ex-plained.

Of the Moral Advantages of Geometry.

Geometry, the first and noblest of sciences, is the basis on which the superstructure of masonry is erected. By geometry, we may curiously trace Nature through her various windings, to her most concealed recesses. By it, we may discover the power, the wisdom and the goodness of the Grand Artificer of the universe, and view with delight the proportions which connect this vast machine.

By it, we may discover how the planets move in their different orbits, and demonstrate their various revolutions. By it we account for the return of sea-sons, and the variety of scenes which each season displays to the discerning eye. Numberless worlds are around us, all framed by the same Divine Artist, which roll through the vast expanse, and are all con-ducted by the same unerring law of nature.

A survey of Nature, and the observations of her beautiful proportions, first determined man to imitate the divine plan, and study symmetry and order. This gave rise to societies, and birth to every useful art. The architect began to design ; and the plans which he laid down, being improved by experience and time, have produced works which are the admi-ration of every age.

The lapse of time, the ruthless hand of ignorance, and the devastations of war, have laid waste and de-stroyed many valuable monuments of antiquity ; on which the utmost exertions of human genius have been employed. Even the temple of Solomon, so

..acious and magnificent, and constructed by so many celebrated artists, escaped not the unsparing ravages of barbarous force. Free-Masonry, notwithstanding, has still survived. The *attentive Ear* receives the sound from the *instructive Tongue:* and the mysteries of free-masonry are safely lodged in the repository of *faithful Breasts.* Tools and instruments of architecture, and symbolic emblems, most expressive, are selected by the fraternity, to imprint on the mind wise and serious truths; and thus, through a succession of ages, are transmitted, unimpaired, the most excellent tenets of our institution.

CHARGE at passing to the Degree of Fellow Craft.

BROTHER—

Being passed to the second degree of masonry we congratulate you on your preferment. The internal, and not the external qualifications of a man, are what masonry regards. As you increase in knowledge, you will improve in social intercourse.

It is unnecessary to recapitulate the duties which, as a mason, you are bound to discharge, or to enlarge on the necessity of a strict adherence to them, as your own experience must have established their value. Our laws and regulations you are strenuously to support; and be always ready to assist in seeing them duly executed. You are not to palliate, or aggravate, the offences of your brethren; but in the decision of every trespass against our rules, you are to judge with candor, admonish with friendship, and reprehend with justice.

The study of the liberal arts, that valuable branch of education, which tends so effectually to polish and adorn the mind, is earnestly recommended to your consideration; especially the science of geometry, which is established as the basis of our art. Geometry, or masonry, originally synonymous terms, being of a divine and moral nature, is enriched with the most useful knowledge : while it proves the wonderful properties of nature, it demonstrates the more important truths of morality.

Your past behavior and regular deportment have merited the honor which we have now conferred; and in your new character, it is expected that you will conform to the principles of the order, by steadily persevering in the practice of every commendable virtue. Such is the nature of your engagement as a fellow craft, and to these duties you are bound by the most sacred ties.

MASTER MASON'S DEGREE.

SECTION FIRST.

THE ceremony of raising to the sublime degree of Master Mason, is particularly specified, and other useful instructions are given in this branch of the ιecture.

The following passage of scripture is introduced during the ceremonies:

ECCL. xii. 1—7.

" Remember now thy Creator in the days of thy youth, while the evil days come not, nor the years draw nigh, when thou shalt say, I have no pleasure in them; while the sun, or the light, or the moon, or the stars, be not darkened, nor the clouds return after the rain; in the day when the keepers of the house shall tremble, and the strong men shall bow themselves, and the grinders cease because they are few, and those that look out of the windows be darkened; and the doors shall be shut in the streets, when the sound of the grinding is low ; and he shall rise up at the voice of the bird, and all the daughters of music shall be brought low. Also, when they shall be afraid of that which is high, and fears shall be in the way, and the almond-tree shall flourish, and the grasshopper shall be a burden, and desire shall fail; because man goeth to his long home, and the mourners go about the streets : or ever the silver cord be loosed, or the golden bowl be broken at the fountain, or the wheel broken at the cistern. Then shall the dust return to the earth as it was ; and the spirit shall return unto God who gave it."

The *working tools* of a master mason are all the implements of masonry indiscriminately, but more especially *the trowel.*

The TROWEL is an instrument made use of by operative masons, to spread the cement which unites a building into one common mass : but we, as free and accepted masons, are taught to make use of it for the more noble and glorious purpose of spreading the cement of BROTHERLY LOVE and affection ; that cement which unites us into one sacred band, or society of friends and brothers, among whom no contention should ever exist, but that noble contention, or rather emulation, of who can best work, or best agree.

SECTION SECOND.

This section recites the historical traditions of the order, and presents to view a finished picture, of the utmost consequence to the fraternity. It exemplifies an instance of virtue, fortitude, and integrity, unparalleled in the history of man.

Prayer at raising a Brother to the sublime Degree of Master Mason

Thou, O God ! knowest our down-sitting and our up-rising, and understandest our thoughts afar off. Shield and defend us from the evil intentions of our enemies, and support us under the trials and afflictions we are destined to en-

dure while travelling through this vale of tears.
Man that is born of a woman, is of few days,
and full of trouble. He cometh forth as a flower,
and is cut down; he fleeth also as a shadow,
and continueth not. Seeing his days are determined, the number of his months are with thee,
thou hast appointed his bounds that he cannot
pass: turn from him that he may rest, till he
shall accomplish his day. For there is hope
of a tree, if it be cut down, that it will sprout
again, and that the tender branch thereof will
not cease. But man dieth and wasteth away;
yea, man giveth up the ghost, and where is he?
As the waters fail from the sea, and the flood
decayeth and drieth up, so man lieth down, and
riseth not up till the heavens shall be no more.
Yet, O Lord! have compassion on the children
of thy creation; administer them comfort in
time of trouble, and save them with an everlasting salvation.

So mote it be. Amen.

SECTION THIRD.

The third section illustrates certain hieroglyphical
emblems, and inculcates many useful lessons, to extend knowledge, and promote virtue. In this branch
of the lecture, many particulars relative to king Solomon's Temple are noticed.

This famous fabric was supported by fourteen
hundred and fifty-three columns, and two thousand
nine hundred and six pilasters; all hewn from the
finest Parian marble. There were employed in its
building, three Grand Masters; three thousand three
hundred overseers of the work; eighty thousand Fellow Crafts, or hewers on the mountains and in the

quarries; and seventy thousand Entered Apprentices, or bearers of burdens.

The Three Steps,

Usually delineated upon the master's carpet, are emblematical of the three principal stages of human life, viz. *youth, manhood,* and *age.* In *youth,* as entered apprentices, we ought industriously to occupy our minds in the attainment of useful knowledge: in *manhood,* as fellow crafts, we should apply our knowledge to the discharge of our respective duties to God, our neighbors, and ourselves; that so, in *age,* as master masons, we may enjoy the happy reflections consequent on a well-spent life, and die in the hope of a glorious immortality.

The Pot of Incense

Is an emblem of a pure heart, which is always an acceptable sacrifice to the Deity; and, as this glows with fervent heat, so should our hearts continually glow with gratitude to the great beneficent Author of our existence, for the manifold blessings and comforts we enjoy.

The Bee Hive

Is an emblem of industry, and recommends the practice of that virtue to all created beings, from the highest seraph in heaven, to the lowest reptile of the dust. It teaches us, that as we came into the world rational and intelligent beings, so we should ever be industrious ones; never sitting down contented while our fellow-creatures around us are in want, when it is in our power to relieve them, without inconvenience to ourselves.

When we take a survey of nature, we view man, in his infancy, more helpless and indigent than the brutal creation: he lies languishing for days, months, and years, totally incapable of providing sustenance for himself, of guarding against the attack of the wild beasts of the field, or sheltering himself from the inclemencies of the weather. It might have pleased the great Creator of heaven and earth, to have made man independent of all other beings : but, as dependence is one of the strongest bonds of society, mankind were made dependent on each other for protection and security, as they thereby enjoy better opportunities of fulfilling the duties of reciprocal love and friendship. Thus was man formed for social and active life, the noblest part of the work of God , and he that will so demean himself, as not to be endeavoring to add to the common stock of know edge and understanding, may be deemed a *drone* in the *hive* of nature, a useless member of society, and unworthy of our protection as masons.

The Book of Constitutions, guarded by the Tyler's Sword,

Reminds us that we should be ever watchful and guarded in our words and actions, particularly when before the enemies of masonry ; ever bearing in remembrance those truly masonic virtues, *silence* and *circumspection.*

The Sword, pointing to a Naked Heart,

Demonstrates that justice will sooner or later overtake us ; and although our thoughts, words and actions, may be hidden from the eyes of men, yet that

ALL-SEEING EYE,

whom the SUN, MOON, and STARS obey, and under whose watchful care even COMETS perform their stupendous revolutions, pervades the inmost recesses of the human HEART, and will reward us according to our merits.

The Anchor and Ark

Are emblems of a well-grounded *hope*, and a well-spent life. They are emblematical of that divine *Ark*, which safely wafts us over this tempestuous sea of troubles, and that *Anchor* which shall safely moor us in a peaceful harbor, where the wicked cease from troubling, and the weary shall find rest.

The Forty-Seventh Problem of Euclid.

This was an invention of our ancient friend and brother, the great Pythagoras, who, in his travels through Asia, Africa, and Europe, was initiated into several orders of priesthood, and raised to the sublime degree of a master mason. This wise philosopher enriched his mind abundantly in a general knowledge of things, and more especially in geometry, or masonry. On this subject, he drew out many problems and theorems; and among the most distinguished, he erected this, which, in the joy of his heart, he called Ευρηκα, (*Eureka*,) in the Grecian language, signifying, *I have found it;* and upon the discovery of which, he is said to have sacrificed a hecatomb. It teaches masons to be general lovers of the arts and sciences.

The Hour-Glass

Is an emblem of human life. Behold! how swiftly the sands run, and how rapidly our lives are drawing to a close! We cannot without astonishment behold the little particles which are contained in this machine;—how they pass away almost imperceptibly! and yet, to our surprise, in the short space of an hour, they are all exhausted. Thus wastes man! To-day, he puts forth the tender leaves of hope; to-morrow, blossoms, and bears his blushing honors thick upon him; the next day comes a frost, which nips the shoot; and when he thinks his greatness is still aspiring, he falls, like autumn leaves, to enrich our mother earth.

The Scythe

Is an emblem of time, which cuts the brittle thread of life, and launches us into eternity.—Behold! what havock the scythe of time makes among the human race! If by chance we should escape the numerous evils incident to childhood and youth, and with health and vigor arrive to the years of manhood; yet, withal, we must soon be cut down by the all-devouring scythe

of time, and be gathered into the land where oui
fathers have gone before us.

Thus we close the explanation of the emblems upon
the solemn thought of death, which, without revelation, is dark and gloomy; but the Christian is suddenly revived by the *ever green* and ever living *sprig*
of Faith in the merits of the Lion of the tribe of
Judah; which strengthens him, with confidence and
composure, to look forward to a blessed immortality;
and doubts not, but in the glorious morn of the resur
rection, his body will rise, and become as incorrupt-
ible as his soul.

Then let us imitate the Christian in his virtuous and
amiable conduct; in his unfeigned piety to God; in
his inflexible fidelity to his trust; that we may welcome the grim tyrant Death, and receive him as a
kind messenger sent from our Supreme Grand Master, to translate us from this imperfect to that all-per-
fect, glorious, and celestial Lodge above, where the
Supreme Architect of the universe presides.

CHARGE at raising to the sublime degree of Master Mason.

BROTHER,

Your zeal for the institution of masonry; the
progress you have made in the mystery; and
your conformity to our regulations, have pointed
you out as a proper object of our favor and esteem.   You are now bound by duty, honor and
gratitude, to be faithful to your trust; to support the dignity of your character on every occasion; and to enforce, by precept and example,
obedience to the tenets of the order.

In the character of a master mason, you are
authorized to correct the errors and irregularities of your uninformed brethren, and to guard
them against a breach of fidelity.   To preserve
the reputation of the fraternity unsullied, must
4*

be your constant care; and for this purpose, it is your province to recommend to your inferiors, obedience and submission; to your equals, courtesy and affability; to your superiors, kindness and condescension. Universal benevolence you are always to inculcate; and by the regularity of your own behavior, afford the best example for the conduct of others less informed. The ancient land-marks of the order, entrusted to your care, you are carefully to preserve; and never suffer them to be infringed, or countenance a deviation from the established usages and customs of the fraternity.

Your virtue, honor and reputation, are concerned in supporting with dignity the character you now bear. Let no motive, therefore, make you swerve from your duty, violate your vows, or betray your trust; but be true and faithful, and imitate the example of that celebrated artist, whom you this evening represent. Thus you will render yourself deserving of the honor which we have conferred, and merit the confidence that we have reposed.

MARK MASTER'S DEGREE.

By the influence of this degree, each operative mason, at the erection of King Solomon's temple, was known and distinguished, by the Senior Grand Warden. If defects were found, the overseers were enabled, without difficulty, to ascertain who was the faulty workman; so that deficiencies might be remedied, without injuring the credit or diminishing the reward of the industrious and faithful of the craft.

CHARGE to be read at Opening.

"Wherefore, brethren, lay aside all malice, and guile, and hypocrisies, and envies, and all evil speakings. If so be ye have tasted that the Lord is gracious; to whom coming, as unto a living stone, disallowed indeed of men, but chosen of God, and precious; ye also, as living stones, be ye built up a spiritual house, an holy priesthood, to offer up sacrifices acceptable to God.

"Brethren, this is the will of God, that with well-doing, ye put to silence the ignorance of foolish men. As free, and not as using your liberty for a cloak of maliciousness; but as the servants of God. Honor all men; love the brotherhood; fear God."

SECTION FIRST.

The first section explains the manner of opening a Mark Master's Lodge; and recapitulates the mystic ceremony of the preparatory circumstance of introducing a candidate. The number of artists employed in building the Temple is specified; and the progress they made in architecture, is remarked; and it ends with a beautiful display of the manner in which one of the principal events originated, which characterizes this degree.

SECTION SECOND.

In the second section is recited the mode of advancing a candidate to this degree—By which the mark master is instructed in the origin and history of the Degree, and in the indispensable obligations he is under to stretch forth his assisting hand for the relief of an indigent and worthy brother, to a certain specified extent. We are here taught to ascribe praise to the meritorious, and to dispense rewards to the diligent and industrious.

The following texts of scripture are introduced and explained.

PSALM cxviii. 22.

" The stone which the builders refused, is become the head stone of the corner."—MATT. xxi. 42. " Did ye never read in the scriptures, The stone which the builders rejected, is become the head of the corner ?"—MARK xii. 10. " And have you not read this scripture, The stone which the builders rejected, is become the head of the corner ?"—LUKE xx. 17. " What is this, then, that is written, The stone which the builders rejected, is become the head of the corner."

ACTS iv. 11.

" This is the stone which was set at nought of you, builders, which is become the head of the corner."

Rev. of St. Jo n, ii. 17.

" To him that overcometh, will I give to eat of the hidden manna; and I will give him a *white stone*, and in the stone a *new name* written, which no man knoweth, saving him that receiveth it."

Rev. iii. 13.

" He that hath *an ear* to hear, let him hear."

2 Chron. ii. 16.

" And we will cut wood out of Lebanon, as much as thou shalt need; and we will bring it to thee in floats by sea to Joppa, and thou shalt carry it up to Jerusalem."

Ezekiel xliv. 1 and 5.

" Then he brought me back the way of the gate of the outward sanctuary, which looketh towards the east, and it was shut. And the Lord said unto me, Son of man, mark well, and behold with thine eyes, and hear with thine ears, all that I say unto thee, concerning all the ordinances of the house of the Lord, and all the laws thereof; and mark well the entering in of the house, with every going forth of the sanctuary."

The *working tools* of a mark master are the chisel and mallet.

The Chisel

Morally demonstrates the advantages of discipline and education. The mind, like the diamond in its original state, is rude and unpolished; but as the effect of the chisel on the

external coat soon presents to view the latent
beauties of the diamond; so education discovers
the latent virtues of the mind, and draws them
forth to range the large field of matter and space,
to display the summit of human knowledge,
our duty to God and to man.

The Mallet

Morally teaches to correct irregularities, and
reduce man to a proper level; so that, by quiet
deportment, he may, in the school of discipline,
learn to be content.—What the mallet is to the
workman, enlightened reason is to the passions:
ıt curbs ambition, it depresses envy, it mode-
rates anger, and it encourages good dispositions;
whence arises among good masons that comely
ɒrder,

> " Which nothing earthly gives, or can destroy,
>   The soul's calm sunshine, and the heart-felt joy."

*CHARGE to be delivered when a candidate is ad-
vanced to the degree of Mark Master.*

BROTHER,

I congratulate you on having been thought
worthy of being advanced to this honorable degree of masonry. Permit me to impress it on
your mind, that your assiduity should ever be
commensurate with your duties, which become
more and more extensive, as you advance in masonry. In the honorable character of mark master mason, it is more particularly your duty to
endeavor to let your conduct in the lodge, and
among your brethren, be such as may stand the
test of the Grand Overseer's square, that you

may not, like the unfinished and imperfect work of the negligent and unfaithful of former times, be rejected and thrown aside, as unfit for that spiritual building, that house not made with hands, eternal in the heavens.

While such is your conduct, should misfor-tunes assail you, should friends forsake you, should envy traduce your good name, and malice persecute you; yet may you have confidence, that among mark master masons you will find friends who will administer relief to your dis-tresses, and comfort your afflictions; ever bear-ing in mind, as a consolation under all the frowns of fortune, and as an encouragement to hope for better prospects, that *the stone which the builders rejected*, [possessing merits to them unknown,] became the chief stone of the corner.

The following song is sung previous to closing.

MARK MASTER'S SONG.

Mark Mas-ters all ap-pear, Be-fore the

Mark Mas-ters all ap-pear, Be-fore the

Chief O'erseer, In concert move; Let him your

Chief O'erseer, In concert move; Let him your

work inspect, For the Chief Architect; If there be

work inspect, For the Chief Architect; If there be

no de-fect, He will ap - prove.

no de-fect, He will ap - prove.

You who have passed the square,
For your rewards prepare,
　　Join heart and hand;
Each with his mark in view,
March with the just and true;
Wages to you are due,
　　At your command.

Hiram, the widow's son,
Sent unto Solomon
　　Our great key-stone;
On it appears the name
Which raises high the fame
Of all to whom the same
　　Is truly known.

Now to the westward move,
Where, full of strength and **love,**
　　Hiram doth stand;
But if impostors are
Mix'd with the worthy there,
Caution them to beware
　　Of the right hand.

Now to the praise of those
Who triumph'd o'er the **foes**
　　Of mason's art:

5

To the praiseworthy three,
Who founded this degree;
May all their virtues be
Deep in our hearts.

Previous to closing, the following Parable is recited.

MATTHEW xx. 1—16.

"For the kingdom of heaven is like unto a
man that is an householder, which went out
early in the morning to hire laborers into his
vineyard. And when he had agreed with the
laborers for a penny a day, he sent them into
his vineyard. And he went out about the third
hour, and saw others standing idle in the
market place, and said unto them, Go ye also
into the vineyard, and whatsoever is right, I
will give you.—And they went their way. And
again he went out about the sixth and ninth
hour, and did likewise. And about the eleventh
hour, he went out and found others standing
idle, and saith unto them, Why stand ye here
all the day idle? They say unto him, Because
no man hath hired us. He saith unto them,
Go ye also into the vineyard, and whatsoever
is right, that shall ye receive. So, when even
was come, the lord of the vineyard saith unto
his steward, Call the laborers, and give them
their hire, beginning from the last unto the first.
And when they came, that were hired about the
eleventh hour, they received every man a
penny. But when the first came, they supposed that they should have received more, and
they likewise received every man a penny.

And when they received it, they murmured against the good man of the house, saying, These last have wrought but one hour, and thou hast made them equal unto us, which have borne the burden and heat of the day. But he answered one of them, and said, Friend. I do thee no wrong; didst thou not agree with me for a penny? Take that thine is, and go thy way; I will give unto this last even as unto thee. Is it not lawful for me to do what I will with my own? Is thine eye evil, because I am good? So the last shall be first, and the first last: for many be called. but few chosen."

PRESENT, OR PAST MASTER'S DEGREE.

This degree treats of the government of our society; the disposition of our rulers; and illustrates their requisite qualifications. It includes the ceremony of opening and closing lodges in the several preceding degrees: it comprehends the ceremonies and forms of installations, consecrations, laying the foundation stones of public buildings, and also at dedications and at funerals, by a variety of particulars explanatory of those ceremonies.

SECTION FIRST.

This section contains the form of a petition for letters of dispensation, or a warrant of constitution for a lodge, empowering them to work. The ceremonies of Constitution and Consecration are considered, with the form of a Grand Procession.

Form of Petition for a Charter or Warrant to establish a new Lodge.

To the Most Worshipful Grand Lodge of the State of ———, the petitioners humbly shew, that they are *ancient, free, and accepted Master Masons.* Having the prosperity of the Fraternity at heart, they are willing to exert their best endeavors to promote and diffuse the genuine principles of Masonry.

For the convenience of their respective dwellings, and for other good reasons, they are desirous of forming a new Lodge in the town of ———, to be named ———. In consequence of this desire, and for the good of the craft, they pray for a *Charter*, or *Warrant*, to empower them to assemble as a legal Lodge, to discharge the duties of masonry, in the several degrees of Entered Apprentice, Fellow Craft, and Master Mason, in a regular and constitutional manner, according to the ancient form of the fraternity, and the laws and regulations of the Grand Lodge. That they have nominated and do recommend A. B. to be the first master, C. D. to be the first senior warden, and E. F. to be the first junior warden of said Lodge that, if the prayer of the petition should be granted, they promise a strict conformity to all the constitutional laws, rules and regulations of the Grand Lodge.

This petition must be signed by at least seven regular masons, and recommended by some lodge contiguous to the place where the new lodge is to be held. It must be delivered to the Grand Secretary, whose duty it is to lay it before the Grand Lodge.

After a charter is granted by the Grand Lodge, the Grand Master appoints a day and hour for constituting and consecrating the new lodge, and for installing the master, wardens, and other officers. The Grand Master has power to appoint some worthy *Past Master*, with full power to consecrate, constitute, and install the petitioners.

Ceremony of Constitution and Consecration.

On the day and hour appointed, the Grand Master and his officers meet in a convenient room near to the

5*

Lodge to be constituted, and open in the third degree. After tne officers in the new lodge are examined, they send a messenger to the Grand Master, with the following message : viz.

MOST WORSHIPFUL,

The officers and brethren of ———— Lodge, who are now assembled at ————, have instructed me to inform you, that the Most Woishipful Grand Lodge was pleased to grant them a Charter, authorizing them to form and open a lodge of free and accepted masons in the town of ————: They are now desirous that their lodge should be consecrated, and their officers installed in *due and ancient form ;* for which purpose they are now met, and await the pleasure of the Most Worshipful Grand Master.

When notice is given, the Grand Lodge walk in procession to the hall of the new Lodge.   When the Grand Master enters, the grand honors are given by the new lodge ; the officers of which resign their seats to the grand officers, and take their several stations on the left.

The necessary cautions are given ; and all, excepting PRESENT or PAST MASTERS of lodges, are requested to retire until the Master of the new lodge is inducted into the *Oriental Chair of Solomon.* He is ther bound to the faithful performanse of .his trust, and invested with the characteristics of the chair.

Upon due notice, the Grand Marshal re-conducts the brethren into the hall ; and all take their places, except the members of the new lodge, who form a procession on one side of the hall.   As they advance, the Grand Master addresses them :

" *Brethren, behold your Master.*"

They make the proper salutations as they pass.

A grand procession is then formed, in the follow
ng order: viz.

Tyler with a drawn Sword

Two Stewards with white Rods;

Entered Apprentices;

Fellow Crafts;

Master Masons;

Stewards;

Junior Deacons;

Senior Deacons;

Secretaries;

Treasurers;

Past Wardens;

Junior Wardens;

Senior Wardens;

Past Masters;

Mark Masters;

Royal Arch Masters;

Select Masters;

Knights Templars;

Masters of Lodges.

Marshals

The New Lodge

Tyler with a drawn Sword

Stewards with white Rods;

Entered Apprentices;

Fellow Crafts;

Master Masons;

Junior and Senior Deacons ·

Secretary and Treasurer;

Two Brethren, carrying the flooring,* or Lodge

Junior and Senior Wardens;

The Holy Writings, carried by the oldest or some
suitable member, not in office;

The W. Master;

Music;

* Carpet.

The Grand Lodge.

Grand Tyler with drawn Sword ;
Grand Stewards with white Rods ;
A Brother carrying a Golden Vessel of Corn ; *
Two Brethren, carrying the Silver Vessels, one of
Wine, the other of Oil ;
Grand Secretaries ;
Grand Treasurers ;
A burning Taper, borne by a Past Master ;
A Past Master bearing the Holy Writings, Square
and Compasses, supported by two Stewards
with white Rods ;
Two burning Tapers, borne by two Past Masters ;
The Tuscan and Composite Orders ;
The Doric, Ionic, and Corinthian Orders ,
Past Grand Wardens ;
Past Deputy Grand Masters ,
Past Grand Masters ;
The Globes ;
Clergy and Orator ;
R. W. Junior and Senior Grand Wardens ;
R. W. Deputy Grand Master ;
The Master of the oldest Lodge, carrying the Book
of Constitutions ;
The M. W. Grand Master ;
The Grand Deacons, on a line seven feet apart, on
the right and left of the Grand Master,
with black Rods ;
Grand Sword Bearer, with a drawn Sword ;
Two Stewards with white Rods.

The Marshals conduct the procession to the church,
or house, where the services are to be performed.
When the front of the procession arrives at the door
they halt, open to the right and left, and face inward

* Wheat.

while the Grand Master and others, in succession, pass through and enter the house.

A platform is erected in front of the pulpit, and provided with seats for the accommodation of the Grand Officers.

The Holy Bible, Square and Compasses, and Book of Constitutions, are placed upon a table in front of the Grand Master: the flooring is then spread in the centre, upon the platform, covered with white satin or linen, and encompassed by the three tapers, and the vessels of *corn, wine* and *oil.*

SERVICES.

1. A piece of Music.
2. Prayer.
3. An Oration.
4. A piece of Music.
5. The Grand Marshal forms the officers and members of the new Lodge in front of the Grand Master. The Deputy Grand Master addresses the Grand Master as follows:

MOST WORSHIPFUL,

A number of brethren, duly instructed in the mysteries of Masonry, having assembled together at stated periods, by virtue of a dispensation granted them for that purpose, do now desire to be *constituted* into a *regular lodge*, agreeably to the ancient usages and customs of the fraternity.

The dispensation and records are presented to the Grand Master, who examines the records, and, if found correct, proclaims:

The records appear to be correct, and are approved. Upon due deliberation, the Grand Lodge have granted the brethren of this new Lodge a charter, establishing and confirming them in the rights and privileges of a *regular constituted Lodge;* which the Grand Secretary will now read.

After the charter is read, the Grand Master then says,

We shall now proceed, according to ancient usage, to constitute these brethren into a regular Lodge.

Whereupon the several officers of the new Lodge deliver up their jewels and badges to their Master, who presents them, with his own, to the Deputy Grand Master; and he to the Grand Master.

The Deputy Grand Master presents the Master Elect to the Grand Master, saying,

MOST WORSHIPFUL,

I present you Brother ———, whom the members of the Lodge, now to be constituted, have chosen for their Master.

The Grand Master asks them if they remain satisfied with their choice. [*They bow in token of assent.*]

The Master elect then presents, severally, his wardens and other officers, naming them and their respective offices. The Grand Master asks the brethren if they remain satisfied with each and all of them. [*They bow as before.*]

The officers and members of the new Lodge form in front of the Grand Master; and the business of *Consecration* commences with solemn music.

6. *Ceremony of Consecration.*

The Grand Master, attended by the Grand Officers and the Grand Chaplain, form themselves in order round the lodge—all devoutly kneeling.

7. A piece of solemn music is performed while the Lodge is uncovered.

After which, the first clause of the Consecration Prayer is rehearsed, which is as follows:

"Great Architect of the universe! Maker and Ruler of all worlds! deign, from thy celestial temple, from realms of light and glory, to bless us in all the purposes of our present assembly! We humbly invoke thee to give us at this, and at all times, *wisdom* in all our doings, *strength* of mind in all our difficulties, and the *beauty* of harmony in all our communications! Permit us, O thou Author of light and life, great Source of love and happiness, to erect this Lodge, and now solemnly to *consecrate* it to the honor of thy glory!

"Glory be to God on high."

[Response by the brethren.]

"As it was in the beginning, is now, and ever shall be; world without end. Amen."

The Deputy Grand Master takes the Golden Vessel of Corn, and the Senior and Junior Grand Wardens take the Silver Vessels of Wine and Oil, and sprinkle the elements of consecration upon the Lodge.

[The Grand Chaplain then continues:]

"Grant, O Lord our God, that those who are now about to be invested with the government of this Lodge, may be endued with wisdom to instruct their brethren in all their duties. May *brotherly love*, *relief*, and *truth*, always prevail among the members of this lodge; and may this bond of union continue to strengthen the Lodges throughout the world!

"Bless all our brethren, wherever dispersed; and grant speedy relief to all who are either oppressed or distressed.

" We affectionately commend to thee, all the members of thy whole family. May they increase in grace, in the knowledge of thee, and in the love of each other.

" Finally: may we finish all our work here below, with thy approbation; and then have our transition from this earthly abode to thy heavenly temple above, there to enjoy light, glory and bliss, ineffable and eternal !

" Glory be to God on high."

[Response by the brethren.]

" As it was in the beginning, is now, and ever shall be. So mote it be. Amen."

8. A piece of solemn music is performed while the Lodge is covered.

9. The Grand Chaplain then dedicates the Lodge in the following terms.

" To the memory of the HOLY ST. JOHNS, we dedicate this Lodge. May every brother revere their character, and imitate their virtues.

" Glory be to God on high."

[Response.]

" As it was in the beginning, is now, and ever shall be, world without end.

" So mote it be. Amen."

10. A piece of music is performed, while the brethren of the new Lodge advance in procession to salute the Grand Lodge, with their hands crossed upon their breasts, and bowing as they pass. They then take their places as they were.

11. The Grand Master then rises, and constitutes the new Lodge in the form following :

" In the name of the Most Worshipful Grand

Lodge, I now constitute and form you, my beloved brethren, into a regular Lodge of free and accepted Masons. From henceforth I empower you to meet as a regular lodge, constituted in conformity to the rites of our order, and the charges of our ancient and honorable fraternity; —and may the Supreme Architect of the universe prosper, direct and counsel you, in all your doings.

[Response.]

" So mote it be. Amen."

SECTION SECOND.

Ceremony of Installation.

The Grand Master, or presiding officer, addresses the Master Elect in the words following, viz.

BROTHER,

Previous to your investiture, it is necessary that you should signify your assent to those ancient charges and regulations, which point out the duty of a Master of a Lodge.

I. You agree to be a good man and true, and strictly to obey the moral law.

II. You agree to be a peaceable subject, and cheerfully to conform to the laws of the country in which you reside.

III. You promise not to be concerned in plots and conspiracies against government; but patiently to submit to the decisions of the supreme legislature.

IV. You agree to pay a proper respect to the civil magistrates to work diligently, live creditably, and act honorably by all men.

6

V. You agree to hold in veneration, the original rules and patrons of the order of masonry,
and their regular successors, supreme and subordinate, according to their stations; and to submit to the awards and resolutions of your
brethren, when convened, in every case cor-
sistent with the constitutions of the order.

VI. You agree to avoid private piques and
quarrels, and to guard against intemperance and
excess.

VII. You agree to be cautions in carriage
and behavior, courteous to your brethren, and
faithful to your lodge.

VIII. You promise to respect genuine brethren, and to discountenance impostors, and all
dissenters from the original plan of masonry.

IX. You agree to promote the general good of
society, to cultivate the social virtues, and to
propagate the knowledge of the art.

X. You promise to pay homage to the Grand
Master for the time being, and to his officers
when duly installed, and strictly to conform to
every edict of the Grand Lodge, or general assembly of masons, that is not subversive of the
principles and groundwork of masonry.

XI. You admit, that it is not in the power of
any men, or body of men, to make innovations
in the body of masonry.

XII. You promise a regular attendance on
the committees and communications of the
Grand Lodge, on receiving proper notice, and
to pay attention to all the duties of masonry, on
convenient occasions.

XIII. You admit, that no new lodge shall be formed without permission of the Grand Lodge : and that no countenance be given to an irregular lodge, or to any person clandestinely initiated therein, being contrary to the ancient charges of the order.

XIV. You admit, that no person can be regularly made a mason in, or admitted a member of, any regular lodge, without previous notice, and due inquiry into his character.

XV. You agree that no visitors shall be received into your lodge, without due examination, and producing proper vouchers of their having been initiated into a regular lodge.

These are the regulations of free and accepted masons.

The presiding officer then addresses the Master as follows :

Do you submit to these charges, and promise to support these regulations, as masters have done in all ages before you ?

The Master is to answer, *I do.*

The presiding officer then addresses him :

BROTHER A. B.

In consequence of your cheerful conformity to the charges and regulations of the order, you are now to be installed Master of this * lodge, in full confidence of your care, skill, and capacity to govern the same.

[The new master is then regularly invested with the insignia of his office, and the furniture and implements of his lodge.]

* If this lodge is installed for the first time, it is called *This new Lodge.*"

The various implements of the profession are emblematical of our conduct in life, and upon this occasion are carefully enumerated.

The *Holy Writings*, that great light in masonry, will guide you to all truth: it will direct your path to the temple of happiness, and point out to you the whole duty of man.

The *Square* teaches us to regulate our actions by rule and line, and harmonize our conduct by the principles of morality and virtue.

The *Compasses* teach us to limit our desires in every station; that, rising to eminence by merit, we may live respected, and die regretted.

The *Rule* directs that we should punctually observe our duty; press forward in the path of virtue, and, neither inclining to the right nor to the left, in all our actions have (eternity) in view.

The *Line* teaches the criterion of moral rectitude, to avoid dissimulation in conversation and action, and to direct our steps to the path which leads to a glorious immortality.

The *Book of Constitutions*, you are to search at all times. Cause it to be read in your lodge, that none may pretend ignorance of the excellent precepts it enjoins.

You will also receive in charge the *By-Laws* of your .odge, which you are to see carefully and punctually executed.

CHARGE upon the Installation of the Master of a Lodge.

WORSHIPFUL MASTER:

Being appointed Master of this lodge, you cannot be insensible of the obligations which devolve on you, as their head; nor of your responsibility for the faithful discharge of the important duties annexed to your appointment.

The honor, reputation, and usefulness of your lodge, will materially depend on the skill and assiduity with which you manage its concerns; while the happiness of its members will be generally promoted, in proportion to the zeal and ability with which you propagate the genuine principles of our institution.

For a pattern of imitation, consider the great luminary of nature, which, rising in the *East*, regularly diffuses light and lustre to all within its circle. In like manner, it is your province to spread and communicate light and instruction to the brethren of your lodge. Forcibly impress upon them the dignity and high importance of masonry, and seriously admonish them never to disgrace it. Charge them to practise out of the lodge, those duties which are taught in it; and by amiable, discreet, and virtuous conduct, to convince mankind of the goodness of the institution; so that, when any one is said to be a member of it, the world may know that he is one to whom the burthened heart may pour out its sorrows; to whom distress may prefer its suit; whose hand is guided by justice, and his heart expanded by benevolence. In short, by a diligent observance of the by-laws of your lodge, the constitutions of masonry, and. above al the *Holy Scriptures*, which are given as a rule and guide to your faith, you will be enabled to acquit yourself with honor and reputation, and lay up a *crown of rejoicing*, which shall continue when time shall be no more.

6*

The subordinate officers are then severally invested by the presiding officer, who delivers each of them a short Charge, as follows : viz.

The Senior Warden.

BROTHER C D.

You are appointed Senior Warden of this lodge, and are now invested with the ensign of your office.

The *Level* demonstrates that we are descended from the same stock, partake of the same nature, and share the same hope ; and though distinctions among men are necessary to preserve subordination, yet no eminence of station should make us forget that we are brethren ; for he who is placed on the lowest spoke of fortune's wheel, may be entitled to our regard ; because a time will come, and the wisest knows not how soon, when all distinction, but that of goodness, shall cease ; and death, the grand leveller of human greatness, reduce us to the same state.

Your regular attendance on our stated meetings, is essentially necessary. In the absence of the master, you are to govern this lodge; in his presence, you are to assist him in the government of it. I firmly rely on your knowledge of masonry, and attachment to the lodge, for the faithful discharge of the duties of this important trust.—*Look well to the West !*

The Junior Warden.

BROTHER E. F.

You are appointed Junior Warden of this lodge, and are now invested with the badge of your office.

The *Plumb* admonishes us to walk uprightly in our several stations; to hold the scales of justice in equal poise; to observe the just medium between intemperance and pleasure : and to make our passions and prejudices coincide with the line of our duty.

To you is committed the superintendence ot the craft, during the hours of refreshment : it is therefore indispensably necessary, that you should not only be temperate and discreet, in the indulgence of your own inclinations, but carefully observe that none of the craft be suffered to convert the purposes of refreshment into intemperance and excess.

Your regular and punctual attendance is particularly requested; and I have no doubt that you will faithfully execute the duty which you owe to your present appointment.—*Look well to the South !*

The Treasurer.

BROTHER G. H.

You are appointed Treasurer of this lodge. It is your duty to receive all monies from the hands of the Secretary, make due entries of the same, and pay them out by order of the Worshipful Master and the consent of the lodge.

1 trust your regard for the fraternity will prompt you to the faithful discharge of the duties of your office.

The Secretary.

BROTHER J. K.

You are appointed Secretary of this lodge. It is your duty to observe all the proceedings of the lodge; make a fair record of all things proper to be written; to receive all monies due the lodge, and pay them over to the Treasurer, and take his receipt for the same.

Your good inclination to masonry and this lodge, I hope, will induce you to discharge your office with fidelity; and by so doing, you will merit the esteem and applause of your brethren.

Senior and Junior Deacons.

BROTHERS L. M. AND N. O.

You are appointed Deacons of this lodge. To you, with such assistance as may be necessary, is entrusted the examination of visitors. —It is also your province to attend on the master and wardens, and to act as their proxies in the active duties of the lodge; such as in the reception of candidates into the different degrees of masonry, and in the immediate practice of our rites. The Square and Compasses, as badges of your office, I trust to your care, no doubting your vigilance and attention.

The Stewards.

BROTHERS P. Q. AND R. S.

You are appointed Stewards of this lodge. The duties of your office are, to assist in the collection of dues and subscriptions; to keep an account of the lodge expenses; to see that the tables are properly furnished at refreshment, and that every brother is suitably provided for:

and generally to assist the deacons and other officers in performing their duties.

Your regular and early attendance will afford the best proof of your zeal and attachment to the lodge.

The Tyler.

BROTHER:

You are appointed Tyler of this lodge; and I invest you with the implement of your office. As the sword is placed in the hands of the Tyler, to enable him effectually to guard against the approach of cowans and evesdroppers, and suffer none to pass or repass but such as are duly qualified; so it should morally serve as a constant admonition to us, to set a guard at the entrance of our thoughts; to place a watch at the door of our lips; to post a sentinel at the avenue of our actions: thereby excluding every unqualified and unworthy thought, word, and deed; and preserving consciences void of offence towards God and towards man.

Your early and punctual attendance will afford the best proof of your zeal for the institution.

CHARGE to the Brethren of the Lodge.

Such is the nature of our constitution, that as some must of necessity rule and teach, so others must of course learn to submit and obey. Humility in both is an essential duty. The officers who are appointed to govern your lodge, are sufficiently conversant with the rules of propriety, and the laws of the institution, to avoid

exceeding the powers with which they are entrusted; and you are of too generous dispositions
to envy their preferment. I therefore trust that
you will have but one aim, to please each other,
and unite in the grand design of being happy,
and communicating happiness.

Finally, my brethren, as this association has
been formed and perfected with so much unanimity and concord, in which we greatly rejoice,
so may it long continue. May you long enjoy
every satisfaction and delight which disinterested friendship can afford. May kindness and
brotherly affection distinguish your conduct, as
men, and as masons. Within your peaceful
walls, may your children's children celebrate
with joy and gratitude, the transactions of this
auspicious solemnity. And may *the tenets of
our profession* be transmitted through your
lodge, pure and unimpaired, from generation to
generation.

12. The Grand Marshal then proclaims the New
Lodge in the following manner, viz.:

In the name of the Most Worshipful Grand
Lodge of the State of ——, I proclaim this new
Lodge by the name of —— Lodge, No. —, to be
legally constituted, consecrated, and the officers
thereof duly installed.

13. A piece of Music is then performed.

14. Benediction.

The procession is then formed, and returns in du
form to the hall whence it set out.

The W. Master having been previously inducted into the *Oriental Chair of Solomon*, all but master masons are caused to retire.

A procession is then formed, and passes three times round the hall; and upon passing the master, pays him due homage by the usual honors, in the different degrees.

During the procession passing round, the following song is sung:

HAIL MASONRY divine!
Glory of ages shine;
   Long may'st thou reign!
Where'er thy lodges stand,
May they have great command
And always grace the land,
   Thou Art divine;

Great fabrics still arise,
And grace the azure skies;
   Great are thy schemes;
Thy noble orders are
Matchless, beyond compare;
No art with thee can share,
   Thou Art divine.

Hiram, the architect,
Did all the craft direct
   How they should build:
Sol'mon, great Israel's king,
Did mighty blessings bring,
And left us room to sing,
   Hail, royal Art!   *Chorus, three times.*

The Grand Master then directs the Grand Marshal to form the procession; when the Grand Lodge walk to their own hall, and both Lodges are closed in due form.

SECTION THIRD.

This section contains the ceremony observed on laying the Foundation Stones of Public Structures.

This ceremony is conducted by the M. W. Grand Master and his officers, assisted by such officers and members of subordinate Lodges, as can conveniently attend. The chief magistrate, and other civil officers of the place where the building is to be erected, also generally attend on the occasion.

At the time appointed, the Grand Lodge is convened in some suitable place. A band of martial music is provided, and the brethren appear in the insignia of the order.

The Lodge is then opened by the Grand Master, and the rules for regulating the procession are read by the Grand Secretary. The Lodge is then adjourned; after which, the procession sets out in *due form*, in the following order:—

Procession at Laying Foundation Stones.

Two Tylers with drawn Swords;
Tyler of the older Lodge with do.,
Two Stewards of the older Lodge;
Entered Apprentices;
Fellow Crafts;
Master Masons;
Past Secretaries;
Past Treasurers;
Past Junior Wardens;
Past Senior Wardens;
Mark Masters;
Past Masters;
Royal Arch Masons;
Select Masters;
Knights Templars;
Masters;
Music;
Grand Tyler with a drawn Sword;
Grand Stewards with white Rods;

Marshal.

A Past Master with a Golden Vessel containing
Corn;
Principal Architect, with Square, Level, and Plumb;
Two Past Masters with Silver Vessels, one contain-
ing Wine, and the other oil;
Grand Secretary and Treasurer,
The Five Orders;
One large Light, borne by a Past Master;
The Holy Bible, Square and Compasses, borne by a
Master of a Lodge, supported by two Stew-
ards on the right and left;
Two large Lights, borne by two Past Masters;
Grand Chaplain;
Clergy and Orator;
Grand Wardens;
Deputy Grand Master;
The Master of the oldest Lodge, carrying the Book
of Constitutions on a velvet cushion;
Grand Deacons with black Rods, on a line seven
feet apart;
Grand Master;
Two Stewards with white Rods;
Grand Sword-Bearer with drawn Sword.

A Triumphal Arch is usually erected at the place
where the ceremony is to be performed. The procession passes through the arch; and the brethren re-
pairing to their stands, the Grand Master and his
officers take their places on a temporary platform,
covered with carpet. The Grand Master commands
silence. An Ode on Masonry is sung; after which,
the necessary preparations are made for laying the
stone, on which is engraved the year of masonry, the
name of the Grand Master, &c. &c.

The stone is raised up, by means of an engine
erected for that purpose, and the Grand Chaplain or
Orator repeats a short prayer.

The Grand Treasurer then, by the Grand Master's
7

command, places under the stone various sorts of coin and medals of the present age. Solemn music is introduced and the stone is let down into its place.

The principal Architect then presents the working tools to the Grand Master, who applies the *plumb*, *square*, and *level*, to the stone, in their proper positions, and pronounces it to be WELL FORMED, TRUE and TRUSTY.

The Golden and Silver Vessels are next brought to the table, and delivered; the former to the Deputy Grand Master, and the latter to the Grand Wardens, who successively present them to the Grand Master; and he, according to ancient ceremony, pours the corn, the wine, and the oil, which they contain, on the stone; saying,

"May the all-bounteous Author of Nature bless the inhabitants of this place with all the necessaries, conveniences and comforts of life; assist in the erection and completion of this building; protect the workmen against every accident, and long preserve this structure from decay: and grant to us all, a supply of the CORN of *nourishment*, the WINE of *refreshment*, and the OIL of *joy!*

"So mote it be. Amen."

He then strikes the stone thrice with the mallet; and the *public grand honors of Masonry are given.* The Grand Master then delivers over to the Architect the various implements of architecture, entrusting him with the superintendence and direction of the work; after which, he reäscends the platform, and an Oration suitable to the occasion is delivered.

A voluntary Collection is made for the needy workmen; and the sum collected is placed upon the stone by the Grand Treasurer.

A suitable Song in honor of Masonry concludes the ceremony; after which, the procession returns to the place whence it set out, and the Lodge is closed in due form.

SECTION FOURTH.

The fourth section contains the ceremony observed at the Dedication of the Free-Masons' Halls.

On the day appointed, the Grand Master and his officers, accompanied by the members of the Grand Lodge, meet in a convenient room near the place where the ceremony is to be performed, and open in *due and ample form*, in the third degree of masonry.

The Master of the Lodge to which the Hall to be dedicated belongs, being present, addresses the Grand Master as follows:

MOST WORSHIPFUL,

The brethren of —— Lodge, being animated with a desire of promoting the honor and interest of the craft, have, at great pains and expense, erected a Masonic Hall, for their convenience and accommodation. They are desirous that the same should be examined by the M. W. GRAND LODGE; and if it should meet their approbation, that it should be solemnly dedicated to masonic purposes, agreeably to *ancient form*.

The Grand Master then directs the Grand Marshal to form the procession, when they move forward to the Hall to be dedicated. On entering, the music will continue while the procession marches three times round the hall.

The lodge, or flooring, is then placed in the centre, and the Grand Master having taken the chair, under a canopy of state, the Grand Officers, and the Masters and Wardens of the Lodges, repair to the places previously prepared for their reception. The three

Lights, and the Gold and Silver Pitchers, with the corn, wine and oil, are placed round the Lodge, at the head of which stands the Altar, with the Holy Bible open, and the Square and Compasses laid thereon, with the Charter, Book of Constitutions, and By-Laws.

An anthem is sung, and an Exordium on Masonry given; after which, the Architect addresses the Grand Master as follows:

MOST WORSHIPFUL,

Having been entrusted with tne superintend-ence and management of the workmen em-ployed in the construction of this edifice; and having, according to the best of my ability, ac-complished the task assigned me; I now re-turn my thanks for the honor of this appoint-ment, and beg leave to surrender up the imple-ments which were committed to my care, when the foundation of this fabric was laid; humbly hoping, that the exertions which have been made on this occasion, will be crowned with your approbation, and that of the Most Wor-shipful Grand Lodge.

To which the Grand Master makes the following reply:

BROTHER ARCHITECT,

The skill and fidelity displayed in the execu-tion of the trust reposed in you, at the com-mencement of this undertaking, have secured the entire approbation of the Grand Lodge· and they sincerely pray, that this edifice may continue a lasting monument of the taste, spirit, and liberality of its founders.

An Ode in honor of Masonry is sung, accompanied with instrumental music.

Th₂ Deputy Grand Master then rises, and says ·

MOST WORSHIPFUL,

The hall in which we are now assembled, and the plan upon which it has been constructed, having met with your approbation, it is the desire of the fraternity that it should now be dedicated, according to ancient form and usage.

Whereupon the Grand Master requests all to retire, but such as are Master Masons. A procession is then formed in the following order, viz.:

Grand Sword-Bearer ;
A Past Master, with a Light ;
A Past Master, with a Bible, Square, and Compasses, on a velvet cushion ;
Two Past Masters, each with a Light ;
Grand Secretary and Treasurer, with Emblems ;
Grand Junior Warden, with Pitcher of Corn :
Grand Senior Warden, with Pitcher of Wine ;
Deputy Grand Master, with Pitcher of Oil ;
Grand Master ;
Two Stewards with rods ;

All the other brethren keep their places, and assist in performing an Ode, which continues during the procession, excepting only at the intervals of dedication. The Lodge being uncovered, the first time passing round it, the Junior Grand Warden presents the Pitcher of Corn to the Grand Master, who pours it out upon the Lodge, at the same time pronouncing,

7*

"In the name of the Great JEHOVAH, to whom ꞵe all honor and glory, I do solemnly dedicate his Hall to MASONRY."

The grand honors are given.

The second time passing round the Lodge, the Grand Senior Warden presents the pitcher of Wine to the Grand Master, who sprinkles 't upon the Lodge, at the same time saying,

"In the name of the HOLY SAINT JOHNS, I do solemnly DEDICATE this Hall to VIRTUE."

The grand honors are twice given.

The third time passing round the Lodge, the Dep uty Grand Master presents the Grand Master with the pitcher of Oil, who sprinkles it upon the Lodge, saying,

"In the name of the whole Fraternity, I do solemnly dedicate this Hall to UNIVERSAL BENEVOLENCE."

The grand honors are thrice given

A solemn Invocation is made to the Throne of Grace, by the Grand Chaplain, and an Anthem sung; after which, the Lodge is covered, and the Grand Master retires to his Chair.

An Oration is then delivered, and the ceremonies conclude with music.

The Grand Lodge is then closed in due and ample form.

SECTION FIFTH.

This section contains the ceremony observed at Funerals, according to ancient custom; together with the Service used on such occasions.

No mason can be interred with the formalities of he order, unless he has been raised to the sublime degree of Master Mason; as no Fellow Craft or Entered Apprentices are entitled to funeral obsequies, nor to attend the masonic procession, on such occasions.

All the brethren, who walk in procession, should observe, as much as possible an uniformity in their dress.   Decent mourning around the left arm, with white stockings, gloves and aprons, are most suitable.

The Funeral Service.

The brethren being assembled at the lodge-room, (or some other convenient place,) the presiding officer opens the Lodge in the third degree, with the usual forms; and having stated the purpose of the meeting, the service begins :—

Master. "What man is he that liveth, and shall not see death? Shall he deliver his soul from the hand of the grave?"

Response. "Man walketh in a vain shadow; he heapeth up riches, and cannot tell who shall gather them."

Master. "When he dieth he shall carry nothing away; his glory shall not descend after him."

Response. "Naked he came into the world, and naked he must return."

Master. "The Lord gave, and the Lord hath taken away : blessed be the name of the Lord !"

The Master then taking the *roll* in his hand, says,

"Let us live and die like the righteous, that our last end may be like his !"

The Brethren answer, "God is our God for ever and ever; he will be our guide even unto death !"

The Master then records the name and age of the deceased upon the *roll*, and says,

"Almighty Father! in thy hands we leave with humble submission the soul of our deceased Brother."

The Brethren answer three times, (giving the *grand honors* each time,)

"The will of God is accomplished! So mote it be. Amen."

The Master then deposits the *roll* in the *archives*, and repeats the following Prayer:—

"Most glorious God! author of all good, and giver of all mercy! pour down thy blessings upon us, and strengthen our solemn engagements with the ties of sincere affection! May the present instance of mortality remind us of our approaching fate, and draw our attention toward thee, the only refuge in time of need! that, when the awful moment shall arrive, that we are about to quit this transitory scene, the enlivening prospect of thy mercy, through the Redeemer, may dispel the gloom of death; and after our departure hence in peace, and in thy favor, may we be received into thine everlasting kingdom, to enjoy, in union with the souls of our departed friends, the just reward of a pious and virtuous life. Amen."

A procession is then formed, which moves to the house of the deceased, and from thence to the place of interment.

Order of Procession at a Funeral.

Tyler with a drawn Sword;

Stewards with white Rods;

Musicians. (if they are masons,) otherwise they follow the Tyler;

Master Masons.

Senior and Junior Deacons;

Secretary and Treasurer;

Senior and Junior Wardens;

Mark Masters;

Past Masters;

Royal Arch Masons;

Select Masters;

Knights Templars;

The Holy Writings, on a cushion, covered with
black cloth, carried by the oldest (or some
suitable) Member of the Lodge;

The Master;

Clergy;

Marshal;

The Body, with the   insignia placed thereon.

Pall Bearers.   Pall Bearers.

When the procession arrives at the church-yard,
the members of the lodge form a circle round the
grave; and the clergymen and officers of the lodge
take their station at the head of the grave, and the
mourners at the foot.   The service is resumed, and
the following Exhortation is given :—

"Here we view a striking instance of the uncertainty of life, and the vanity of all human pursuits. The last offices paid to the dead, are only useful as lectures to the living: —from them we are to derive instruction, and to consider every solemnity of this kind as a summons to prepare for our approaching dissolution.

"Notwithstanding the various mementos of mortality, with which we daily meet; notwith-standing Death has established his empire over all the works of nature; yet, through some unaccountable infatuation, we forget that we are born to die; we go on from one design to another, add hope to hope, and lay out plans for the employment of many years, till we are suddenly alarmed with the approach of Death, when we least expect him, and at an hour which we probably conclude to be the meridian of our existence.

"What are all the externals of majesty, the pride of wealth, or charms of beauty, when Nature has paid her just debt?—Fix your eyes on the last scene, and view life stript of her ornaments, and exposed in her natural mean-ness; you will then be convinced of the futil-ity of those empty delusions. In the grave, all fallacies are detected, all ranks are levelled, and all distinctions are done away.

"While we drop the sympathetic tear over the grave of our deceased friend, let charity incline us to throw a veil over his foibles whatever they may have been, and not withhold from his memory the praise that his virtues may have claimed. Suffer the apologies of human nature to plead in his behalf. Perfection on earth has never been attained;—the wisest, as well as the best of men, have erred.

"Let the present example excite our most serious thoughts, and strengthen our resolutions of amendment. As life is uncertain, and all earthly pursuits are vain, let us no longer postpone the all-important concern of preparing for eternity; but embrace the happy moment, while time and opportunity offer, to provide against the great change, when all the pleasures of this world shall cease to delight, and the reflections of a virtuous and holy life yield the only comfort and consolation. Thus our expectations will not be frustrated, nor we hurried unprepared into the presence of an all-wise and powerful Judge, to whom the secrets of all hearts are known.

"Let us, while in this state of existence, support with propriety the character of our profession, advert to the nature of our solemn ties, and pursue with assiduity the sacred tenets of our order. Then, with becoming reverence, let us seek the favor of the ETERNAL GOD, through the merits of his SON our Saviour, so that when the awful moment of Death arrives, be it soon or late, we may be enabled to prosecute our journey without dread or apprehension, to that far distant country, whence no traveller returns."

The following invocations are then made by the Master:

Master. "May we be true and faithful; and may we live and die in love!"
Answer. "So mote it be."
Master. "May we profess what is good and always act agreeably to our profession!"
Answer. "So mote it be."
Master. "May the Lord bless us and prosper us, and may all our good intentions be crowned with success!"
Answer. "So mote it be."
Master. "Glory be to God in the highest; on earth peace! good will towards men!"
Answer. "So mote it be, now, from henceforth, and for evermore. Amen."

The apron is taken off from the coffin and handed to the Master—the coffin is deposited in the grave—and the Master says:—

" This Lamb Skin, or white leather Apron, is an emblem of Innocence, and the badge of a Mason, more ancient than the golden fleece or Roman eagle; more honorable than the star and garter, when worthily worn. [*The Master then deposits it in the grave.*] This emblem I now deposit in the grave of our deceased Brother. By this we are reminded of the universal dominion of Death. The arm of Friendship cannot oppose the King of Terrors nor the charms of innocence elude his grasp. This grave, that coffin, this circle of mourning friends, remind us that we too are mortal:

soon shall our bodies moulder to dust. Then how important for us that we should know that our REDEEMER liveth, and that he shall stand at the latter day upon the Earth. [*The Master, holding the evergreen in his hand, continues,*] This *evergreen* is an emblem of our faith in the immortality of the soul. By this we are reminded that we have an immortal part within us, which shall survive the grave, and which shall never, never, never die. Though like our Brother whose remains now lie before us, we shall soon be clothed in the habiliments of DEATH and deposited in the silent tomb, yet through the mediation of a divine and ascended Savior, we may confidently hope that our souls will bloom in Eternal Spring."

The brethren then move in procession round the place of interment, and severally drop the sprig of evergreen into the grave; after which, *the public grand honors are given.*

The Master then continues the ceremony at the grave, in the following words:

"From time immemorial, it has been the custom among the fraternity of free and accepted masons, at the request of a brother, to accompany his corpse to the place of interment, and there to deposit his remains with the usual formalities.

"In conformity to this usage, and at the request of our deceased brother, whose mem-

8

ory we revere, and whose loss we now deplore, we have assembled in the character of masons, and to offer up to his memory, before the world, the last tribute of our affection; thereby demonstrating the sincerity of our past esteem, and our steady attachment to the principles of the order.

"The great Creator having been pleased, out of his mercy, to remove our brother from the cares and troubles of a transitory existence, to a state of eternal duration, and thereby to weaken the chain, by which we are united man to man; may we, who survive him, anticipate our approaching fate, and be more strongly cemented in the ties of union and friendship; that, during the short space allotted to our present existence, we may wisely and usefully employ our time; and, in the reciprocal intercourse of kind and friendly acts, mutually promote the welfare and happiness of each other.

"Unto the grave we have resigned the body of our deceased friend, earth to earth, dust to dust, ashes to ashes, there to remain until the trump shall sound on the resurrection morn. We can cheerfully leave him in the hands of a Being who has done all things well; who is glorious in holiness, fearful in praises, doing wonders.   Then let us all so improve this solemn warning, that on the great day of account we may receive from the compassionate Judge, the welcome invitation, "Come, ye blessed of my Father, inherit the kingdom prepared for you from the foundation of the world."

"So mote it be. Amen."

"Almighty and eternal God, in whom we live and move, and have our being—and before whom all men must appear in the judgment day to give an account of their deeds in life; we, who are daily exposed to the flying shafts of death, and now surround the grave of our fallen brother; most earnestly beseech thee to impress deeply on our minds the solemnities of this day, as well as the lamentable occurrence that has occasioned them. Here may we be forcibly reminded, that in the midst of life we are in death, and that whatever *elevation* of character we may have attained; however *upright* and *square* the course we have pursued; yet shortly must we all submit as victims of its destroying power, and endure the humbling *level* of the tomb, until the last loud trump shall sound the summons of our *resurrection* from mortality and *corruption.*

"May we have thy divine assistance, O merciful God, to redeem our misspent time; and in the discharge of the important duties thou hast assigned us in the erection of our moral edifice, may we have *wisdom* from on high to direct us, *strength* commensurate with our *task* to support us, and the *beauty* of holiness to adorn and render all our performances acceptable in the sight: and when our work is done, and our bodies mingle with the *mother earth,* may our souls, disengaged from their cumbrous dusι flourish and bloom in eternal day; and enjoy that rest which thou hast prepared for all good and faithful servants, in that spiritual house, not made with hands, eternal in the heavens, through the great Redeemer. Amen."

"So mote it be. Amen."

The procession then returns in form to the place whence it set out, where the necessary duties are complied with, and the lodge is closed in the third degree.

NOTE. *If the Grand Master attends, and presides at any ceremony, it is said to be performed in* AMPLE FORM;—*if a subordinate officer of the Grand Lodge, in* DUE FORM;—*if vested in the master of a subordinate Lodge, in* FORM

MOST EXCELLENT MASTER'S DEGREE.

None but those who have been inducted into the *Oriental Chair of Solomon*, by the unanimous suffrages of their brethren, can be admitted to this 'egree of masonry.

When the temple of Jerusalem was finished, and the cap-stone celebrated, with great joy, King Solomon admitted to this degree, only those who had proved themselves worthy, by their virtue, skill, and inflexible fidelity to the craft. The duties incumbent on a Most Excellent Master are such, that he should have a perfect knowledge of all the preceding degrees.

The following Psalm is read at opening.

PSALM xxiv.

"The earth is the Lord's and the fulness thereof; the world, and they that dwell therein. For he hath founded it upon the seas, and established it upon the floods.—Who shall ascend into the hill of the Lord? or who shall stand in his holy place? He that hath clean hands and a pure heart; who hath not lifted up his soul unto vanity, nor sworn deceitfully. He shall receive the blessing from the Lord, and righteousness from the God of his salvation. This is the generation of them that seek him, that seek

8*

thy face, O Jacob: Selah. Lift up your heads, O ye gates; and be ye lifted up, ye everlasting doors, and the King of Glory shall come in. Who is this King of Glory? The Lord, strong and mighty; the Lord, mighty in battle. Lift up your heads O ye gates; even lift them up, ye everlasting doors, and the King of Glory shall come in. Who is this King of Glory? The Lord of Hosts, he is the King of Glory. Selah."

The following Psalm is read during the ceremony of receiving a candidate in this degree.

Psalm cxxii.

"I was glad when they said unto me, Let us go into the house of the Lord. Our feet shall stand within thy gates, O Jerusalem. Jerusalem is builded as a city that is compact together: whither the tribes go up, the tribes of the Lord, unto the testimony of Israel, to give thanks unto the name of the Lord. For there are set thrones of judgment, the thrones of the house of David.

"Pray for the peace of Jerusalem: they shall prosper that love thee. Peace be within thy walls, and prosperity within thy palaces. For my brethren and companions' sakes, I will now say, Peace be within thee. Because of the house of the Lord our God, I will seek thy good."

The following song is sung with solemn ceremony.

MOST EXCELLENT MASTER'S SONG.

Andante Moderato.

ALL hail to the morning, That bids us re-joice;

ALL hail to the morning, That bids us re-joice;

The tem-ple's com-ple-ted, Ex-alt high each voice.

The tem-ple's com-ple-ted, Ex-alt high each voice.

Cres.

The capstone is finish'd, Our la - bour is o'er;

The capstone is finish'd, Our la - bour is o'er;

The sound of the ga-vel shall hail us no more.

The sound of the ga-vel shall hail us no more.

For.

To the Power Almighty, who ev-er has gui-ded

To the Power Almighty, who ev-er has gui-ded

The tribes of old   Is-rael, ex - alt-ing their fame,

The tribes of old   Is-rael, ex - alt-ing their fame;

To Him, who hath govern'd our hearts un - di - vided,

To Him, who hath govern'd our hearts un - di - vided,

Fortiss.

Let's send forth our voices to praise his great Name.

Let's send forth our voices to praise his great Name.

Companions assemble
  On this joyful day;
(The occasion is glorious,
  The key-stone to lay :
Fulfill'd is the promise,
  By the ANCIENT OF DAYS,
To bring forth the cap-stone
  With shouting and praise

[*Ceremonies.*]

There is no more occasion for level or plumb-line
For trowel or gavel, for compass or square ·
Our works are completed, the ark safely seated,
And we shall be greeted as workmen most rare.

Now those that are worthy,
  Our toils who have shar'd,
And prov'd themselves faithful,
  Shall meet their reward.
Their virtue and knowledge
  Industry and skill,
Have our approbation,
  Have gained our good will.

We accept and receive them, Most Excellent Masters
Invested with honors, and power to preside ;
Among worthy crafts-men, wherever assembled,
The knowledge of masons to spread far and wide.

ALMIGHTY JEHOVAH !
  Descend now and fill
This Lodge with thy glory,
  Our hearts with good will !
Preside at our meetings,
  Assist us to find
True pleasure in teaching
  Good will to mankind.

Thy *wisdom* inspired the great institution,
Thy *strength* shall support it till nature expire ;
And when the creation shall fall into ruin,
Its *beauty* shall rise through the midst of the fire

The ceremony closes with the following passage:

2 Chron. vii. 1—4.

Now when Solomon had made an end of praying, the fire came down from heaven, and consumed the burnt offering and sacrifices; and the glory of the Lord filled the house. And the priest could not enter into the house of the Lord, because the glory of the Lord had filled the Lord's house.

And when all the children of Israel saw how the fire came down, and the glory of the Lord upon the house, they bowed themselves with their faces to the ground upon the pavement, and worshipped, and praised the Lord, saying, For he is good; for his mercy endureth forever.

The following Psalm is read at closing.

Psalm xxiii.

"The Lord is my shepherd; I shall not want. He maketh me to lie down in green pastures · he leadeth me beside the still waters. He restoreth my soul; he leadeth me in the paths of righteousness for his name's sake. Yea, though I walk through the valley of the shadow of death, I will fear no evil: for thou art with me; thy rod and thy staff they comfort me. Thou preparest a table before me in the presence of mine enemies; thou anointest my head with oil; my cup runneth over. Surely goodness and mercy shall follow me all the days of my life, and I will dwell in the house of the Lord for ever."

CHARGE to a Brother who is received and acknowl edged as a most excellent master.

" BROTHER,

" Your admittance to this degree of masonry, is a proof of the good opinion the brethren of this lodge entertain of your masonic abilities Let this consideration induce you to be careful of forfeiting, by misconduct, and inattention to our rules, that esteem which has raised you to the rank you now possess.

" It is one of your great duties as a most excellent master, to dispense light and truth to the uninformed mason ; and I need not remind you of the impossibility of complying with this obligation without possessing an accurate acquaintance with the lectures of each degree.

" If you are not already completely conversant in all the degrees heretofore conferred on you, remember, that an indulgence, prompted by a belief that you will apply yourself with double diligence to make yourself so, has induced the brethren to accept you.

" Let it therefore be your unremitting study, to acquire such a degree of knowledge and in formation, as shall enable you to discharge with propriety, the various duties incumbent on you, and to preserve unsullied, the title now conferred upon you, of a MOST EXCELLENT MASTER."

A Description of Solomon's Temple.

This structure, for beauty, magnificence, and expense, exceeded any building which was ever erected. It was built of large stones of white marble, curiously

hewn, and so artfully joined together, that they appeared like one entire stone. Its inner *Walls, Beams,
Posts, Doors, Floors,* and *Ceilings,* were made of
cedar and olive wood, and planks of fir; which were
entirely covered with plates of gold, with various
beaut'ful engravings, and adorned with precious jewels of many splendid colors. The nails which fas-
tened those plates were also of gold, with heads of
curious workmanship. The roof was of olive wood
covered with gold; and when the sun shone thereon
the reflection from it was of such a *refulgent splen-
dour,* that it dazzled the eyes of all who beheld it.
The court in which the temple stood, and the courts
without, were adorned on all sides with stately buildings, and cloisters; and the gates entering therein,
were exquisitely beautiful and elegant. The vessels
consecrated to the perpetual use of the temple, were
suited to the magnificence of the edifice in which
they were deposited and used.

Josephus states, that there were one hundred and
forty thousand of those vessels, which were made of
gold and one million three hundred and forty thou
sand of silver; ten thousand vestments for the priests
made of silk, with purple girdles; and two millions
of purple vestments for the singers. There were also
two hundred thousand trumpets, and forty thousand
other musical instruments, made use of in the temple,
and in worshipping God.

According to the most accurate computation of the
number of talents of gold, silver, and brass, laid out
upon the temple, the sum amounts to six thousand
nine hundred and four millions, eight hundred and
twenty-two thousand and five hundred pounds sterling; and the jewels are reckoned to exceed this sum
The gold vessels are estimated at five hundred and
forty-five millions, two hundred and ninety-six thousand, two hundred and three pounds, and four shillings sterling; and the silver ones, at four hundred
and thirty-nine millions, three hundred and forty-four
thousand pounds sterling; amounting in all, to nine
hundred and eighty-four millions, six hundred and

9

thirty thousand, two hundred and thirty pounds, four
shillings. In addition to this, there were expenses for
workmen, and for materials brought from Mount Libanus, and the quarries of Zeradatha. There were
ten thousand men per month in Lebanon, employed
in falling and preparing the timbers for the craftsmen
to hew them; seventy thousand to carry burdens;
eighty thousand to hew the stones and timber; and
three thousand three hundred overseers of the work;
who were all employed for seven years; to whom,
besides their wages and diet, King Solomon gave, as
a free gift, six millions, seven hundred and thirty-
three thousand, nine hundred and seventy-seven
pounds.

The treasure left by David, towards carrying on
this noble and glorious work, is reckoned to be nine
hundred and eleven millions, four hundred and six-
teen thousand, two hundred and seven pounds; to
which, if we add King Solomon's annual revenue,
his trading to Ophir for gold, and the presents made
him by all the earth, as mentioned 1 Kings x. 24, 25,
we shall not wonder at his being able to carry on so
expensive a work; nor can we, without impiety,
question its surpassing all other structures, since we
are assured that it was built by the immediate direction of HEAVEN.

ROYAL ARCH DEGREE.

This degree is more august, sublime, and important, than all which precede it. It impresses on our minds a belief of the being and existence of the Supreme Grand High Priest of our Salvation; who is without beginning of days or end of years; and forcibly reminds us of the reverence due to his Holy Name.

In this degree is brought to light many essentials which are of importance to the craft, that were concealed in darkness for the space of four hundred and seventy years; and without a knowledge of which the masonic character cannot be complete.

SECTION FIRST.

This section explains the mode of government in this degree; it designates the appellation, number and situation of the several officers, and points out the purpose and duty of their respective stations. The various colors of their banners are designated, and the morals to which they allude are introduced and explained.

The following passage of scripture is read at opening:

2 Thess. iii. 6—18.

Now we command you, brethren, in the name of our Lord Jesus Christ, that ye withdraw from every brother that walketh disorderly, and not after the tradition which ye received of us.

For yourselves know how ye ought to follow
us: for we behaved not ourselves disorderly
among you; neither did we eat any man's
bread for nought; but wrought with labor and
travail night and day, that we might not be
chargeable to any of you; not because we have
not power, but to make ourselves an ensample
unto you to follow us. For even when we
were with you, this we commanded you, that
if any would not work, neither should he eat.
For we hear that there are some which walk
among you disorderly, working not at all, but
are busybodies. Now them that are such we
command and exhort, by our Lord Jesus Christ,
that with quietness they work, and eat their
own bread. But ye, brethren, be not weary in
well doing. And if any man obey not our
word by this epistle, note that man, and have
no company with him, that he may be ashamed.
Yet count him not as an enemy, but admonish
him as a brother. Now the Lord of peace himself give you peace always by all means. The
Lord be with you all.

The salutation of Paul with mine own hand,
which is the token in every epistle: so I write.
The grace of our Lord Jesus Christ be with you
all. Amen.

SECTION SECOND.

This section contains much valuable historical information, and exhibits to our view, in striking col
ors, that prosperity and happiness are ever the ulti
mate consequences of virtue and justice; while disgrace and ruin invariably follow the practices of vice
and immorality.

The following charges and passages of Scripture are introduced during the ceremony of Exaltation.

ISAIAH xliii. 16.

"I will bring the blind by a way that they knew not; I will lead them in paths that they have not known; I will make darkness light before them, and crooked things straight. These things will I do unto them, and will not forsake them."

Prayer used at the Exaltation of a Royal Arch Mason.

O thou eternal and omnipotent JEHOVAH, the glorious and everlasting I AM, permit us, thy frail, dependent and needy creatures, in the name of our *Most Excellent and Supreme High Priest,* to approach thy divine majesty. And do thou, who sittest *between the Cherubim,* incline thine ear to the voice of our praises, and of our supplication; and vouchsafe to commune with us from off the *mercy seat.* We humbly adore and worship thy unspeakable perfections, and thy unbounded goodness and benevolence. We bless thee, that when man had sinned, and fallen from his innocence and happiness, thou didst still leave unto him the powers of reasoning, and the capacity of improvement and of pleasure. We adore thee, that amidst the pains and calamities of our present state so many means of refreshment and satisfaction are afforded us, while travelling the *rugged path of life.* And O, thou who didst aforetime appear unto thy servant Moses *in a flame of fire, out of the midst of a bush,* enkindle,

9*

we beseech thee, in each of our hearts a flame
of devotion to thee, of love to each other, and
of benevolence and charity to all mankind.
May the *veils* of ignorance and blindness be removed from the eyes of our understandings,
that we may behold and adore thy mighty and
wondrous works.   May the *rod* and staff of thy
grace and power continually support us, and
defend us from the rage of all our enemies, and
especially from the subtilty and malice of that
old *serpent*, who with cruel vigilance seeketh
our ruin.   May the *leprosy* of sin be eradicated
from our *bosoms ;* and may *Holiness to the Lord*
be engraven upon all our thoughts, words and
actions.   May the *incense* of piety ascend continually unto thee, from off the *altar* of our
hearts, and *burn day and night*, as a sweet-
smelling savor unto thee.   May we daily *search*
the records of *truth*, that we may be more and
more instructed in our duty ; and may we
share the blessedness of those who hear the
sacred word and keep it.   And finally, O merciful Father, when we shall have passed
through the outward *veils* of these earthly
courts, when the earthly house of this *tabernacle* shall be dissolved, may we be admitted
into the *Holy of Holies* above, into the presence
of the *Grand Council* of Heaven, where the
Supreme *High Priest* for ever presides, for ever
reigns.   Amen.   *So mote it be.*

Exodus iii. 1—6.

" Now Moses kept the flock of Jethro his
father-in-law, the priest of Midian; and he led

the flock to the back side of the desert, and came to the mountain of God, even to Horeb. And the angel of the Lord appeared unto him in a flame of fire, out of the midst of a bush; and he looked, and behold the bush burned with fire, and the bush was not consumed.

"And when the Lord saw that he turned aside to see, God called to him out of the bush, and said, Moses, Moses! And he said, Here am I. And he said, Draw not nigh hither: put off thy shoes from off thy feet, for the place whereon thou standest is holy ground. Moreover he said, I am the God of thy father, the God of Abraham, the God of Isaac, and the God of Jacob. And Moses hid his face: for he was afraid to look upon God."

2 Chron. xxxvi. 11—20.

"Zedekiah was one-and-twenty years old, when he began to reign, and he reigned eleven years in Jerusalem. And he did that which was evil in the sight of the Lord his God, and humbled not himself before Jeremiah the prophet, speaking from the mouth of the Lord. And he also rebelled against king Nebuchadnezzar, and stiffened his neck, and hardened his heart, from turning unto the Lord God of Israel. Moreover, all the chief of the priests and the people transgressed very much, after all the abominations of the heathen, and polluted the house of the Lord, which he had hallowed in Jerusalem. And the Lord God of their fathers sent to them by his messengers, because he had compassion on his people, and on his dwelling place. But they mocked the messengers of God, and despised his word, and misused his prophets, until the wrath of the Lord arose against his people, till there was no remedy.

Therefore he brought upon them the king of the Chaldees, who slew their young men with the sword, in the house of their sanctuary, and had no compassion upon young men or maidens, old men, or him that stooped for age; he gave them all into his hand. And all the vessels of the house of God, great and small, and the treasures of the house of the Lord, and the treasures of the king, and his princes: all these he brought to Babylon.

And they burnt the house of God, and brake down the wall of Jerusalem, and burnt all the palaces thereof with fire, and destroyed all the goodly vessels thereof. And them that had escaped from the sword, carried he away to Babylon;—where they were servants to him and his sons, until the reign of the kingdom of Persia.

EZRA i. 1—3.

Now, in the first year of Cyrus, King of Persia, the Lord stirred up the spirit of Cyrus, King of Persia, that he made a proclamation throughout all his kingdom, and put it also in writing, saying, Thus saith Cyrus, King of Persia, the Lord God of Heaven hath given me all the kingdoms of the earth, and he hath charged me to build him an house at Jerusalem, which is in Judah.—Who is there among you of all his people? His God be with him. and let him go up to Jerusalem, which is in Judah and build the house of the Lord God of Israel, which is in Jerusalem.

Exodus iii. 13, 14.

And Moses said unto God, Behold, when I come unto the children of Israel, and shall say unto them, The God of your fathers hath sent me unto you; and they shall say to me, What is his name? what shall I say unto them?

And God said unto Moses, I AM THAT I AM: And thus thou shalt say unto the children of Israel, I AM hath sent me unto you.

Psalm cxli.

Lord, I cry unto thee: make haste unto me; give ear unto my voice. Let my prayer be set forth before thee as incense, and the lifting up of hands as the evening sacrifice. Set a watch, O Lord, before my mouth; keep the door of my lips. Incline not my heart to any evil thing, to practise wicked works with men that work iniquity. Let the righteous smite me, it shall be a kindness; let him reprove me, it shall be an excellent oil. Mine eyes are unto thee, O God the Lord; in thee is my trust; leave not my soul destitute. Keep me from the snares which they have laid for me, and the gins of the workers of iniquity. Let the wicked fall into their own nets, while that I withal escape.

Psalm cxlii.

I cried unto the Lord with my voice; with my voice unto the Lord did I make my supplication. I poured out my complaint before him: I shewed before him my trouble. When my spirit was overwhelmed within me, then thou knewest my path: in the way wherein I walked, have they privily laid a snare for me. I looked on my right hand and beheld, but there was no man that would know me: refuge failed me: no man cared for my soul. I cried unto thee, O Lord: I said, Thou art my refuge, and my portion in the land of the living. Attend unto my cry; for I am brought very low: deliver me from my persecutors; for they are stronger than I. Bring my soul out of darkness, that I may praise thy name.

Psalm cxliii.

Hear my prayer, O Lord; give ear to my supplication. In thy faithfulness answer me, and in thy righteousness. And enter not into judgment with thy servant; for in thy sight shall no man living be justified. For the enemy hath persecuted my soul; he hath made me to dwell in darkness. Therefore is my spirit overwhelmed within me; my heart within me is desolate. Hear me speedily, O Lord; my spirit faileth; hide not thy face from me, lest I be like them that go down into the pit. Cause me to hear thy loving kindness in the morning; for in thee do I trust: cause me to know the way wherein I should walk; for I lift up my soul unto thee. Teach me to lo thy will, for thou art my God: bring my soul out of trouble, and of thy mercy cut off mine enemies, for I am thy servant.

Exodus iv. 1—10.

"And Moses answered and said, But behold, they wil. not believe me, nor hearken unto my voice; for they will say, The Lord hath not appeared unto thee And the Lord said unto him, What is that in thine hand? And he said, A rod. And he said, Cast it on the ground; and he cast it on the ground, and it became a serpent; and Moses fled from before it. And the Lord said unto Moses, Put forth thine hand, and take it by the tail. And he put forth his hand and caught it, and it became a rod in his hand. That they may believe that the Lord God of your fathers, the God of Abraham, the God of Isaac, and the God of Jacob, hath appeared unto thee.

"And the Lord said furthermore unto him, Put now thine hand into thy bosom; and he put his hand into his bosom; and when he took it out, behold his hand was leprous as snow. And he said, Put thine hand into thy bosom again; and he put his hand into his bosom again; and he plucked it out of his bosom, and, behold, it was turned again as his other flesh. And it shall come to pass, if they will not believe thee, neither hearken to the voice of the first sign, that they will believe the voice of the latter sign.

"And it shall come to pass, if they will not believe also these two signs, neither hearken unto thy voice, that thou shalt take of the water of the river, and pour it upon the dry land: and the water which thou takest out of the river, shall become blood upon the dry and.'¹

HAGGAI iL 2—4, 23.

Speak now to Zerubbabel, the son of Shealtiel governor of Judah, and to Joshua, the son of Josedec the high priest, and to the residue of the people, saying, Who is left among you, that saw this house in her first glory? and how do you see it now? is it not, in your eyes, in comparison of it, as nothing? Yet now be strong, O Zerubbabel; and be strong, O Joshua, son of Josedec, the high priest; and be strong, all ye people of the land, saith the Lord, and work: for I am with you, saith the Lord of Hosts.

"In that day, will I take thee, O Zerubbabel, my servant, the son of Shealtiel, saith the Lord, and will make thee as a signet: for I have chosen thee."

ZECHARIAH iv. 9, 10.

The hands of Zerubbabel have laid the foundation of this house; his hands shall also finish it; *and thou shalt know that the Lord of hosts hath sent me unto you.* For who hath despised the day of small things? for they shall rejoice, and shall see the plummet in the hand of Zerubbabel, with those seven.

AMOS ix. 11.

"In that day will I raise up the tabernacle of David that is fallen, and close up the breaches thereof, and I will raise up his ruins, and I will buil'd it as in days of old."

The following passages of scripture are read by the High Priest.

GENESIS i. 1—3.

In the beginning God created the heaven and the earth. And the earth was without form and void; and darkness was upon the face of the deep; and the Spirit of God moved upon the face of the waters. And God said, Let there be light; and there was light.——— DEUT. xxxi. 24—26. And it came to pass, when Moses had made an end of writing the words of this law in a book, until they were finished, that Moses commanded the Levites which bare the ark of the covenant of the Lord, saying, Take this book of the law, and put it in the side of the ark of the covenant of the Lord your God, that it may be there for a witness against thee.—EXODUS xx. 21. And thou shalt put the mercy seat above, upon the ark; and in the ark thou shalt put the testimony that I shall give thee.——EXODUS xvi. 32—34. And Moses said, This is the thing which the Lord commandeth, Fill an omer of the manna, to be kept for your generations; that they may see the bread wherewith I have fed you in the wilderness, when I brought you forth from the land of Egypt. And Moses said unto Aaron, Take a pot, and put an omer full of manna therein, and lay it up before the Lord, to be kept for your generations. As the Lord commanded Moses, so Aaron laid it up before the testimony to be kept.——NUMBERS xvii. 10. And the Lord said unto Moses, Bring Aaron's rod again before the testimony, to be kept for a token.——HEBREWS ix. 2—5.

10

For there was a tabernacle made; the first, wherein was the candlestick, and the table, and the shew-bread, which is called the sanctuary. And after the veils, the tabernacle, which is called the Holiest of all; which had the golden censer, and the ark of the covenant, overlaid round about with gold, wherein was the golden pot that had manna, and Aaron's rod that budded, and the tables of the covenant; and over it, the cherubims of glory, shadowing the mercy seat; of which we cannot now speak particularly.

Exodus vi. 2, 3.

"And God spake unto Moses, and said unto him, I am the Lord: and I appeared unto Abraham, unto Isaac, and unto Jacob, by the name of God Almighty; but by my name JEHOVAH was I not known to them."

The High Priest will then recite the following passage, previous to investing the candidate with an important secret of the degree.

John i. 1—5.

"In the beginning was the Word: and the Word was with God, and the Word was God. The same was in the beginning with God. All things were made by him: and without him was not any thing made that was made In him was life, and the life was the light of men. And the light shineth in darkness, and the darkness comprehendeth it not."

The following remarks relative to King Solomon's Temple, cannot be uninteresting to a Royal Arch Mason.

This famous fabric was situated on Mount Moriah, near the place where Abraham was about to offer up his son Isaac, and where David met and appeased the destroying angel, who was visible over the *threshing floor of Ornan the Jebusite.* It was begun in the fourth year of the reign of Solomon; the third after the death of David; four hundred and eighty years after the passage of the Red Sea, and on the second day of the month Zif, being the second month of the sacred year, which answers to the 21st of April, in the year of the world two thousand nine hundred and ninety-two; and was carried on with such prodigious speed, that it was finished, in all its parts, in little more than seven years.

By the masonic art, and the wise regulations of Solomon, this famous edifice was erected without the sound of the axe, hammer, or any tool of iron; for the stones were all hewed, squared, and numbered, in the quarries of Zeradathah, where they were raised; the timbers were fitted and prepared in the forest of Lebanon, and conveyed by sea in floats to Joppa, and from thence by land to Jerusalem; where the fabric was erected by the assistance of wooden instruments prepared for that purpose. And when the building was finished, its several parts fitted with that exact nicety, that it had more the appearance of being the handy work of the Supreme Architect of the Universe, than of human hands.

In the year of the world, 3029, King Solomon died, and was succeeded by his son Rehoboam. Soon after this, instigated and led on by Jeroboam the son of Nebat, ten of the tribes revolted from Rehoboam, and set up a separate kingdom, with Jeroboam at their head. In this manner were the tribes of Israel divided, and under two distinct governments, for two hundred and fifty-four years. The ten revolted tribes became weak and degenerated; their country was laid waste, and their government overthrown and extirpated by Salmanezer, King of Assyria. After a series of changes and

events, Nebuchadnezzar, King of Babylon, having
besieged Jerusalem, and raised towers all round the
city, so that, after defending it for the space of a
year and a half, it was, in the eleventh year of the
reign of Zedekiah, King of Judah, surrendered and
delivered at midnight to the officers of Nebuchadnezzar, who sacked and destroyed the temple, and
took away all the holy vessels, together with those
two famous brazen pillars; and the remnant of the
people that escaped the sword, carried he away cap-
tives to Babylon, where they remained servants to
him and his successors, until the reign of Cyrus,
King of Persia. Cyrus, in the first year of his
reign, being directed by that divine power which
invisibly led him to the throne of Persia, issued his
famous edict for the liberation of the Hebrew cap-
tives, with permission that they should return to
their native country, and rebuild the city and *house
of the Lord.* Accordingly, the principal people of
the tribes of Judah and Benjamin, with the Priests
and Levites, immediately departed for Jerusalem,
and commenced the great and glorious work.

CHARGE to a newly Exalted Companion.

WORTHY COMPANION,

By the consent and assistance of the members
of this Chapter, you are now exalted to the sublime and honorable degree of Royal Arch Mason. The rites and mysteries developed in this
degree, have been handed down through a
chosen few, unchanged by time, and uncon-
trolled by prejudice; and we expect and trust,
they will be regarded by you with the same
veneration, and transmitted with the same scrupulous purity to your successors.

No one can reflect on the ceremonies of gaining admission into this place, without being forcibly struck with the important lessons which
they teach. Here we are necessarily led to con-

template, with gratitude and admiration, the sacred Source from whence all earthly comforts flow. Here we find additional inducements to continue steadfast and immoveable in the discharge of our respective duties; and here we are bound by the most solemn ties, to promote each other's welfare, and correct each other's failings, by advice, admonition, and reproof. As it is our earnest desire, and a duty we owe to our companions of this order, that the admission of every candidate into this chapter, should be attended by the approbation of the most scrutinizing eye, we hope always to possess the satisfaction of finding none among us, but such as will promote, to the utmost of their power, the great end of our institution. By paying due attention to this determination, we expect you will never recommend any candidate to this Chapter, whose abilities, and knowledge of the preceding degrees, you cannot freely vouch for, and whom you do not firmly and confidently believe, will fully conform to the principles of our order, and fulfil the obligations of a Royal Arch Mason. While such are our members, we may expect to be united in one object, without lukewarmness, inattention or neglect; but zeal, fidelity and affection, will be the distinguishing characteristics of our society, and that satisfaction, harmony and peace may be enjoyed at our meetings, which no other society can afford.

Closing Prayer.

By the *wisdom* of the Supreme High Priest, may we be directed; by his *strength*, may we
10*

be enabled; and by the *beauty* of virtue, may we be incited, to perform the obligations here enjoined on us ; to keep inviolably the mysteries here unfolded to us; and invariably to practise all those duties out of the Chapter, which are inculcated in it

[Response.]

So mote it be   **Amen.**

ROYAL MASTER'S DEGREE.

THIS degree cannot be legally conferred on any but Royal Arch Masons, who have taken all the preceding degrees; and it is preparatory to that of the Select Master. Although it is short, yet it contains some valuable information, and it is intimately connected with the degree of Select Master. It also enables us with ease and facility to examine the privileges of others to this degree; while, at the same time, it proves ourselves.

The following passages of scripture, &c. are considered to be appropriate to this degree.

1 KINGS vii. 48—50, and 40.

And Solomon made all the vessels that pertained unto the house of the Lord; the altar of gold, and the table of gold, whereupon the shew-bread was; and the candlesticks of pure gold; five on the right side, and five on the left, before the oracle; with the flowers, and the lamps, and the tongs of gold; and the bowls, and the snuffers, and the basons, and the spoons, and the censers, of pure gold; and the hinges of gold, both for the doors of the inner house, the most holy place, and for the doors of the house, to wit, of the Temple. So Hiram made an end of doing all the work, that he had made King Solomon, for the house of the Lord.

REV. xxii. 12—14.

And behold I come quickly; and my reward is with me, *, give every man according as his work shall be. I am Alpha and Omega, the begin· ning and the end, the first and the last. Blessed are they that do his commandments, that they may have a right to the tree of life, and may enter in through the gates into the city.

1 KINGS vi. 27.

And he set the cherubims within the inner house; and they stretched forth the wings of the cherubims, so that the wing of the one touched the one wall; and the wing of the other cherub touched the other wall; and their wings touched one another in the midst of the house.

The Ark, called the glory of Israel, which was seated in the middle of the holy place, under the wings of the cherubim, was a small chest, or coffer, three feet nine inches long, two feet three inches wide, and three feet three inches high. It was made of wood, excepting only the mercy seat, but overlaid with gold, both inside and out. It had a ledge of gold surrounding it at the top, into which the cover, called the mercy seat, was let in. The mercy seat was of solid gold, the thickness of a hand's breadth: at the two ends of it were two cherubims, looking inwards towards each other with their wings ex· panded; which embracing the whole circumference of the mercy seat, they met on each side, in the mid· the; all of which, the Rabbins say, was made out of the same mass, without any soldering of parts

Here the Shekinah, or Divine Presence, rested, and was visible in the appearance of a cloud over it. From hence the Bathkoll issued, and gave answers when God was consulted. And hence it is that God is said, in the scriptures, to dwell between the cherubim; that is, between the cherubim on the mercy seat, because there was the seat or throne of the visible appearance of his glory among them.

SELECT MASTER'S DEGREE

This degree is the summit and perfection of ancient masonry; and without which the history of the Royal Arch Degree cannot be complete. It rationally accounts for the concealment and preservation of those essentials of the craft, which were brought to light at the erection of the second Temple, and which lay concealed from the masonic eye four hundred and seventy years.

Many particulars relative to those few who, for their superior skill, were selected to complete an important part of King Solomon's Temple, are explained.

And here too is exemplified an instance of *justice* and *mercy*, by our ancient patron, towards one of the craft, who was led to disobey his commands, by an over *zealous* attachment for the institution. It ends with a description of a particular circumstance, which characterizes the degree.

The following Psalm is read at opening:

Psalm lxxxvii.

"His foundation is in the holy mountains. The Lord loveth the gates of Zion more than all the dwellings of Jacob. Glorious things are spoken of thee, O city of God. Selah. I will make mention of Rahab and Babylon, to them that know me. Behold Philistia and Tyre, with Ethiopia; this man was born there. And of Zion it shall be said, This and that man was born in her; and the highest himself shall establish her. The Lord shall count, when he writeth up the people, that this man was born there. Selah. As well the singers, as the players on instruments, shall be there: all my springs are in thee."

The following passages of scripture are introduced and explained:

1 KINGS iv. 1, 5 and 6.

So King Solomon was king over all Israel. Azariah, the son of Nathan, was over the officers; and Zabud, the son of Nathan, was principal officer, and the king's friend; and Ahishar was over the household; and Adoniram. the son of Abda, was over the tribute.

1 KINGS v. 17, 18.

And the king commanded, and they brought great stones, costly stones, and hewed stones, to lay the foundation of the house. And Solomon's builders and Hiram's builders did hew them, and the stone-squarers; so they prepared timber and stones to build the house.

1 KINGS viii. 13, 14.

And King Solomon sent and fetched Hiram out of Tyre. He was a widow's son, of the tribe of Naphtali; and his father was a man of Tyre, a worker of brass; and he was filled with wisdom and understanding, and cunning, to work all works in brass.

EZEKIEL xxvii. 9.

The ancients of Gebal, and the wise men thereof, were in thee thy calkers· all the ships of the sea, with their mariners, were in thee, to occupy thy merchandize.

DEUT. xxxi. 24—26.

And it came to pass, when Moses had made an end of writing the words of this law in a book, until they were finished, that Moses commanded the Levites, which bore the ark of the covenant of the Lord, saying, Take this book of the law, and put it in the side of the ark of the covenant of the Lord your God, that it may be there for a witness against thee.

EXODUS xvi. 33, 34.

And Moses said unto Aaron, Take a pot, and put an omer full of manna therein, and lay it up before the Lord, to be kept for your generations. As the Lord commanded Moses, so Aaron laid it up before the testimony to be kept.

NUMBERS xvii. 10.

And the Lord said unto Moses, Bring Aaron's rod again before the testimony, to be kept for a token.

NUMBERS vii. 89.

And when Moses was gone into the tabernacle of the congregation, to speak with him, then he heard the voice of one speaking unto him from off the mercy seat, that was upon the ark of the testimony, from between the two cherubims; and he spake unto him.

EXODUS xxv. 40.

And look that thou make them after their pattern, which was shewed thee in the mount.

Charge to a Select Master

COMPANION,

Having attained to this degree, you have passed the *circle of perfection* in ancient masonry. In the capacity of Select Master, you must be sensible that your obligations are increased in proportion to your privileges. Let it be your constant care to prove yourself worthy of the confidence reposed in you, and of the high honor conferred on you, in admitting you to this select degree. Let uprightness and integrity attend your steps; let *justice* and *mercy* mark your conduct; let *fervency* and *zeal* stimulate you in the discharge of the various duties incumbent on you; but suffer not an idle or impertinent *curiosity* to lead you astray, or betray you into danger. Be *deaf* to every insinuation which would have a tendency to weaken your resolution, or tempt you to an act of *disobedience.* Be voluntarily *dumb* and *blind,* when the exercise of those faculties would endanger the peace of your mind or the probity of your conduct; and let *silence* and *secrecy*, those cardinal virtues of a Select Master, on all necessary occasions, be scrupulously observed. By a steady adherence to the important instructions contained in this degree, you will merit the approbation of the select number with whom you are associated, and will enjoy the high satisfaction of having acted well your part in the important enterprise in which you are engaged; and after having *wrought your regular hours,* may you be admitted to participate in all the privileges of a *Select Master.*

11

ORDER OF HIGH PRIESTHOOD

THIS order appertains to the office of High Priest of a Royal Arch Chapter; and no one can be legally entitled to receive it, until he has been duly elected to preside as High Priest in a regular Chapter of Royal Arch Masons. This order should not be conferred when a less number than three duly qualified High Priests are present. Whenever the ceremony is performed in due and ample form, the assistance of at least nine High Priests, who have received it, is requisite.

Though the High Priest of every regular Royal Arch Chapter, having himself been duly qualified, can confer the order, under the preceding limitation as to number; yet it is desirable, when circumstances will permit, that it should be conferred by the Grand High Priest of the Grand Royal Arch Chapter, or such Present or Past High Priest as he may designate for that purpose. A convention, notified to meet at the time of any convocation of the Grand Chapter, will afford the best opportunity of conferring this important and exalted degree of masonry, with appropriate solemnity. Whenever it is conferred, the following directions are to be observed.

A candidate desirous of receiving the order of High Priesthood, makes a written request to his predecessor in office, or when it can be done, to the Grand High Hriest, respectfully requesting that a convention of High Priests may be called, for the purpose of conferring on him the order. When the convention meets, and is duly organized, a certificate of the due election of the candidate to the office of High Priest, must be produced. This certificate is signed by his predecessor in office, attested by the Secretary of the Chapter. On examination of this certificate, the qualifications of the candidate are ascertained. The solemn ceremonies of conferring the order upon him, then ensue. When ended, the presiding officer directs the Secretary of the convention to make a record of the proceedings, and return it to the Secretary of the Grand Chapter, to be by him laid before the Grand High Priest, for the information of all whom it may concern. The convention of High Priests is then dissolved in due form.

It is the duty of every Companion, as soon after his election to the office of High Priest, as is consistent with his personal convenience, to apply for admission to the order of High Priesthood, that he may be fully qualified properly to govern his Chapter.

The following passages of scripture are made use of during the ceremonies appertaining to this order.

GENESIS xiv. 12—24.

And they took Lot, Abraham's brother's son, (who dwelt in Sodom,) and his goods, and departed. And there came one that had escaped, and told Abram, the Hebrew; for he dwelt in the plain of Mamre, the Amorite, brother of Eschol, and brother of Aner; and these were confederate with Abram. And when Abram heard that his brother was taken captive, he armed his trained servants, born in his own house, three hundred and eighteen, and pursued them unto Dan. And he divided himself against them, he and his servants, by night and smote them, and pursued them unto Hobah, which is on the left hand of Damascus. And he brought back all the goods and also brought again his

brother Lot, and his goods, and the women
also, and the people. And the king of Sodom
went out to meet him, (after his return from the
slaughter of Chedorlaomer, and of 'he kings
that were with him,) at the valley of Shevah,
which is the king's dale. And Melchisedek
king of Salem, brought forth bread and wine
and he was the priest of the Most High God
And he blessed him, and said, Blessed be Abram
of the Most High God, who hath delivered
thine enemies into thy hand. And he gave him
tithes of all. And the king of Sodom said to
Abram, Give me the persons, and take the
goods to thyself. And Abram said to the king
of Sodom, I have lifted up mine hand to the
Lord, the Most High God, the possessor of
heaven and earth, that I will not take from a
thread even to a shoe-latchet; and that I will
not take any thing that is thine, lest thou
shouldest say, I have made Abram rich: save
only that which the young men have eaten,
and the portion of the men which went with
me, Aner, Eshcol and Mamre, let them take
their portion.

NUMBERS vi. 22—26.

And the Lord spake unto Moses, saying,
Speak unto Aaron, and unto his sons, saying,
On this wise, ye shall bless the children of
Israel, saying unto them, The Lord bless thee,
and keep thee; the Lord make his face to shine
upon thee, and be gracious unto thee; the Lord
lift up his countenance upon thee, and give thee
peace.

Heb. vii. 1—6.

For this Melchisedek, king of Salem, priest of the Most High God, (who met Abram returning from the slaughter of the kings, and blessed him; to whom also Abraham gave a tenth part of all; first being, by interpretation, King of Righteousness, and after that also, King of Salem, which is, King of Peace: without father, without mother, without descent; having neither beginning of days, nor end of life; but made like unto the Son of God,) abideth a priest continually. Now consider how great this man was, unto whom even the patriarch Abraham gave the tenth of the spoils. And verily, they that are of the sons of Levi, who receive the office of the priesthood, have a commandment to take tithes of the people, according to the law, that is, of their brethren, though they come out of the loins of Abraham.

"For he testifieth, Thou art a priest for ever, after the order of Melchisedek.

"And inasmuch as not without an oath, he was made priest.

"For those priests (under the Levitical law) were made without an oath; but this with an oath, by him that said unto him, The Lord sware, and will not repent, Thou art a priest for over, after the order of Melchisedek."

CEREMONIES AND CHARGES UPON THE INSTALLATION OF THE OFFICERS OF A ROYAL ARCH CHAPTER.

The Grand Officers will meet at a convenient place and open.

2. *The subordinate Chapter will meet in the outer*

11*

courts of their Hall, and form an avenue for the reception of the Grand Officers.

3. *When formed, they will dispatch a committe to the place where the Grand Officers are assembled, to inform the Grand Marshal that the Chapter is prepared to receive them ;— The Grand Marshal will announce the committee, and introduce them to the Grand Officers.*

4. *The Grand Officers will move in procession, conducted by the committee, to the Hall of the Chapter, in the following order :*

Grand Tyler ;
Two Grand Stewards ;
Representatives of subordinate Chapters, according to seniority, by threes triangular ;
Three Great Lights ;
Orator, Chaplain, and other Clergy ;
Grand Secretary, Grand Treasurer, and Grand Roya
Arch Captain ;
Grand P. Sojourner, Grand Captain of the Host, an
Deputy Grand High Priest ;
Grand Scribe, Grand King, and Grand High Priest
(Grand Marshal on the left of the Procession.)

N. B. The Grand P. Sojourner, Grand Captain of the Host, and Grand Royal Arch Captain, are appointed pro tempore.

When the Grand High Priest enters, the grand honors are given.

5. *The Grand Secretary will then call over the names of the officers elect ; and the Grand High Priest will ask whether they accept their respective offices. If they answer in the affirmative, he then asks the members whether they remain satisfied with their choice.* If they answer in the affirmative, he directs their offi cers to approach the sacred volume, and become quali

fied for Installation, agreeably to the 4th section of the 4th article of the General Grand Royal Arch Constitution.

6. The Grand Marshal will then form the whole in procession, and they will march through the *veils* into the inner apartment, where they will surround the altar, which is previously prepared in *ample form* for the occasion.

7. All present will kneel, and the following prayer will be recited.

Prayer.

"Almighty and Supreme High Priest of Heaven and Earth! Who is there in heaven but thee! and who upon earth can stand in competition with thee! Thy OMNISCIENT Mind brings all things in review, past, present and to come; thine OMNIPOTENT Arm directs the movements of the vast creation; thine OMNIPRESENT Eye pervades the secret recesses of every heart; thy boundless beneficence supplies us with every comfort and enjoyment; and thine unspeakable perfections and glory surpass the understanding of the children of men! Our Father, who art in heaven, we invoke thy benediction upon the purposes of our present assembly. Let this Chapter be established to thine honor: let its officers be endowed with wisdom to discern, and fidelity to pursue, its true interests; let its members be ever mindful of the duty they owe to their God, the obedience they owe to their superiors, the love they owe to their equals, and the good will they owe to all mankind. Let this Chapter be consecrated

to thy glory, and its members ever exemplify
their love to God by their beneficence to men.

"Glory be to God on high."

Response. "Amen! So mote it be."

They are then qualified in due form.

All the Companions, except High Priests and Past
High Priests, are then desired to withdraw, while the
new High Priest is solemnly bound to the performance of his duties; and after the performance of
other necessary ceremonies, not proper to be written
they are permitted to return.

8. *The whole then repair to their appropriate stations; when the Grand Marshal will form a general
procession, in the following order.*

> Three Royal Arch Stewards, with Rods;
> Tyler of a Blue Lodge;
> Entered Apprentices;
> Fellow Crafts;
> Master Masons;
> Stewards of Lodges, having Jewels;
> Deacons having Jewels;
> Secretaries having Jewels;
> Treasurers having Jewels;
> Wardens having Jewels;
> Mark Master Masons,
> M. E. Masters;
> Royal Arch Masons by three;
> Royal Masters by three;
> Select Masters by three;
> Orders of Knighthood;
> Tyler of the new Chapter;
> Members of the new Chapter, by three;
> Three Masters of Veils;

Captain of the Host:

Secretary, Treasurer, R. A. Captain, and
P. Sojourner carrying the Ark;
A Companion carrying the Pot of Incense;
Two Companions carrying Lights;
Scribe, High Priest and King;
Grand Chapter, as before prescribed.

On arriving at the church, or house where the ser-
n es are to be performed, they halt, open to the right
an l left, and face inward, while the Grand Officers
and others in succession, pass through and enter the
house.

*9. The officers and members of the new Chapter, and
also of the Grand Chapter, being seated, the Grand
Marshal proclaims silence, and the ceremonies com-
mence.*

1?. *An Anthem or Ode is to be performed.*

11. *An Oration or Address is to be delivered.*

12. *An Ode or Piece of Music.*

**[13. The Deputy Grand High Priest then rises
and informs the Grand High Priest, that " a number
of Companions, duly instructed in the sublime mysteries, being desirous of promoting the honor, and
propagating the principles of the Art, have applied
to the Grand Chapter for a warrant to constitute a
new Chapter of Royal Arch Masons, which having
been obtained, they are now assembled for the purpose
of being constituted, and having their officers installed
in due and ancient form.]*

*[14. The Grand Marshal will then form the offi-
cers and members of the new Chapter in front of the*

---

* NOTE. Those paragraphs which are enclosed within brack-
ets, apply exclusively to cases when new Chapters are constituted, and their officers installed for the first time. The rest
apply equally to such cases, as well as to annual Installations

Grand Officers; after which, the Grand High Priest directs the Grand Secretary to read the warrant.]

[15. *The Grand High Priest then rises and says, " By virtue of the high powers in me vested, I do form you, my respected Companions into a regular Chapter of Royal Arch Masons. From henceforth you are authorized and empowered to open and hold a Lodge of Mark Masters, Past Masters, and Most Excellent Masters, and a Chapter of Royal Arch Masons; and to do and perform all such things as thereunto may appertain; conforming, in all your doings, to the General Grand Royal Arch Constitution, and the general regulations of the State Grand Chapter. And may the God of your fathers be with you, guide and direct you in all your doings."*]

16. *The furniture, clothing, jewels, implements, utensils, &c. belonging to the Chapter, (having been previously placed in the centre, in front of the Grand Officers, covered,) are now uncovered, and the new Chapter is dedicated in due and ancient form.*

17. *The Dedication then follows: the Grand Chaplain saying,*

" To our Most Excellent Patron, ZERUB-BABEL, we solemnly dedicate this Chapter. May the blessing of our Heavenly High Priest descend and rest upon its members, and may their felicity be immortal.

" Glory be to God on high."

[Response by the Companions.]

" As it was in the beginning, is now, and **ever** shall be, world without end ! Amen.

" So mote it be."

18. *The Grand Marshal then says, "I am directed to proclaim, and I do hereby proclaim this Chapter, by the name of —— Chapter, duly consecrated, constituted and dedicated. This,"* &c. &c.

19. *An Ode.*

20. *The Deputy Grand High Priest will then present the first officer of the new Chapter to the Grand High Priest, saying,*

MOST EXCELLENT GRAND HIGH PRIEST,

I present you my worthy Companion —— ——, nominated in the warrant, to be installed High Priest of this [new] Chapter. I find him to be skilful in the royal art, and attentive to the moral precepts of our forefathers, and have therefore no doubt but he will discharge the duties of his office with fidelity.

The Grand High Priest then addresses him as follows:

MOST EXCELLENT,

I feel much satisfaction in performing my duty on the present occasion, by installing you into the office of High Priest of this [new] Chapter. It is an office highly honorable to all those who diligently perform the important duties annexed to it. Your reputed masonic knowledge, however, precludes the necessity of a particular enumeration of those duties. I shall therefore only observe, that by a frequent recurrence to the constitution, and general regulations, and constant practice of the several sublime lectures and charges, you will be best able to fulfi them; and I am confident that the Companions who are chosen to preside with you, will give strength to your endeavors, and support your exertions. I shall now propose certain questions to you, relative to the duties of your office, and to which I must request your unequivocal answer.

1. Do you solemnly promise that you will redouble your endeavors to correct the vices, purify the morals, and promote the happiness of those of your Companions, who have attained this sublime degree?

2. That you will never suffer your Chapter to be opened, unless there be present nine regular Royal Arch Masons?

3. That you will never suffer either more or less than three brethren to be exalted in your Chapter at one and the same time?

4. That you will not exalt any one to this degree, who has not shown a charitable and humane disposition; or who has not made a considerable proficiency in the foregoing degree?

5. That you will promote the general good of our order, and on all proper occasions, be ready to give and receive instructions, and particularly from the General and State Grand Officers?

6. That, to the utmost of your power, you will preserve the solemnities of our ceremonies and behave, in open Chapter with the most

profound respect and reverence, as an example to your Companions?

7. That you will not acknowledge or have intercourse with any Chapter that does not work under a constitutional warrant or dispensation?

8. That you will not admit any visitor into your Chapter, who has not been exalted in a Chapter legally constituted, without his being first formally healed?

9. That you will observe and support such bye-laws as may be made by your Chapter, in conformity to the General Grand Royal Arch Constitution, and the general regulations of the Grand Chapter?

10. That you will pay respect and due obedience to the instructions of the General and State Grand Officers, particularly relating to the several Lectures and Charges, and will resign the chair to them, severally, when they may visit your Chapter?

11. That you will suppor and observe the General Grand Royal Arch Constitution, and the General Regulations of the Grand Royal Arch Chapter, under whose authority you act?

Do you submit to all these things, and do you promise to observe and practise them faithfully?

These questions being answered in the affirmative the Companions all kneel in due form, and the Grand High Priest or Grand Chaplain repeats the following, or some or other suitable prayer.

" Most holy and glorious Lord God, the Great High Priest of Heaven and Earth,

" We approach thee with reverence, and implore thy blessing on the Companion appointed to preside over this new assembly, and now prostrate before thee ;—fill his heart with thy fear, that his tongue and actions may pronounce thy glory. Make him steadfast in thy service ; grant him firmness of mind; animate his heart, and strengthen his endeavors; may he teach thy judgments and thy laws ; and may the incense he shall put before thee, upon thine altar, prove an acceptable sacrifice unto thee. Bless him, O Lord, and bless the work of his hands.— Accept us, in mercy; hear thou from Heaven thy dwelling-place, and forgive our transgressions.

"Glory be to God the Father ; as it was in the beginning," &c.

[Response.]
" So mote it be."

21. *The Grand High Priest will then cause the High Priest elect to be invested with his clothing, badges, &c.; after which he will address him as follows, viz.*

MOST EXCELLENT,

In consequence of your cheerful acquiescence with the charges, which you have heard recited, you are qualified for installation as the High Priest of this Royal Arch Chapter; and it is incumbent upon me, on this occasion, to point out some of the particulars appertaining to your office, duty and dignity.

All legally constituted bodies of Royal Arch Masons, are called Chapters; as regular bodies of masons of the preceding degrees, are called Lodges. Every Chapter ought to assemble for work, at least once in three months; and must consist of a High Priest, King, Scribe, Captain of the Host, Principal Sojourner, Royal Arch Captain, three Grand Masters of the Veils, Treasurer, Secretary, and as many members as may be found convenient for working to advantage.

The officers of the chapter officiate in the lodges, holden for conferring the preparatory degrees, according to rank, as follows: viz.

The High Priest, as Master.

The King, as Senior Warden.

The Scribe, as Junior Warden.

The Captain of the Host, as Marshal or Master of Ceremonies.

The Principal Sojourner, as Senior Deacon.

The Royal Arch Captain, as Junior Deacon.

The Master of the first Veil, as Junior Overseer.

The Master of the second Veil, as Senior Overseer.

The Master of the third Veil, as Master Overseer.

The Treasurer, Secretary, Chaplain, Stewards, and Tyler, as officers of corresponding rank.

The High Priest of every Chapter has it in special charge, to see that the by-laws of his Chapter, as well as the General Grand Royal Arch Constitution, and all the regulations of the

Grand Chapter, are duly observed : that all the officers of his Chapter perform the duties of their respective offices faithfully, and are examples of diligence and industry to their companions;—that true and accurate records of all the proceedings of the chapter are kept by the secretary;—that the treasurer keeps and renders exact and just accounts of all the monies and other property belonging to the Chapter;— that the regular returns be made annually to the Grand Chapter;—and that the annual dues to the Grand Chapter be regularly and punctually paid. He has the right and authority of calling his Chapter together at pleasure, upon any emergency or occurrence, which in his judgment may require their meeting. It is his privilege and duty, together with the king and scribe, to attend the meetings of the Grand Chapter, either in person or by proxy ; and the well-being of the institution requires that his duty should on no occasion be omitted.

The office of High Priest is a station highly honorable to all those, who diligently perform the important duties annexed to it. By a frequent recurrence to the constitution and general regulations, and a constant practice of the several sublime lectures and charges, you wil be best enabled to fulfil those duties; and I am confident that the companions, who are chosen to preside with you, will give strength to your endeavors, and support to your exertions.

Let the *Mitre* with which yoɩ are invested.
remind you of the dignity of the office you
ɪɪstain, and its inscription impress upon your
ᴍind a sense of your dependence upon God;—
ᴛhat perfection is not given unto man upon
ᴇarth, and that perfect holiness belongeth alone
ᴜnto the Lord.

The *Breast-Plate*, with which you are deco-
ᴛated, in imitation of that upon which were
ᴇngraven the names of the twelve tribes, and
worn by the High Priest of Israel, is to teach
ʏou that you are always to bear in mind your
ᴛesponsibility to the laws and ordinances of the
ɪnstitution, and that the honor and interests of
ʏour Chapter and its members, should be al-
ᴡays near your heart.

The *various colors* of the *Robes* you wear,
are emblematical of every grace and virtue
which can adorn and beautify the human mind;
each of which will be briefly illustrated in the
course of the charges to be delivered to your
subordinate officers.

You will now take charge of your officers,
standing upon their right, and present them
severally in succession to the Deputy Grand
High Priest, ᴏy whom they will be presented
to me for installation.

22. *The High Priest of the Chapter will then
present his second officer to the Deputy Grand High
Priest, who will present him to the Grand High
Priest in the words of the Constitution. The Grand
High Priest will then ask him whether he has at-*

tended to the ancient charges and regulations before recited to his superior officer : if he answers in the affirmative, he is asked whether he fully and freely assents to the same : if he answers in the affirmative, the Grand High Priest directs his deputy to invest him with his clothing, &c. and then addresses him as follows, viz

CHARGE to the Second Officer, or King.

EXCELLENT COMPANION,

The important station to which you are elected in this Chapter, requires from you exemplary conduct; its duties demand your most assiduous attention; you are to second and support your chief in all the requirements of his office; and should casualties at any time prevent his attendance, you are to succeed him in the performance of his duties.

Your badge (the Level surmounted by a crown) should remind you, that although you are the representative of a King, and exalted by office above your Companions, yet that you remain upon a level with them, as respects your duty to God, to your neighbor, and to yourself; that you are equally bound with them, to be obedient to the laws and ordinances of the institution, to be charitable, humane and just, and to seek every occasion of doing good.

Your office teaches a striking lesson of humility. The institutions of political society teach us to consider the king as the chief of

created beings, and that the first duty of his
subjects, is to obey his mandates :—but the
institutions of our sublime degrees, by placing
the King in a situation subordinate to the
High Priest, teaches us that our duty to God
is paramount to all other duties, and should
ever claim the priority of our obedience to
man; and that however strongly we may be
bound to obey the laws of civil society, yet
that those laws, to be just, should never intermeddle with matters of conscience, nor dictate
articles of faith.

The *Scarlet Robe*, an emblem of imperial
dignity, should remind you of the paternal
concern you should ever feel for the welfare of
your Chapter, and the *fervency* and *zeal* with
which you should endeavor to promote its prosperity.

In presenting to you the Crown, which is an
emblem of royalty, I would remind you, that
to reign sovereign in the hearts and affections
of men, must be far more grateful to a generous
and benevolent mind, than to rule over their
lives and fortunes; and that to enable you to
enjoy this preëminence with honor and satisfaction, you must subject your own passions
and prejudices to the dominion of reason and
charity.

You are entitled to the second seat in the
council of your Companions.   Let the bright
example of your illustrious predecessor in the

Grand Council at Jerusalem, stimulate you to the faithful discharge of your duties; and when the King of kings shall summon you into his immediate presence, from his hand may you receive a *crown of glory,* which shall never fade away.

23. *The King will then retire to the line of officers, and the Scribe will be presented in the manner before mentioned. After his investiture, the Grand High Priest will address him as follows, viz.*

CHARGE to the Third Officer, or Scribe.

EXCELLENT COMPANION,

The office of Scribe, to which you are elected, is very important and respectable. In tne absence of your superior officers, you are bound to succeed them, and to perform their duties. The purposes of the institution ought never to suffer for want of intelligence in its proper officers; you will therefore perceive the necessity there is of your possessing such qualifications as will enable you to accomplish those duties which are incumbent upon you, in your appropriate station, as well as those which may occasionally devolve on you, by the absence of your superiors.

The *Purple Robe,* with which you are invested, is an emblem of *union,* and is calculated to remind you that the harmony and unanimity of the Chapter should be your constant aim; and to this end you are studiously to avoid all occasions of giving offence, or countenancing anything that may create divisions or dissensions. You are, by all means in your power, to endeavor to establish a permanent union and good understanding among all orders and degrees of masonry; and, as the glorious sun, at its meridian height, dispels the mist and clouds which obscure the horizon, so may your exertions tend to dissipate the gloom of jealousy and discord, whenever they may appear.

Your badge (*a Plumb-rule surmounted by the Turban,*) is an emblem of rectitude and vigilance; and while you stand as a watchman upon the tower, to guard your Companions against the approach of those enemies of human felicity, *intemperance* and *excess*, let this faithful monitor ever remind you to walk uprightly in your station; admonishing and animating your Companions to fidelity and industry while at labor, and to temperance and moderation while at refreshment. And, when the Great Watchman of Israel, whose eye never slumbers nor sleeps, shall relieve you from your post on earth, may he permit you in heaven to participate in that food and refreshment which is

"Such as the saints in glory love,
And such as angels eat."

24. *The Scribe will then retire to the line of officers, and the next officer be presented as before.*

CHARGE to the Fourth Officer, or Captain of the Host.

COMPANION,

The office with which you are entrusted is of high importance, and demands your most zealous consideration. The preservation of the most essential traits of our ancient customs, usages, and landmarks, are within your province; and it is indispensably necessary, that the part assigned to you, in the immediate practice of our rites and ceremonies, should be perfectly understood and correctly administered.

Your office corresponds with that of marshal, or master of ceremonies. You are to superintend all processions of your Chapter, when moving as a distinct body, either in public or private; and as the world can only judge of our private discipline by our public deportment, you will be careful that the utmost order and decorum be observed on all such occasions. You will ever be attentive to the commands of your chief, and always near at hand to see them duly executed. I invest you with the badge of your office, and presume that you will give to your duties all that study and attention which their importance demands.

25. *He will then retire to the line of officers, and the next officer will be presented.*

CHARGE to the Fifth Officer, or Principal Sojourner.

COMPANION,

The office confided to you, though subordinate in degree, is equal in importance to any in the Chapter, that of your chief alone excepted. Your office corresponds with that of *senior deacon,* in the preparatory degrees. Among the duties required of you, the preparation and introduction of candidates are not the least. As in our intercourse with the world, experience teaches that first impressions are often the most durable, and the most difficult to eradicate; so it is of great importance, in all cases, that those impressions should be correct and just: hence it is essential that the officer, who brings the blind by a way that they knew not, and leads them in paths that they have not known, should always be well qualified to make darkness light before them, and crooked things straight.

Your *Robe of Office* is an emblem of humility; and teaches that in the prosecution of a laudable undertaking, we should never decline taking any part that may be assigned us, although it may be the most difficult or dangerous.

The *rose-colored tesselated Border,* adorning the robe, is an emblem of ardor and perseverance, and signifies, that when we have engaged in a virtuous course, notwithstanding all the impediments, hardships, and trials, we may be des-

tined to encounter, we should endure them all
with fortitude, and ardently persevere unto the
end; resting assured of receiving, at the ter-
mination of our labors, a noble and glorious reward. Your past exertions will be considered
as a pledge of your future assiduity in the faithful discharge of your duties.

26. *He will then retire to the line of officers, and
the next officer is presented.*

*CHARGE to the Sixth Officer, or Royal Arch
Captain.*

COMPANION,

The well-known duties of your station require but little elucidation. Your office in the
preparatory degrees corresponds with that of
junior deacon. It is your province, conjointly
with the Captain of the Host, to attend the examination of all visitors, and to take care that
none are permitted to enter the Chapter, but
such as have *travelled the rugged path* of trial,
and evinced their title to our favor and friendship. You will be attentive to obey the commands of the Captain of the Host, during *the
introduction of strangers among* the workmen;
and should they be permitted to pass your post,
may they by him be introduced into the presence of the Grand Council.

The *White Banner*, entrusted to your care, is
emblematical of that purity of heart and recti-

tude of conduct which ought to actuate all those who pass the white veil of the sanctuary. I give it to you strongly in charge, never to suffer any one to pass your post, without the *signet of truth.*

I present you the badge of your office, in expectation of your performing your duties with intelligence, assiduity and propriety.

27. *He then retires, and the Three Grand Masters of the Veils are presented together.*

CHARGE *to the Master of the Third Veil.*

COMPANION,

I present you with the *Scarlet Banner*, which is the ensign of your office, and with a sword to protect and defend the same. The rich and beautiful color of your banner is emblematical of *fervency* and *zeal;* it is the appropriate color of the Royal Arch degree; it admonishes us, that we should be fervent in the exercise of our devotions to God, and zealous in our endeavors to promote the happiness of man.

CHARGE *to the Master of the Second Veil.*

COMPANION,

I invest you with the *Purple Banner*, which is the ensign of your office, and arm you with a sword, to enable you to maintain its honor.

The color of your banner is produced by a due mixture of *blue* and *scarlet;* the former of

13

which is the characteristic color of the *symbolic* or *first three degrees of masonry*, and the latter, that of the *royal arch degree.*   It is an emblem of *union,* and is the characteristic color of the intermediate degrees.   It admonishes us to cultivate and improve that spirit of union and har· mony, between the brethren of the symbolic degrees and the companions of the sublime degrees, which should ever distinguish the members of a society founded upon the principles of everlasting truth and universal philanthropy.

CHARGE to the Master of the First Veil.

Companion,

I invest you with the *Blue Banner,* which is the ensign of your office, and a sword for its defence and protection.   The color of your banner is one of the most durable and beautiful in nature.   It is the appropriate color adopted and worn by our ancient brethren of the three symbolic degrees, and is the *peculiar characteristic* of an institution which has stood the test of ages, and which is as much distinguished by the durability of its materials or principles, as by the beauty of its superstructure.   It is an emblem of universal *friendship* and benevolence; and instructs us that in the mind of a mason those virtues should be as expansive as the blue arch of heaven itself.

CHARGE to the three Masters of the Veils, as Overseers.

COMPANIONS,

Those who are placed as overseers of any work, should be well qualified to judge of its beauties and deformities, its excellencies and defects; they should be capable of estimating the former, and amending the latter. This consideration should induce you to cultivate and improve all those qualifications with which you are already endowed, as well as to persevere in your endeavors to acquire those in which you are deficient. Let the various *colors* of the *banners* committed to your charge, admonish you to the exercise of the several virtues of which they are emblematic; and you are to enjoin the practice of those virtues upon all who shall present themselves, or the *work* of their hands *for* your *inspection.* Let no work receive your approbation, but such as is calculated to adorn and strengthen the masonic edifice. Be industrious and faithful in practising and disseminating a knowledge of the *true and perfect work*, which alone can stand the test of the *Grand Overseer's Square*, in the great day of trial and retribution. Then, although every *rod* should become a *serpent*, and every serpent an enemy to this institution, yet shall their utmost exertions to destroy its reputation, or sap its foundation, become as impotent as the *leprous hand*, or as *water spilled upon the ground*, which cannot be gathered up again.

28. *They then retire and the Treasurer is pre-sented.*

CHARGE *to the Treasurer.*

COMPAN ON,

You are elected Treasurer of this Chapter, and I have the pleasure of investing you with the badge of your office. The qualities which should recommend a Treasurer, are *accuracy* and *fidelity;* accuracy in keeping a fair and minute account of all receipts and disburse-ments; fidelity, in carefully preserving all the property and funds of the Chapter, that may be placed in his hands, and rendering a just ac-count of the same, whenever he is called upon for that purpose. I presume that your respect for the institution, your attachment to the in-terests of your Chapter, and your regard for a good name, which is better than precious oint-ment, will prompt you to the faithful discharge of the duties of your office.

29. *He then retires, and the Secretary is pre sented.*

CHARGE *to the Secretary.*

COMPANION,

I with pleasure invest you with your badge as Secretary of this Chapter. The qualities which should recommend a Secretary, are, *promptitude* in issuing the notifications and or-ders of his superior officers; *pu ictuality* in at-tending the convocations of the Chapter; *cor-*

rectness in recording their proceedings; *judgment* in discriminating between what is proper and what is improper to be committed to writing; *regularity* in making his annual returns to the Grand Chapter; *integrity* in accounting for all monies that may pass through his hands; and *fidelity* in paying the same over into the hands of the treasurer. The possession of these good qualities, I presume, has designated you a suitable candidate for this important office; and I cannot entertain a doubt that you will discharge its duties beneficially to the Chapter, and honorably to yourself. And when you shall have completed the record of your transactions here below, and finished the term of your probation, may you be admitted into the celestial Grand Chapter of saints and angels and find your name *recorded* in the *book of life eternal*.

30. *He then retires, and the Chaplain is presented.*

CHARGE to the Chaplain.

'' E. AND REV. COMPANION,

" You are appointed Chaplain of this Chapter; and I now invest you with this circular jewel, the badge of your office. It is emblematical of eternity, and reminds us that here is not our abiding place. Your inclination will undoubtedly conspire with your duty, when you perform in the Chapter those solemn services which created beings should constantly render to their infinite CREATOR; and which,

13*

when offered by one whose holy profession is, 'to point to heaven and lead the way,' may, by refining our morals, strengthening our virtues, and purifying our minds, prepare us for admission into the society of those above, whose happiness will be as endless as it is perfect."

31. *He then retires and the Stewards are pre-sented.*

CHARGE *to the Stewards.*

COMPANIONS,

You being elected Stewards of this Chapter, I with pleasure invest you with the badges of your office. It is your province to see that every necessary preparation is made for the convenience and accommodation of the Chapter, previous to the time appointed for meeting. You are to see that the clothing, implements and furniture of each degree respectively, are properly disposed, and in suitable array for use, whenever they may be required, and that they are secured, and proper care taken of them, when the business of the Chapter is over. You are to see that necessary refreshments are provided, and that all your companions, and particularly visitors, are suitably accommodated and supplied. You are to be frugal and prudent in your disbursements, and to be careful that no extravagance or waste is committed in your department; and when you have faithfully fulfilled your stewardship here below, may you receive from Heaven the happy greeting of "Well done, good and faithful servants."

32. *They then retire, and the Tyler is presented.*

CHARGE to the Tyler.

COMPANION,

You are appointed Tyler of this Chapter, and I invest you with the badge, and this implement of your office. As the sword is placed in the hands of the Tyler, to enable him effectually to guard against the approach of all *cowans and eavesdroppers*, and suffer none to pass or repass but such as are *duly qualified;* so it should morally serve as a constant admonition to us to set a guard at the entrance of our thoughts; to place a watch at the door of our lips; to post a sentinel at the avenue of our actions; thereby excluding every unqualified and unworthy thought, word and deed; and preserving consciences void of offence towards God and towards man.

As the first application from visitors for admission into the Chapter is generally made to the Tyler at the door, your station will often present you to the observation of strangers; it is therefore essentially necessary that he who sustains the office with which you are entrusted, should be a man of good morals, steady habits, strict discipline, temperate, affable and discreet. I trust that a just regard for the honor and reputation of the institution will ever induce you to perform with fidelity the trust reposed in you ; and when the door of this earthly tabernacle shall be closed, may you find an abun dant entrance through the gates into the temple and city of our God.

33. *He will then retire, and then follows an*

ADDRESS to the High Priest.

M. E. COMPANION,

Having been honored with the free suffrages of the members of this Chapter, you are elected to the most important office which is within their power to bestow. This expression of their esteem and respect should draw from you corresponding sensations; and your demeanor should be such as to repay the honor they have so conspicuously conferred upon you, by an honorable and faithful discharge of the duties of your office. The station you are called to fill, is important, not only as it respects the correct practice of our rites and ceremonies, and the internal economy of the Chapter over which you preside ; but the public reputation of the institution will be generally found to rise or fall according to the skill, fidelity and discretion, with which its concerns are managed, and in proportion as the characters and conduct of its principal officers are estimable or censurable.

You have accepted a trust, to which is attached a weight of responsibility that will require all your efforts to discharge honorably to yourself, and satisfactorily to the Chapter. You are to see that your officers are capable and faithful in the exercise of their offices. Should they lack ability, you are expected to supply their defects; you are to watch carefully the progress of their performances, and to see that the long established customs of the institution suffer no derangement in their hands. You are to have a careful eye over the general conduct of the Chapter; see that due order and subordination are observed on all occasions; that the members are properly instructed; that due solemnity be observed in the practice of our rites; that no improper levity be permitted at any time, but more especially at the *introduction of strangers among the workmen.*

In fine, you are to be an example to your officers and members, which they need not hesitate to follow; thus securing to yourself the favor of Heaven, and the applause of your brethren and companions.

ADDRESS to the Officers generally.

COMPANIONS IN OFFICE,

Precept and example should ever advance with equal pace. Those moral duties which you are required to teach unto others, you should never neglect to practise yourselves.

Do you desire that the demeanor of your equals and inferiors towards you, should be marked with deference and respect? Be sure that you omit no opportunity of furnishing

them with examples in your own conduct towards your superiors.   Do you desire to obtain
instruction from those who are more wise or
better informed than yourselves?   Be sure that
you are always ready to impart of your knowledge to those within your sphere, who stand in
need of, and are entitled to receive it.   Do
you desire distinction among your companions?
Be sure that your claims to preferment are
founded upon superior attainments; let no am-
bitious passion be suffered to induce you to
envy or supplant a companion who may be
considered as better qualified for promotion
than yourselves; but rather let a laudable emulation induce you to strive to excel each other
in improvement and discipline: ever remembering, that he, who faithfully performs his duty,
even in a subordinate or private station, is as
justly entitled to esteem and respect, as he who
is invested with supreme authority.

ADDRESS to the Chapter at large.

COMPANIONS,

The exercise and management of the sublime
degrees of masonry in your Chapter hitherto.
are so highly appreciated, and the good reputation of the Chapter so well established, that I
must presume these considerations alone, were
there no others of greater magnitude, would be
sufficient to induce you to preserve and to perpetuate this valuable and honorable character.
But when to this is added the pleasure which

every philanthropic heart must feel in doing good, in promoting good order, in diffusing light and knowledge, in cultivating Masonic and Christian charity, which are the great objects of this sublime institution, I cannot doubt that your future conduct, and that of your successors, will be calculated still to increase the lustre of your justly esteemed reputation.

May your *chapter* become *beautiful* as the *temple*, *peaceful* as the *ark*, and *sacred* as its *most holy place*. May your oblations of *piety* and *praise* be *grateful* as the *incense ;* your love *warm* as its *flame*, and your charity diffusive as its fragrance. May your hearts be *pure* as the *altar*, and your conduct *acceptable* as the *offering*. May the exercises of your *charity* be as constant as the returning wants of the distressed *widow* and helpless *orphan*. May the approbation of Heaven be your encouragement, and the testimony of a good conscience your support : may you be endowed with every good and perfect gift, while *travelling* the *rugged path* of life, and finally be *admitted within the veil* of heaven to the full enjoyment of life eternal. So mote it be. Amen.

34. *The officers and members of the Chapter will then pass in review in front of the Grand Officers, with their hands crossed on their breasts, bowing as they pass.*

35. *The Grand Marshal will then proclaim the Chapter, by the name of* ———, *to be regularly contituted, and its officers duly installed.*

36. *The ceremonies conclude with an Ode, or ap-propriate piece of music.*

37. *The procession is then formed, when they re-turn to the place from whence they set out*

38. *When the Grand officers retire, the Chapter will form an avenue for them to pass through, and salute them with the grand honors. The two bodies then separately close their respective Chapters.*

CONSTITUTION

OF THE

GENERAL GRAND ROYAL ARCH CHAPTER

OF THE

UNITED STATES OF AMERICA.

ARTICLE 1.

OF THE GENERAL GRAND CHAPTER.

SECT. 1. There shall be a General Grand Chapter of Royal Arch Masons for the United States of America, which shall be holden as is hereinafter directed, and shall consist of a General Grand High Priest, Deputy General Grand High Priest, General Grand King, General Grand Scribe, Secretary, Treasurer, Chaplain, and Marshal; and likewise of the several Grand and Deputy Grand High Priests, Kings, and Scribes, for the time being, of the several State Grand Chapters, under the jurisdiction of this General Grand Chapter; and of the Past General Grand High Priests, Deputy General Grand High Priests, Kings, and Scribes, of the said General Grand Chapter; and the aforesaid officers, or their proxies, shall be the only members and voters in said General Grand Chapter. And no person shall be

14

constituted a proxy, unless he be a present or past officer of this or a State Grand Chapter.

SECT. 2. The General Grand Chapter shall meet septennially, on the second Thursday in September, for the choice of officers, and other business : dating from the second Thursday in September, A. D. 1805, at such place as may, from time to time, be appointed.

SECT. 3. A special meeting of the General Grand Chapter shall be called whenever the General Grand High Priest, Deputy General Grand High Priest, General Grand King, and General Grand Scribe, or any two of them may deem it necessary; and also whenever it may be required by a majority of the Grand Chapters of the States aforesaid, provided such requisition be made known in writing, by the said Grand Chapters respectively, to the General Grand High Priest, Deputy General Grand High Priest, King or Scribe.—And it shall be the duty of the said General Officers, and they are each of them severally authorized, empowered and directed, upon receiving official notice of such requisition from a majority of the General Grand Chapters aforesaid, to appoint a time and place of meeting, and notify each of the State Grand Chapters thereof accordingly.

SECT. 4. I. shall be incumbent on the General Grand High Priest, Deputy General Grand High Priest, General Grand King, and General Grand Scribe, severally to improve and perfect themselves in the sublime Arts, and work of Mark Masters, Past Masters, Most Excellent Masters, and Roya Arch Masons; to make themselves Masters of the several Masonic Lectures and Ancient Charges;—to consult with each other, and with the Grand and Deputy Grand High Priests, Kings and Scribes of the several States aforesaid, for the purpose of adopting measures suitable and proper for diffusing a knowledge of the said Lectures and Charges, and an uniform mode of *working*, in the several Chapters and Lodges throughout this jurisdiction; and the better to effect this laudable purpose, the aforesaid General Grand Officers are severally hereby authorized, and empowered, to visit and preside in any and every Chapter of Royal Arch Masons, and lodge of Most Excellent, Past, or Mark Master Masons, throughout the said States, and to give such instructions and directions as the good of the Fraternity may require; always adhering to the ancient landmarks of the order.

SECT. 5. In all cases of the absence of any Officer from any body of masons, instituted or holden by virtue of this Constitution, the officer next in rank shall succeed his superior; unless through courtesy said Officer should decline in favor of a past superior Officer present.—And in case of the absence of all the Officers from any legal meeting of either of the bodies aforesaid, the members present, according to seniority, and abilities, shall fill the several Offices.

SECT. 6. In every Chapter or Lodge of Masons, instituted or holden by virtue of this Constitution, all questions (except upon the admission of members or candidates) shall be determined by a majority of votes; the presiding Officer for the time being, being entitled to vote, if a Member; and in case the votes should at any time be equally divided, the presiding Officer as aforesaid, shall give the casting vote.

SECT. 7. The General Grand Royal Arch Chapter shall be competent (on concurrence of two thirds of its members present) at any time hereafter, to revise, amend and alter this Constitution.

SECT. 8. In case any casualty should, at any time hereafter, prevent the septennial election of Officers, the several General Grand Officers shall sustain their respective offices until successors are duly elected and qualified.

SECT. 9. The General Grand High Priest, Deputy General Grand High Priest, General Grand King, and General Grand Scribe, shall severally have power and authority to institute new Royal Arch Chapters, and Lodges of the subordinate degrees, in any State in which there is not a Grand Chapter regularly established. But no new Chapter shall be instituted in any State wherein there is a Chapter or Chapters holden under the authority of this Constitution, without a recommendation from the Chapter nearest the residence of the petitioners.— The fees for instituting a new Royal Arch Chapter with the subordinate degrees, shall be ninety dollars; and for a new Mark Master's Lodge, twenty dollars; exclusive of such compensation to the Grand Secretary, as the Grand Officers aforesaid may deem reasonable.

ARTICLE II.

OF THE STATE GRAND ROYAL ARCH CHAPTERS.

SECT. 1. The STATE GRAND CHAPTERS shall sev·
erally consist of a Grand High Priest, Deputy Grand
High Priest, Grand King, Grand Scribe, Grand Secretary, Grand Treasurer, Grand Chaplain, and Grand
Marshal, and likewise of the High Priests, Kings and
Scribes, for the time being, of the several Chapters
over which they shall respectively preside, and of
the Past Grand and Deputy Grand High Priests,
Kings and Scribes of the said Grand Chapters; and
the said enumerated officers (or their proxies) shall
be the only members and voters in the said Grand
Chapters respectively.

SECT. 2. The State Grand Chapters shall severally be holden at least once in every year, at such
times and places as they shall respectively direct;
and the Grand or Deputy Grand High Priests respectively, for the time being, may at any time call
a special meeting, to be holden at such place as they
shall severally think proper to appoint.

SECT. 3. The Officers of the State Grand Chapters shall be chosen annually, by ballot, at such time
and place as the said Grand Chapters shall respectively direct.

SECT. 4. The several State Grand Chapters (subject to the provisions of this Constitution) shall have
the sole government and superintendence of the several Royal Arch Chapters, and Lodges of most Excellent, Past and Mark Master Masons, within their re-

14*

spective jurisdictions; to assign their limits and settle controversies that may happen between them; —and shall have power, under their respective seals, and the sign manual of their respective Grand or Deputy Grand High Priests, Kings and Scribes, (or their legal proxies,) attested by their respective Secretaries, to constitute new Chapters of Royal Arch Masons, and Lodges of Most Excellent, Past, and Mark Master Masons, within their respective jurisdictions.

SECT. 5. The Grand and Deputy Grand High Priests severally, shall have the power and authority, whenever they shall deem it expedient, (during the recess of the Grand Chapter of which they are officers,) to grant Letters of Dispensation, under their respective hands, and private seals, to a competent number of petitioners (possessing the qualifications required by the 9th Section of the 2d Article,) empowering them to open a Chapter of Royal Arch Masons, and Lodge of Most Excellent, Past and Mark Master Masons, for a certain specified term of time: provided, that the said term of time shall not extend beyond the next meeting of the Grand Chapter of the State in which such Dispensation shall be granted; and provided further, that the same fees as are required by this Constitution for Warrants, shall be first deposited in the hands of the Grand Treasurer.—And in all cases of such Dispensations, the Grand or Deputy Grand High Priests respectively, who may grant the same, shall make report thereof, at the next stated meeting of the Grand Chapter of their respective jurisdictions, when the said Grand Chapters, respectively, may either continue or recall the said Dispensations, or may grant the petitioners a warrant of Constitution : And in case such warrant shall be granted, the fees first deposited, shall be credited in payment for the same ; but if a warrant should not be granted, nor the dispensation continued, the said fees shall be refunded to the petitioners, except only such part thereof as shall have been actually expended by means of their application.

SECT. 6. The several State Grand Chapters shall possess authority, upon the institution of new Royal Arch Chapters, or Lodges of Mark Masters, within their respective jurisdictions, to require the payment of such fees as they may deem expedient and proper ; which said fees shall be advanced and paid into the Treasury before a warrant or charter shall be issued.

SECT. 7. No warrant shall be granted, for instituting Lodges of Most Excellent or Past Masters, independent of a Chapter of Royal Arch Masons.

SECT. 8. The Grand Chapters severally, shall have power to require from the several Chapters and Lodges under their respective jurisdictions, such reasonable proportion of sums, received by them for the exaltation or advancement of candidates, and such certain annual sums from their respective members, as by their ordinances or regulations shall hereafter be appointed ; all which said sums or dues shall be made good, and paid annually, by the said Chapters and Lodges respectively, into the Grand Treasury of the Grand Chapter under which they hold their authority, on or before the first day of the respective annual meetings of the said Grand Chapters.

SECT. 9. No warrant for the institution of a new Chapter of Royal Arch Masons shall be granted, except upon the petition of nine regular Royal Arch Masons; which petition shall be accompanied by a certificate from the Chapter nearest to the place where the new Chapter is intended to be opened, vouching for the moral characters, and masonic abilities of the petitioners, and recommending to the Grand Chapter under whose authority they act, to grant their prayer. And no warrant for the institution of a Lodge of Mark Master Masons shall be granted, except upon the petition of (at least) five regular Mark Master Masons, accompanied by vouchers from the nearest Lodge of that degree, similar to those required upon the institution of a Chapter.

SECT. 10. The Grand Secretaries of the State Grand Chapters, shall severally make an annual communication to each other, and also to the General Grand Secretary, containing a list of Grand Officers, and all such other matters as may be deemed necessary for the mutual information of the said Grand Chapters. And the said Grand Secretaries shall also regularly transmit to the General Grand Secretary, a copy of all their by-laws and regulations.

SECT. 11. Whenever there shall have been three or more, Royal Arch Chapters instituted in any State, by virtue of authority derived from this Constitution, a Grand Chapter may be formed in such State, (with the approbation of one or more of the General Grand Officers,) by the High Priests, Kings nd Scribes of the said Chapters, who shall be authorized to elect the Grand Officers. Provided always, that no new State Grand Chapter shall be formed until after the expiration of one year from the establishment of the junior Chapter in such State.

SECT. 12. The several Grand and Deputy Grand High Priests, Kings and Scribes, for the time being, of the several State Grand Chapters, are bound to the performance of the same duties, and are invested with the same powers and prerogatives, throughout their respective jurisdictions, as are prescribed to the General Officers, in the 4th Section, 1st Article, of this Constitution.

SECT. 13. The jurisdiction of the several State Grand Chapters, shall not extend beyond the limits of the State in which they shall respectively be holden.

ARTICLE III.

OF THE SUBORDINATE CHAPTERS AND LODGES

SECT. 1. All legally constituted assemblies of Royal Arch Masons are called CHAPTERS; as regular bodies of Mark Masters, Past Masters, and Most Excellent Masters, are called LODGES. Every Chapter ought to assemble for work at least once in every three months; and must consist of an High Priest, King, Scribe, Captain of the Host, Principal Sojourner, Royal Arch Captain, three Grand Masters, Secretary, Treasurer, and as many Members as may be found convenient for working to advantage.

SECT. 2. Every Chapter of Royal Arch Masons, and Lodge of Mark Master Masons, throughout this jurisdiction, shall have a warrant of Constitution from the Grand Chapter of the State in which they may respectively be holden, or a Warrant from one of the General Grand Officers. And no Chapter or Lodge shall be deemed legal without such warrant; and Masonic communication (either public or private) is hereby interdicted and forbidden, between any Chapter or Lodge under this jurisdiction, or any member of either of them, and any Chapter, Lodge or Assembly, that may be so illegally formed, opened or holden, without such warrant, or any or either of their members, or any person exalted or advanced in such illegal Chapter or Lodge. But nothing in this Section shall be construed to affect any Chapter or Lodge which was established before the adoption of the Grand Royal Arch Constitution at Hartford, (on the 27th day of January, A. D. 1798.)

SECT. 3. Whenever a Warrant is issued for instituting a Chapter of Royal Arch Masons, with a power in said Warrant to open and hold a Lodge of Most Excellent, Past, and Mark Master Masons, the High Priest, King and Scribe, for the time being, of such Chapter, shall be the Master and Wardens in said Lodges, according to seniority.

SECT. 4. All applications for the exaltation or advancement of Candidates, in any Chapter or Lodge, under this jurisdiction, shall lie over, at least one meeting, for the consideration of the members.

SECT. 5 No mason shall be a member of **two**

separate and distinct bodies, of the same denomination, at one and the same time.

SECT. 6. No Chapter shall be removed, without the knowledge of the High Priest, nor any motion made for that purpose in his absence; but if the High Priest be present, and a motion s made and seconded, for removing the Chapter to some more convenient place, (within the limits prescribed in their Warrant,) the High Priest shall forthwith cause notifications to be issued to all the members, informing them of the motion for removal, and of the time and place when the question is to be determined; which notice shall be issued at least ten days previous to the appointed meeting. But if the High Priest (after motion duly made and seconded as aforesaid) should refuse or neglect to cause the notices to be issued as aforesaid, the officer next n rank, who may be present at the next regular .neeting following, (upon motion made and seconded ior that purpose,) may in like manner issue the said notices.

SECT. 7. All Mark Master Masons' Lodges shall be regulated, in cases of removal, by the same rules as are prescribed in the foregoing Section for the removal of Chapters.

SECT. 8. The High Priest, and other Officers, of every Chapter, and the Officers of every Lodge of Mark Master Masons, shall be chosen annually, bv ballot.

SECT. 9 The High Priest of every Chapter has it in special charge, as appertaining to his office, duty and dignity, to see that the by-laws of his Chapter, as well as the General Grand Royal Arch Con-

stitution, and the General Regulations of the Grand
Chapter, be duly observed ; that all the other Officers
of his Chapter perform the duties of their respective
offices faithfully, and are examples of diligence and
industry to their companions ;—that true and exact
records be kept of all the proceedings of the Chapter
by the Secretary, that the Treasurer keep and render exact and just accounts of all the monies belonging to the Chapter ; that regular returns be made by
the Secretary, annually, to the Grand Chapter, of all
admissions of candidates or members ; and that the
annual dues to the Grand Chapter be regularly and
punctually paid. He has the special care and charge
of the Warrant of his Chapter.—He has the right
and authority of calling his Chapter at pleasure, upon
any emergency or occurrence which in his judgment
may require their meeting ; and he is to fill the chair
when present. It is likewise his duty, together with
his King and Scribe, to attend the meetings of the
Grand Chapter (when duly summoned by the Grand
Secretary) either in person, or by proxy.

SECT. 10. For the preservation of secrecy and good
harmony, and in order that due decorum may be observed while the Chapter is engaged in business, a
worthy Royal Arch Mason is to be appointed from
time to time for tyling the Chapter. His duty is
fixed by custom, and known in all regular Chapters.
He may be elected annually, but is to continue in
office only during good behavior, and is to be paid
for his services.

SECT. 11. All Lodges of Mark Master Masons are
bound to observe the two preceding articles, as far as
they can be applied to the government of a *Lodge.*

Sect. 12. No Chapter shall confer the degrees of Mark Master Mason, Past Master, Most Excellen Master, and Royal Arch Mason, upon any Brother for a less sum than Twenty Dollars.—And no Lodge of Mark Master Masons shall advance a Brother to that degree, for a less sum than Four Dollars.

Sect. 13. When either of the officers or Members of the General Grand Chapter, or any of the State Grand Chapters, cannot personally attend their respective meetings, they shall severally have the authority to constitute a proxy, which proxy shall have the same right to a seat and vote as his constituent.

ARTICLE IV.

OF CONSTITUTING NEW CHAPTERS.

Sect. 1. [See Order of High Priesthood, from page 122 to 156.]

Sect. 2. At the institution of all Lodges of Mark Master Masons, under this jurisdiction, the same ceremonies as are prescribed in the foregoing section, are to be observed, as far as they will apply to that degree.

Sect. 3. Whenever it shall be inconvenient for the General Grand Officers, or the Grand or Deputy Grand High Priests, respectively, to attend in person, to constitute a new Chapter or Lodge, and install the Officers, they shall severally have power and authority to appoint some worthy High Priest, or Past High Priest, to perform the necessary ceremonies.

Sect. 4. The Officers of every Chapter and Lodge under this jurisdiction, before they enter upon the exercise of their respective Offices, and also the mem-

15

bers of all such Chapters and Lodges, and every candidate upon his admission into the same, shall take
the following obligation, viz. " I, A. B., do promise
and swear, that I will support and maintain the
General Grand Royal Arch Constitution."

I HEREBY certify that the foregoing is a true copy
of the General Grand Royal Arch Constitution for
the United States of America, as altered, amended
and ratified, at a meeting of the General Grand
Chapter, begun and holden at New York, in the State
of New York, on the 6th day of June, A. D. 1816.

 Witness

  JOHN ABBOT, *G. G. Secretary.*

A LIST OF

GRAND LODGES AND GRAND CHAPTERS,

*Their Annual place of Meeting, with the number of
Subordinate Lodges and Chapters.*

MAINE.

Grand Lodge—Annual Communication held at Portland.
Grand Chapter— " Convocation "
Number of Subordinate Lodges, 58. Number of Subordinate Chapters, 11.

NEW HAMPSHIRE.

Grand Lodge—Annual Communication held at Portsmouth.
Grand Chapter— " ,Convocation " Concord.
Number of Subordinate Lodges, 18. Number of Subordinate Chapters, 10.

MASSACHUSETTS.

Grand Lodge—Annual Communication held at Masonic
Temple, Boston.
Grand Chapter— " Convocation "
Number of Subordinate Lodges, 27. Number of Subordinate Chapters ——.

RHODE ISLAND.

Grand Lodge—Annual Communication held at Providence.
Grand Chapter— " Convocation "
Number of Subordinate Lodges, 19. Number of Subordinate Chapters, 7.

CONNECTICUT.

Grand Lodge—Annual Communication held alternately
at New Haven and Hartford.
Grand Chapter—Annual Convocation " "
Number of Subordinate Lodges, 36. Number of Subordinate Chapters, 16.

VERMONT.

Grand Lodge—Annual Communication held at Montpelier.
Grand Chapter— " Convocation " "
Number of Subordinate Lodges, ——. Number of Subordinate Chapters, ——.

NEW YORK.

Grand Lodge—Annual Communication held in the city of New York.

Grand Chapter— "   Convocation   "   "

Number of Subordinate Lodges, 114. Number of Subordinate Chapters, 36.

NEW JERSEY.

Grand Lodge—Annual Communication held at Trenton

Grand Chapter— "   Convocation   "   "

Number of Subordinate Lodges, 17. Number of Subordinate Chapters, 6.

PENNSYLVANIA.

Grand Lodge—Annual Communication held at Philadelphia.

Grand Chapter—Annual Convocation   "   "

Number of Subordinate Lodges, 267. Number of Subordinate Chapters, 17.

DELAWARE.

Grand Lodge—Annual Communication held at Wilmington.

Grand Chapter— "   Convocation   "   "

Number of Subordinate Lodges, ——. Number of Subordinate Chapters, ——.

MARYLAND.

Grand Lodge—Annual Communication held at Baltimore.

Grand Chapter— "   Convocation   "   "

Number of Subordinate Lodges, 47. Number of Subordinate Chapters, 15.

DISTRICT OF COLUMBIA.

Grand Lodge—Annual Communication held at Washington.

Grand Chapter— "   Convocation   "   "

Number of Subordinate Lodges, 15. Number of Subordinate Chapters, ——. Under the Grand Chapter of Maryland.

VIRGINIA.

Grand Lodge—Annual Communication held at Richmond!

Grand Chapter— "   Convocation   "   "

Number of Subordinate Lodges, 155. Number of Subordinate Chapters, 15.

NORTH CAROLINA.

Grand Lodge—Annual Communication held at Raleigh

Grand Chapter— "   Convocation   "   "

Number of Subordinate Lodges, 108. Number of Subordinate Chapters, 27.

SOUTH CAROLINA.

Grand Lodge—Annual Communication held at Charleston.
Grand Chapter— " Convocation " "
Number of Subordinate Lodges, 65. Number of Subor
dinate Chapters, 13.

GEORGIA.

Grand Lodge—Annual Communication held at Macon.
Grand Chapter— " Convocation " "
Number of Subordinate Lodges, 43. Number of Subor
dinate Chapters, 17.

FLORIDA.

Grand Lodge—Annual Communication held at Tallahassa.
Grand Chapter— " Convocation " "
Number of Subordinate Lodges, 15. Number of Subor-
dinate Chapters, 4.

ALABAMA.

Grand Lodge—Annual Communication held at Tuscaloosa.
Grand Chapter— " Convocation " "
Number of Subordinate Lodges, 59. Number of Subor-
dinate Chapters, 21.

LOUISIANA.

Grand Lodge—Annual Communication held at N. Orleans.
Grand Chapter— " Convocation " "
Number of Subordinate Lodges, 23. Number of Subor-
tinate Chapters, 13.

MISSISSIPPI.

Grand Lodge—Annual Communication held at Natchez.
Grand Chapter— " Convocation " "
Number of Subordinate Lodges, 51. Number of Subor-
dinate Chapters, 6.

ARKANSAS.

Grand Lodge—Annual Communication held at Little Rock.
Grand Chapter— " Convocation " "
Number of Subordinate Lodges, 12. Number of Subor-
dinate Chapters, 4.

MISSOURI.

Grand Lodge—Annual Communication held at St. Louis.
Grand Chapter— " Convocation " "
Number of Subordinate Lodges, 74. Number of Subor-
dinate Chapters, 5.

TENNESSEE.

Grand Lodge—Annual Communication held at Nashville.
Grand Chapter— " Convocation " "
Number of Subordinate Lodges, 108. Number of Sub-
ordinate Chapters, 7.

KENTUCKY.

Grand Lodge—Annual Communication held at Lexington.
Grand Chapter— "   Convocation   "   "
Number of Subordinate Lodges, 142. Number of Sub-
ordinate Chapters, 15.

INDIANA.

Grand Lodge—Annual Communication held at Indian-
apolis.
Grand Chapter— "   Convocation   "   "
Number of Subordinate Lodges, 57. Number of Subor
dinate Chapters, 4.

ILLINOIS.

Grand Lodge—Annual Communication held at Jacksom-
ville.
Grand Chapter— "   Convocation   "   "
Number of Subordinate Lodges, 28. Number of Subordinate Chapters, ——.

OHIO.

Grand Lodge—Annual Communication held at Columbus.
Grand Chapter— "   Convocation   "   "
Number of Subordinate Lodges, 97. Number of Subor-
dinate Chapters, 18.

MICHIGAN.

Grand Lodge—Annual Communication held at Detroit.
Grand Chapter— "   Convocation   "   "
Number of Subordinate Lodges, 9. Number of Subordi-
nate Chapters, ——.

WISCONSIN.

Grand Lodge Annual Communication held at Madison.
Grand Chapter-   "   Convocation   "   "
Number of Subordinate Lodges, 10. Number of Subor-
dinate Chapters, ——.

IOWA.

Grand Lodge—Annual Communication held at Iowa.
Grand Chapter— "   Convocation   "   "
Number of Subordinate Lodges, 4. Number of Subordi-
nate Chapters, ——.

TEXAS.

Grand Lodge—Annua. Communication held at Washington.
Grand Chapter— "   Convocation   "   "
Number of Subordinate Lodges, 25. Number of Subordinate Chapters, 5.

MASONIC SONGS.

ENTERED APPRENTICE'S SONG.

JUST straight from his home, See yon candidate come,

JUST straight from his home, See yon candidate come

Pre - par'd for the time and oc - ca - sion;

Pre - par'd for the time and oc - ca - sion;

Of all that can harm, We will him dis-arm.

Of all that can harm, We will him dis-arm.

That he no way may hurt a Free Ma - son.

That he no way may hurt a Free Ma - son.

His eyes cannot search
Out the way of his march,
Nor yet where his steps he must place on :
When him we receive,
He cannot perceive
How he came to be made a **Free Mason.**

Then he'll danger defy,
And on Heaven rely
For strength to support the occasion,
With the blessing of prayer
He banishes fear,
And undaunted is made a Free Mason.

When he makes his demand,
By the master's command,
To know if he's fit for the station,
Around he is brought,
Ere he get what he sought
From a free and an accepted **Mason.**

When girded with care,
By the help of the square,
The emblem of truth and of **reason,**
In form he is placed,
While to him are rehearsed
The mysteries of a Free Mason ;

Then full in his sight
Doth shine the grand light,
To illumine the works which we trace **on ;**
And now, as his due,
He's clothed in full view
With the badge of an accepted **Mason.**

Now hark ! we enlarge
On the duties and charge,
Where his conduct and walk he must place **on ;**
Then our rites we'll fulfil,
And show our good will
To a free and an accepted Mason.

FELLOW CRAFT'S SONG.

When earth's foun-da - tion first was laid,

By the Al - migh - ty Ar-tist's hand;

'Twas then our per-fect, our perfect laws were made,

Es - tablish'd by his strict command.

Chorus.

Hail! mys-te-rious, Hail, glorious Mason - ry.

Hail! mys-te-rious, Hail, glorious Mason - ry!

Hail! mys-te-rious, Hail, glorious Mason - ry!

That makes us ev - - er great and free.

That makes us ev - - er great and free.

That makes us ev - - er great and free.

In vain mankind for shelter sought,
    In vain from place to place did roam,
Until from Heaven, from Heaven he was taught
    To plan, to build, to fix his home

Illustrious hence we date our Art,
    And now in beauteous piles appear,
We shall to endless, to endless time impart,
    How worthy and how great we are.

Nor we less fam'd for every tie,
    By which the human thought is bound;
Love, *truth*, and *friendship*, and friendship socially
    Join all our hearts and hands around.

Our actions still by Virtue blest,
    And to our precepts ever true,
The world admiring, admiring shall request
    To learn, and our bright paths pursue.

MASTER'S SONG.

BY A BROTHER.

Andante.

In   har - mo - ny   the   so - cial band

Are   met   a - round   the   fount o' *light,*

To spend be-neath the Mas-ter's hand

In de-cent joy the fes - tive night;

Let each in truth and hon-our bright

Be pres-ent at the *se - cret hall,*

And on his heart in si-lence write

The sa - cred *Word* that binds us all.

Beneath the blue and starry zone,
Whose arch high swelling girds the po'e,
The Master on his *orient throne*
Unfolds to view the mystic roll;
At once the pure fraternal soul
Bends to the *sign* with sacred awe
And reads upon the letter'd scroll
In words of light, the unutter'd *law*

16

Let us our hearts and hands entwine
And form one perfect wreath of *love ;*
Then kneeling at the voice divine
That spake to mortals from above,
Put on the meekness of the dove,
And the white robes of *charity,*
And in unerring wisdom prove
Our brethren with the single eye.

Be there no darkling scow. of hate
Upon the calm unruffled brow,
But each in innocence elate
To Virtue's brightness only bow:
Blest guardian of all pleasures!   Thou
Be ever at our Master's side,
And mark with radiant finger how
Thy *words* can be our only guide.

By thee conducted we ascend
The *steps* that lead alone to Heaven
And where the mounting arches end
To each the *sign* of *worth* is given ;
Then mantled by the shades of even
We meet beneath the unclouded sky,
And bind the links no power hath riven,
In which we swear to live and die.

Let us these favored hours employ,
These moments of the social night
To sing the silver song of joy,
And make the chain of *union* bright
So may we even here unite
To spend the hours in mercy given,
Led by the *tokens* which invite
Alone to happiness and Heaven.

MASTER'S SONG.

BY BROTHER T. S. WEBB.

SOLO. Moderato.

I sing the Ma - son's glo - ry,

Whose pry - ing' mind doth burn,

Un - - to com - plete per - fec - tion

Our mys - te - ries to learn;

Not those who vis - it, Lodg - es

To eat and drink their fill,

Not   those who   at   our   meet-ings

Hear   lec - tures 'gainst their   will,

DUET. Mezza Voce.

But   on - ly those whose plea-sure,

At   ev'ry lodge can   be, T'improve themselves by

lec - tures, . In   glo-rious Ma-son - ry.

TRIO. CHORUS. For.

Hail! glorious Mason-ry! Hail! glorious Ma-son-ry!

Hail! glorious Mason-ry! Hail! glorious Ma-son-ry!

T'improve themselves by lectures, In glorious Masonry.

T'improve themselves by lectures, In glorious Masonry.

The faithful, worthy brother,
Whose heart can feel for grief,
Whose bosom with compassion
Steps forth to its relief,

16*

Whose soul is ever ready,
   Around him to diffuse
The principles of Masons,
   And guard them from abuse ,

Chorus.   These are thy sons, whose pleasure,
   At every lodge, will be,
T' improve themselves by lectures
   In glorious Masonry.
          Hail ! glorious Masonry

King Solomon, our patron,
   Transmitted this command—
" The faithful and praise-worthy
   True light must understand ;
And my descendants, also,
   Who're seated in the *East*,
Have not fulfilled their duty,
   Till light has reached the *West.*"

Chorus.   Therefore, our highest pleasure,
   At every lodge, should be,
T' improve ourselves by lectures
   In glorious Masonry.
          Hail ! glorious Masonry.

The duty and the station,
   Of master in the chair,
Obliges him to summon
   Each brother to prepare ;
That all may be enabled,
   By slow, though sure degrees,
To answer in rotation,
   With honor and with ease.

Chorus.   Such are thy sons, whose pleasure,
   At every lodge, will be,
T' improve themselves by lectures
   In glorious Masonry.
          Hail ! glorious Masonry

THE MASON'S ADIEU.

WORDS BY BURNS.

ADIEU, a heart warm, fond a - dieu,

Ye bro - thers of our mys - tic tie;

Ye fa-vour'd and en - - light - en'd few,

Com pan ions of my so - cial joy;

Though I to for - eign lands must hie,

Pur - - su - - ing for - tune's slipp' - ry ba';

With melt - ing heart and brim - ful eye,

I'll mind you still when far a - wa'.

Oft have I met your social band,
To spend a cheerful, festive night,
Oft, honour'd with supreme command
Presiding o'er the sons of light:
And by that hieroglyphic bright,
Which none but craftsmen ever saw,
Strong mem'ry on my heart shall write
Those happy scenes when far awa'.

May freedom, harmony, and love,
Cement you in the grand design,
Beneath th' Omniscient Eye above,
The glorious Architect divine:
That you may keep th' unerring line
Still guided by the plummet's law,
'Till order bright completely shine,
Shall be my prayer when far awa'

And you, farewell, whose merits claim
Justly that highest badge to wear,
May heaven bless your noble name,
To Masonry and friendship dear:
My last request permit me then,
When yearly you're assembled a',
One round, I ask it with a tear,
To him, your friend that's far awa'

And you, kind-hearted sisters, fair,
I sing farewell to all your charms,
Th' impression of your pleasing air
With rapture oft my bosom warms.
Alas! the social winter's night
No more returns while breath I draw,
'Till sisters, brothers, all unite,
In that Grand Lodge that's far awa'.

ODE FOR GRAND VISITATION.

WORDS BY R. T. PAINE, ESQ.

Allegro ma non Presto.

SWEET Min-strel who to mortal ears, Canst

SWEET Min-strel who to mortal ears, Canst

SWEET Min-strel who to mortal ears, Canst

tell the Art, which guides the spheres, Bless'd Ma-son-

tell the Art, which guides the spheres, Bless'd Ma-son-

tell the Art, which guides the spheres, Bless'd Ma-son-

Pia.

ry, all hai. With nature's birth thy laws be - gan

ry, all hail!

ry, all hail! With nature's birth thy laws be - gan

To rule on earth fra - ter - nal man, And still   in

To rule on earth fra - ter - nal man, And still   in

For.

heav'n prevail, With nature's birth   thy laws began

With nature's   birth   thy laws be-gan

heav'n prevail, With nature's birth   thy laws be-gan

To rule on earth fra - ter - nal man, And

To rule on earth fra - ter - nal man,

To rule on earth fra - ter - nal man, And

still in heav'n pre - vail.

And still in heav'n pre - vail.

still in heav'n pre - vail.

17

O'er matter's modes thy mystic **sway**
Can fashion Chaos' devious way,
   To order's lucid maze ;
Can rear the cloud-assaulting tow'r,
And bid the worm, that breathes its **nour,**
   Its humble palace raise.

From nascent life to being's pride,
The surest boon thy laws provide,
   When wayward fate beguiles ;
The tears thou shed'st for human **woe,**
In falling shine like Iris' bow,
   And beam an arch of smiles.

Come, Priest of Science, truth **array'd,**
And with thee bring each tuneful **maid,**
   Thou lov'st on Shinar's plains ;
Revive Creation's primal **plan,**
Subdue this wilderness of **man,**
   Bid social *virtue* reign.

HYMN FOR CONSECRATION.

HAIL! u - ni - ver-sal Lord, By

HAIL! u - ni - ver-sal Lord, By

Heav'n and earth a - dor'd, All hail, great God!

Heav'n and earth a - dor'd, All hail, great God!

Be - fore thy throne we bend, To

Be - fore thy throne we bend, To

us thy grace ex - tend, And to our

us thy grace ex - tend, And to our

pray'r at - tend!   All   hail, great God!

pray'r at - tend!   All   hail, great God!

O, hear our prayer to-day,
Turn not thy face away,
   O Lord our God!
Heaven, thy dread dwelling place
Cannot contain thy Grace,
Remember now our race,
   O Lord our God!

God of our fathers, hear,
And to our cry be near,
   Jehovah, God!
The Heavens eternal bow,
Forgive in mercy now
Thy suppliants here, O Thou,
   Jehovah, God!

17*

Tc thee our hearts do draw,
On them O write thy law,
    Our Saviour, God!
When in this Lodge we're met,
And at thine altar set,
O, do not us forget,
    Our Saviour, God!

ODE FOR DEDICATION.

BY J. H

AL-MIGH - TY   FATHER! God of Love!

Bassoon.

Sa - cred   e - - - ter - - nal King   of

Kings!   From   thy   ce - les - tial

courts   a - bove, Send beams   of

grace   on   se - raph's   wings,   O,

may   they,   gilt   with   light   di-

vine,   Shed   on   our   hearts   in

spir – ing   rays; While   bend – ing

at this Sa - cred shrine, While

bend - ing at this sa - - - cred shrine,

We of - fer mys-tic songs of praise.

Faith! with divine and heav'nward eye,
  Pointing to radiant realms of bliss,
Shed here thy sweet benignity,
  And crown our works with happiness;
Hope! too, with bosom void of fear,
  Still on thy steadfast anchor lean,
O! shed thy balmy influence nere,
  And fill our breasts with joy serene.

And thou, fair Charity! whose smile
  Can bid the heart forget its woe,
Whose hand can misery's care beguile,
  And kindness' sweetest boon bestow,
Here shed thy sweet soul-soothing ray;
  Soften our hearts, thou Power divine!
Bid the warm gem of pity play,
  With sparkling lustre, on our shrine.

Thou, who art thron'd 'midst dazzling light,
  And wrapp'd in dazzling robes of gold,
Whose flowing locks of silv'ry white
  Thy age and honor both unfold,
Genius of Masonry! descend,
  And guide our steps by thy strict law;
O! swiftly to our temple bend,
  And fill our breasts with solemn awe.

GLEE.

Allegro ma non Presto. Pia.

Hail! mys - te - rious, glo - rious sci ence,

Cres.

Hail! mys - te - rious, glo-rious sci-ence,

Hail! mys - te - rious, glo-rious sci ence,

For,

Hail! mys - te - rious, glo - rious sci-ence,

Hail! mys - te - rious, glo - rious science,

Which to dis - cord bids de - fi - ance,

Which to dis - cord bids de - fi - ance,

Har - mo - ny a - lone reigns here,

Har - mo - ny a - lone reigns here,

Har - mo - ny a - - lone reigns here.

Har - mo - ny a - - lone reigns here.

Mezzo For.

Come let's sing - - - -

Come let's sing to Him that

ris'd us From the rug - ged path that maz'd us,

18

Pia.

To   the   light   that   we   re - vere,

To   the   light   that   we   re - vere,

For.

To the light that   we   re - vere.

To the light that   we   re - vere.

Pia.

Hail, mys-ter' - ous,

Hail, mys-ter' - ous,   glor' - ous   sci-ence,

For.

Hail, myster'ous,   Hail, myster ous,

Hail, myster'ous, glor'-ous sci-ence,Hail,myster'ous

glor' - ous sci-ence,Which to dis-cord gives de-

glor' - ous sci-ence,Which to dis-cord gives de-

Pia.

fi - ance, Har - mo - ny a - lone reigns here.

fi - ance, Har - mo - ny a - lone reigns here.

For.

Har - mo - ny a - - - lons reigns here.

Har - mo - ny a - - -.one reigns here.

ODE TO CHARITY

Music, see page **178**

OFFSPRING of Heav'n, mankind's best friend,
Bright Charity, inspire the lay;
On these celestial shores descend,
And quit the realms of cloudless day:
Chorus. To Thee our constant vows are paid,
Thy praise we hymn, Angelic Maid.

When Vulcan rages unconfin'd,
And Neptune mourns his baffled pow'r;
When flames aspiring with the wind,
To Heaven's high arch resistless tow'r:
Chorus 'Tis thou our hearts with pity's glow,
Inspir'st to feel for human wo.

The house a dismal ruin lies,
Where mirth late tun'd her lyre of joy;
And tears of anguish fill your eyes,
Poor orphan girl, and houseless boy:—
Chorus.   But thou, sweet maid, with pity's glow,
Inspir'st each heart to sooth their wo

Come then, all-bounteous as thou art,
And hide thee from our sight no more;
Touch ev'ry soul, expand each heart,
That breathes on freedom's chosen shore:
Chorus.   Columbia's sons with pity's glow
Inspire to feel for human wo.

———◆———

CHARITY

A HYMN

Andante. Mezzo For.

O   Cha - ri - ty! thou heaven-ly   grace,

O   Cha - ri - ty! thou heaven-ly   grace,

18*

All ten - der, soft, and kind; A friend

All ten - der, soft, and kind; A friend

to all the hu - man race,

to all the hu - man race,

To all that's good and kind.

To all that's good and kind.

Pia.

The man of cha - ri - ty ex-

The man of cha - ri - ty ex-

tends, To all his lib' - ral hand;

tends, To all his lib' - ral hand;

For.

His kin-dred, neighbours, foes, and friends,

His kin-dred, neighbours, foes, and friends,

His   pit - y   may com - mand.

His   pit - y   may com - mand.

He aids the poor in their distress—
  He hears when they complain;
With tender heart delights to bless
  And lessen all there pain:
The sick, the prisoner, poor, and blind,
  And all the sons of grief,
In him a benefactor find,
  He loves to give relief.

'Tis love, that makes religion sweet,
  'Tis love, that makes us rise,
With willing mind and ardent feet,
  To yonder happy skies: ·
Then let us all in love abound,
  And Charity pursue!
Thus shall we be with glory crown'd,
  And love as angels do,

MASONIC HYMN.

FIRST VOICE. Andante.

GREAT Ar-chi-tect! su-preme, di - vine,

SECOND VOICE.

GREAT Ar-chi-tect! su-preme, di - vine,

BASS.

Whose wis - dom plann'd the grand de - sign

Whose wis - dom plann'd the grand de - sign

And gave to na - ture biith!

And gave to na - ture birth!

Pia.

Whose word with light a - dorn'd the skies,

Whose word with light a - dorn'd the skies,

Cres.

Gave mat - ter form, bade or - der rise,

Gave mat - ter form, bade or - der rise,

For.

And bless'd the new-born earth;

And bless'd the new-born earth;

CHORUS.

'Till love shall cease, 'till or - der dies,

'Till love shall cease, 'till or - der dies,

To Thee ma - son - ic praise shall rise.

To Thee ma - son - ic praise shall rise.

Repeat the last Chorus.

O, bless this love-cemented band,
Form'd and supported by the hand,
    For Charity's employ;
To shield the wretched from despair,
To spread through scenes of grief and care,
    Reviving rays of joy
Chorus   'Till love, &c.

The lib'ral Arts, by Thee design'd,
To polish, comfort, aid mankind,
    We labour to improve;
While we adore Jehovah's name,
Pour on our hearts the melting flame,
    And mould our souls to love.
Chorus.   'Till love, &c.

FUNERAL HYMN

MUSIC BY HANDEL

Un - veil thy bo - som faith - ful

Un - veil thy bo - som faith - ful

tomb, Take this new trea - sure to

tomb, Take this new trea - sure to

thy trust, And give these sa - cred

thy trust, And give these sa - cred

re - lics room, To slum ber

re - lics room, To slum - ber

In the si - lent dust,

In the si - lent dust,

And give these sa - cred

And give these sa - cred

re - lics room   To slum ber

re - .ics room   To slun ber

in the si - lent dust.

in the si - lent dust.

Nor pain, nor grief, nor anxious fear,
Invade thy bounds; no mortal woes
Can reach the silent sleepers here,
And Angels watch their soft repose.

So Jesus slept; God's dying Son,
Past through the grave, and blest the bed;
Rest here, dear Saint, 'till from His throne
The morning break, and pierce the shade.

Break from his throne, illustrious Morn!
Attend, O Earth, his sov'reign Word!
Restore thy trust, a glorious form,
He must ascend to meet his Lord

MOST EXCELLENT MASTER'S ODE.

MUSIC BY A. BROWN.

ALL things in darkness lay, The *Word* went forth,

Up sprung ce-les-tial day,   At na-ture's birth;

The heaven - ly *Arch* sub-lime - ly bent a - bove,

And on the *key stone* blaz'd E-TERNAL LOVE.

19*

Heaven's favourite, man was made
   In beauty fair,
Crime chang'd blest Eden's shade
   To black despair;
Love from the sacred Arch came gently down,
Rais'd man from death, to an immortal crown.

Love, then, in chorus sing,
   Hail Love divine.
Masons your *Cassia* bring
   To deck his shrine;
Christians unite while Angels join in song,
All Earth and Heaven the glorious strain prolong.

ROYAL ARCH SONG.

BY A COMPANION.

MUSIC BY J. WHITAKER.

JOY! the sa - cred *Law* is found, Now the
Tem - ple stands com - plete, Glad - ly let us ga - ther
round, Where the Pon - tiff holds his seat. Now he

spreads the vol - ume wide, Ope-ning forth its leaves to day, And the Mon-arch by his side, Ga - zes on the bright dis - play.

Joy! the secret *vault* is found;
Full the *sunbeam* falls within,
Pointing darkly under ground,
To the treasure we would wir.
They have brought it forth to light,
And again it cheers the earth;
All its leaves are purely bright,
Shining in their newest worth.

This shall be the sacred *mark*
Which shall guide us to the skies,
Bearing, like a *holy ark*,
All the hearts who love to rise;
This shall be the *corner stone*
Which the builders threw away,
But was found the only one
Fitted for the *arch's* stay.

This shall be the *gavel* true,
At whose sound the crowd shall bend,
Giving to the *law* its due ;
This shall be the faithful friend ;
This tne token, which shall bring
Kindness to the sick and poor,
Hastening on, on angel's wing,
To the lone and *darksome door*.

This shall crown the mighty *arch*,
When the temple springs on high,
And the brethren bend their march
Wafting *incense* to the sky.
Then the solemn strain shall swell
From the bosom and the tongue,
And the Master's glory tell
In the harmony of song.

Here the exile, o'er the waste
Trudging homeward, shall **repose** ;
All his toils and dangers past,
Here his long sojourning close.
Entering through the sacred *veils*
To the holy cell he bends ;
Then as sinking Nature fails,
Hope in glad fruition ends.

ROYAL ARCH SONG.

Andante Pomposo.

WHEN or' - ent Wis-dom beam'd se - rene,

And pil - lar'd Strength a - rose;

When beau - ty ting'd the glow - ing scene,

And Faith her man - sion chose; Ex - ult ing

bands the fa - bric view'd, Mys - ter'-ous

pow'rs a - dor'd; And high the Trip-ple

Un - ion stood, And high the Trip - ple

Un - ion stood, That gave the mys - tic

word, - - - - - That gave the mys - tic

word, - - - - - And high the Trip - ple

Un - ion stood, That gave the mys - tic word.

Pale Envy withered at the sight,
And, frowning o'er the pile,
Called *Murder* up from realms of night,
To blast the glorious toil.
With ruffian outrage joined, in woe
They formed the league abhorred;
And wounded Science felt the blow,
That crushed the *Mystic Word*.

Concealment, from sequestered cave,
On sable pinions flew;—
And o'er the sacrilegious grave,
Her veil impervious threw.
The associate band, in solemn state,
The awful loss deplored;
And *Wisdom* mourned the ruthless fate
That whelmed the *Mystic Word*.

At length, through Time's expanded sphere,
Fair Science speeds her way;
And warmed by *Truth's* refulgence, clear
Reflects the kindred ray.
A second fabric's towering height,
Proclaims the *sign* restored;
From whose foundation, brought to light,
Is drawn the *Mystic Word*.

To depths obscure, the favored *Trine*,
A dreary course engage;
Till, through the *Arch*, the ray divine
Illumes the *sacred page*.
From the wide wonders of this blaze,
Our ancient sign's restored;—
The *Royal Arch* alone displays
The long lost *Mystic Word*.

ROYAL ARCH SONG.

Andante Moderato

AL - MIGH-TY SIRE! our heaven-ly king!

Be - fore whose sa - cred name we bend, Ac-

cept the prais - es which we sing, And to our

hum - ble pray'r at - tend; Thou, who didst

Per - sia's king command A pro - cla-ma-tion

to ex - tend, that Is rael's sons might quit

20

the   land, Their ho - ly   Tem-ple   to   at - tend

CHORUS. For.

All hail! great Architect divine! This u-ni-ver-sal

All hail! great Architect divine! This u-ni-ver-sal

frame is thine,   This   u - ni - ver-sal frame is thine,

frame is thine,   This   u - ni - ver-sal frame is thine,

This u - ni-ver-sal frame is thine.

This u - ni-ver-sal frame is thine.

That sacred place, where Three in One
Compris'd thy comprehensive name;
And when the bright meridian Sun
Was seen thy glory to proclaim,
Thy watchful eye, a length of time,
The wond'rous circle did attend;
The glory and the power be thine,
Which shall from age to age descend.

Chorus.   All hail, &c.

On thy Omnipotence we rest,
Secure of thy protection here;
And hope hereafter to be blest,
When we have left this world of care
Grant us, great God, thy powerful aid
To Guide us through this vale of tears;
For where thy goodness is display'd,
Peace sooths the mind, and pleasure cheers.

Chorus.   All hail, &c.

Inspire us with thy grace divine;
Thy sacred law our guide shall be,
To every good our hearts incline,
From every evil keep us free.
Our glad hosannas, Sovereign King!
Thy welcome here shall e'er proclaim,
And heaven's eternal arches ring
With thy revealed, holy Name:

Chorus.   All hail! great Architect divine!
This universal frame is thine.

SELECT MASTER'S SONG.

BY A COMPANION.

HUNGARIAN

The *vault arches* o'er and night broods a - round,

Not   a whisper   is heard thro' the depth of the *cave;*

All hearts in the *si-lence* of   *se-cre-cy*   bound,

Are reading the words the great Architect gave.

U - ni-ted they lis-ten the voice of the *Law*,

The guide to our reason, the spur of the soul,

And they feel in the sounds a sweet myste-ry draw

Their hearts to the *Spirit* who utter'd the whole.

Now the work is completed and all are combin'd,
To close in the secret and deep-hidden cell
The words which are treasur'd as light to the mind,
Like the waters of truth in their close-cover'd well.
Here safely secured they shall live on the rock,
When the storm rages o'er it and levels the wall,
And still in the rage of the *conqueror's* shock,
The arches shall neither be shaken nor fall.

We have laid in its secret and silent retreat
The treasures that Kings shall exult to behold;
And the *pilgrim* shall hasten with ardour to meet
This gift, valued higher than jewels or go.d:
Ages roll on their way and no foot shall be heard
In search of this roll to enlighten the world;
But a hand shall be found to recover the *Word*,
And then shall the standard of *truth* be unfurled.

20*

We are seated in silence, and nothing can find
Its way to our distant and mystical cave;
And the *watchman* who guards not, our mandate shall bind
In the deeper concealment of *death* and the *grave;*
Be faithful and true, ever firm to your trust,
In the lesson we give in the council of light,
And the herald shall summon you forth from the dust,
Above in the meeting of souls to unite.

SELECT MASTER'S ANTHEM.

(*See Music, page* 213.)

"LET there be light," th' Almighty spoke;
Refulgent streams from chaos broke,
   To illume the rising earth!
Well pleased the great JEHOVAH stood;
The Power Supreme pronounced it good,
   And gave the planets birth!

Chorus. In choral numbers masons join,
        To bless and praise this light divine.

Parent of light! accept our praise!
Who shedd'st on us thy brightest rays
   The light that fills the mind:
By *choice selected*, lo! we stand,
By friendship joined, a social band!
   That *love*, that *aid* mankind!

Chorus. In choral numbers, &c.

The *widow's* tear, the *orphan's* cry,
All wants our ready hands supply,
 As far as power is given;
The naked clothe, the *prisoner free*,
These are thy works, sweet *Charity!*
 Revealed to us from Heaven.
Chorus In choral numbers masons join,
   To bless and praise this light **divine.**

SONG.

WRITTEN BY N. H. WRIGHT.

Allegretto. Mezza Voce.

AH! why should the heart be de — press'd,

When its fond - ness is treat - ed with scorn?

The couch that with ro - ses is dress'd,

In its soft - ness con-ceals a rude thorn.

In   its   soft - ness con-ceals   a   rude thorn,

In   its soft - ness con - ceals   a   rude thorn,

The   couch that with ro - ses   is   dress'd

In   its   softness conceals a rude   thorn.

The bright eye of beauty may beam
With a light like the meteor glare;
But her victim may wake from his dream,
And hope may be chang'd to despair.

Like the rainbow, which shines from the cloud
Her allurements awhile may deceive;
'Till joy is enwrapp'd in a shroud,
And the mourner is left but to grieve.

But Friendship has charms which endure,
Its birth was in regions above ;
'T is a passion, like heaven, most pure
For it sprang from the fountain of love

Then let not the heart be depress'd
If one treat its fondness with scorn ;
It may find in a Brother's warm breast
The rose that conceals not a thorn.

MASONIC ODE.

EMPIRES and kings have pass'd away
  Into oblivion's mine ;
And tow'ring domes have felt decay,
    Since auld lang syne.

But MASONRY, the glorious art,
  With wisdom's ray divine ;
'T was ever so, the Hebrew cries,
    In auld lang syne.

Behold the occidental chair
  Proclaims the day's decline—
Hiram of Tyre was seated there,
    In auld lang syne.

The *South* proclaims refreshment nigh
  High twelve's the time to dine ;
And *beauty* decked the southern sky,
    In auld lang syne.

Yes, Masonry, whose temple here
   Was built by hands divine,
Shall ever shine as bright and clear,
    As auld lang syne.

Then, brethren, for the worthy *three*,
   Let us a wreath entwine,
The three great heads of Masonry
    In auld lang syne.

Remembering oft that worthy one,
   With gratitude divine,
The Tyrian youth—the widow's son
   Of auld lang syne

EPILOGUE.

As lately, brethren, from the Lodge I came,
Warm'd with our royal order's purest flame
Absorb'd in thought ;—before my ravish'd eyes,
I saw the Genius, MASONRY, arise :
A curious hieroglyphic robe he wore,
And in his hand the sacred volume bore :
On one side was divine Astræa placed,
And soft-eyed Charity the other graced ;
Humanity, the gen'ral friend, was there,
And Pity, aropping the pathetic tear ;
There too was Order ;—there, with rosy mien,
Blithe Temp'rance shone, and white robed Truth was seen.
There, with a key suspended to his breast,
Silence appear'd ; his lips his finger prest :
With these, soft warbling an instructive song,
Sweet music, gaily smiling, tripped along.
Wild laughter, clam'rous noise, and mirth ill bred,
The brood of folly, at his presence fled.
The Genius spoke,—" My son, observe my train,
Which, of my order diff'rent parts explain.
Look up—behold the bright ASTRÆA there,
She will direct thee how to use the Square.
PITY will bid thee grieve, with those who grieve,
Whilst CHARITY will prompt thee to relieve ;
Will prompt thee every comfort to bestow,
And draw the arrow from the breast of woe ;
HUMANITY will lead to honor's goal,
Give the large thought, and form the gen'rous soul.
Will bid thee thy fraternal love expand,
To virtue of *all* faiths,—and ev'ry land.
ORDER will kindly teach her laws of peace,
Which discord stop, and social joys increase ;

TEMP'RANCE instruct thee all excess t' avoid,
By which fair fame is lost and health destroy'd :
TRUTH warn thee ne'er to use perfidious art,
And bid thy tongue be rooted in thy heart ;
SILENCE direct thee never to disclose,
Whate'er thy brethren in thy breast repose ;
For thee shall MUSIC strike the harmonious lyre,
And whilst she charms the ear, *morality* inspire.
These *all* observe ;—and let thy conduct show,
What real blessings I on man bestow."

He said, and disappear'd ;—and Oh ! may we,
Who wear this honor'd badge, accepted, free,
To ev'ry grace and virtue temples raise,
And by our useful works our Order praise.

HISTORY OF FREE MASONRY.

THAT we may be enabled to discover Free Ma
sonry under those various forms which it has assumed in different countries, and at different times
before it received the name it now bears, it will
be necessary to give a short description of the nature of this institution, without developing those
mysteries, or revealing those ceremonial observances, which are known only to the brethren of the
Order.

Free Masonry is an ancient and respectable institution, embracing individuals of every nation,
of every religion, and of every condition in life.
Wealth, power, and talents, are not necessary to
the person of a Free Mason. An unblemished
character and a virtuous conduct, are the only
qualifications which are requisite for admission
into the order. In order to confirm this institution, and attain the ends for which it was origi
nally formed, every candidate must come under a
solemn engagement never to divulge the mysteries

21

and ceremonies of the Order, nor communicate to the uninitiated, those important precepts with which he may be entrusted, and those proceedings and plans in which the Fraternity may be engaged.

After the candidate has undergone the neces sary ceremonies, and received the usual instruc tions, appropriate words and significant signs are imparted to him, that he may be enabled to dis tinguish his Brethren of the Order, from the un initiated public, and convince others that he is en titled to the privileges of a Brother.

If the newly admitted member be found quali fied for a higher degree, he is promoted, after due intervals of probation, till he has received that Masonic knowledge which enables him to hold the highest office of trust to which the Fraternity can raise its members.

Object of Free Masonry.

In all ages it has been the object of Free Masonry, not only to inform the minds of its members by instructing them in the sciences and useful arts, but to better their hearts by enforcing the precepts of religion and morality. In the course of the ceremonies of initiation, brotherly love, loyalty and other virtues, are inculcated in hieroglyphic symbols; and the candidate is often reminded, that there is an eye above which observeth the workings of his heart, and is ever fixed upon the thoughts and the actions of men.

Regular and appointed meetings of the Frater·
nity are held in lodges constructed for this pur·
pose. Temperance, harmony, and joy, charac·
terise these mixed assemblies. All distinction of
rank seems to be laid aside, all difference in re·
ligious and political sentiments are forgotten; and
those petty quarrels, which disturb the quiet of
private life, cease to agitate the mind, and every
one strives to give happiness to his brother.
Such are the general features of an institution,
which has produced a great division in the sentiments
of the learned, respecting its origin and tendency.

Origin of Free Masonry.

Whilst some, a little over anxious for the dig·
nity of their order, have represented it as co·
eval with the world,* or, arising from the constitu·
tion of Pythagoras ;† others, from opposite motives,
have maintained it to be the invention of English
Jesuits,‡ or, that it arose during the Crusades,§
or, as M. Barruel, that it is a continuation of the
Templars.‖ Without adopting any of these un·
tenable opinions, or attempting to discover the
precise period when Free Masonry arose, I shall

* Anderson's History and Constitution of Free Masonry,
p. 1. Desagulier's Constitutions, p. 1. Smith's Use and
Abuse of Free Masonry, p. 27. Preston's Illustrations of
Masonry, p. 6, 10th edition.

† Anthologia Hibernica for January, March, April, and
June, 1794.

‡ Manuscript of Bode of Germany, in the possession of
M. Mounier.

§ Leyden's Preliminary Dissertation to the Complaynt of
Scotland, p. 67, 71.

‖ Memoirs of Jacobinism, vol. 2, p. 377, 378, &c.

deem it sufficient to show that it car) ;.;.; ;.y claim to an early origin, and that it ;.;.; ;.;.;ted from that period to the present day, un';.;r different forms, and different appellations.

We shall have occasion to consider Free Masonry, when connected with the idolatry of the heathens, when devoted to the church of Rome, and when flourishing under the milder influence of the reformed religion; for, as every human institution is subject to great and numerous variations, so Free Masonry is affected by the progress of civilization, by the nature of the government under which it exists, and by the peculiar opinions and habits of its members.

In the early ages of society, the pursuit of science must have been a secondary consideration, and whatever was found necessary to a safe and comfortable existence, must have been made a primary concern. As architecture, however, could only be preceded by agriculture itself, it must have been in this science that the first efforts of human skill were tried, and in which man must have first experienced success in extending his dominion over the works of nature. The first architects, therefore, would be philosophers; and the information which was acquired individually, would be imparted to others of the same profession; and an association would naturally be formed for the mutual communication of knowledge, and the mutual improvement of its members.

In order to preserve among themselves that information which they alone collected, to excite in others a higher degree of respect for their profession, and to prevent the intrusion of those who were ignorant of architecture, appropriate words and signs would be communicated to the members of the institution, and significant ceremonies would be performed at their initiation, that their engagement to secrecy might be imposed upon their minds, and greater regard excited for the information they were to receive. Nor is this mere speculation: there exist at this day, in the deserts of Egypt, monuments of architecture, which must have been reared in those early ages which precede the records of authentic history; and the erection of those stupendous fabrics, must have required an acquaintance with the mechanical arts, which is not in the possession of modern architects. It is an undoubted fact, also, that there existed, in those days, a particular association of men, to whom scientific knowledge was confined, and who resembled the society of Free Masons in everything but the name.

In Egypt, and those countries of Asia which lie contiguous to that favored kingdom, the arts and sciences were first cultivated with success, and it is here where Free Masonry would flourish, and here only can we discover marks of its existence in the remotest ages.

It is extremely probable that the first and only object of the society of Masons, was the mutual communication of knowledge connected with their profession, and th at those only would gain admittance into their order, whose labors were
21*

subsidiary to those of the architect. But, when the ambition or vanity of the Egyptian priests, prompted them to erect huge and expensive fabrics, for celebrating the worship of their gods, or per-petuating the memory of their Kings, they would naturally desire to participate in that scientific knowledge, which was possessed by the architects they employed ; and as the sacerdotal order sel-dom fail among a superstitious people, to gain the objects of their ambition, they would in this case succeed, and be initiated into the mysteries, and instructed in the science, of Free Masons.

When the Egyptian priests had procured admis-sion into the Society of Free Masons, they con-nected the mythology of their country, and their metaphysical speculations concerning the nature of God, and the condition of man, with an associa-tion formed for the exclusive purpose of scientific improvement, and produced that combination of science and theology, which, in after ages, formed such a conspicuous part of the principles of Free Masonry. The knowledge of the Egyptians was carefully concealed from the vulgar ; and when the priests did condescend to communicate it to the learned of other nations, it was conferred in symbols and hieroglyphics, accompanied with particular rites and ceremonies, marking the value of the gift they bestowed.

What those ceremonies were which were per-formed at initiations into the Egyptian mysteries, we are unable at this distance of time to deter-mine. But as the Eleusinian and other mysteries

had their origin in Egypt, we may perhaps discover the qualities of the fountain by examining
the nature of the stream. It is well known that
Greece was peopled by a colony from Egypt, conducted thither by Inacus, about nineteen hundred
and seventy years before the Christian era, and
that about three centuries afterwards, he was followed by Cecrops, Cadmus and Danaus.* The
Egyptians introduced the arts and sciences into
that country, and sowed those seeds of improvement, which, in future ages, exalted Greece to such
pre-eminence among the nations.

After the Egyptian colonies had obtained a secure settlement in their new territories, they constituted, after the manner of their ancestors, particular festivals, or mysteries, in honor of those
who had benefitted their country by arts or by
arms.

The Eleusinian Mysteries.

In the reign of Ericthonius, about fifteen hundred years before the commencement of our era,†
the Eleusinian mysteries were instituted, in honor
of Ceres, who came into Greece and instructed
Triptolemus in the knowledge of a future state.‡

About the same time the Panathenea were in-

* Voyage du Jeune Anacharsis en Grece, 4to, tom. 1, p. 2.
Cecrops arrived in Attica in 1657, B. C.   Cadmus came from
Phœnicia to Beotia in 1594, and Danaus to Argolis in 1586.
B. C
† Robertson's Greece, p. 58, 59.
‡ Isocrates Paneg. t. 1, p. 132.

stituted in honor of Minerva, and the Dionysian
mysteries in honor of Bacchus, who invented theatres,* and instructed the Greeks in many useful
arts, but particularly in the culture of the vine.†
That the Eleusinian and Dionysian mysteries
were intimately connected with the progress of
the arts and sciences, is manifest from the very
end for which they were formed; and that they
were modeled upon the mysteries of Isis and
Osiris, celebrated in Egypt, is probable from the
similarity of their origin, as well as the consen·
of their ancient authors.‡ And if there is ar
plausibility in our former reasoning concerning
the origin of knowledge in Egypt, it will follow
that the Dionysia and the mysteries of Eleusis,
were societies of Free Masons, formed for scien·
tific improvement, though tinctured with the doc·
trines of Egyptian mythology. But it is not
from conjecture only that this conclusion may be
drawn; the striking similarity among the exter·
nal forms of these secret associations, and the still
more striking similarity of the objects they had in
view, are strong proofs that they were only differ·
ent streams, issuing from a common fountain.
Those who were initiated into the Eleusinian mysteries, were bound, by the most awful engagements,
to conceal the instructions they received, and the
ceremonies that were performed.§

* Polodor. Virg. de Rerum Invent. lib. 3, cap. 13.
† Robertson's Greece, p. 59.
‡ L. Apuleii Metamorph. lib. xi.
§ Andoc. de Myst. p. 7. Meursius in Eleus. Myst. cap. 20

None were admitted as candidates, till they arrived at a certain age ; and particular persons were appointed to examine and prepare them for the rites of initiation.* Those whose conduct was found irregular, or who had been guilty of atrocious crimes were rejected as unworthy of initiation , while the successful candidates were instructed by significant symbols, in the principles of religion,† were exhorted to quell every turbulent appetite and passion,‡ and to merit, by the improvement of their minds and the purity of their hearts, those ineffable benefits which they were still to receive.§ Significant words were communicated to the members ; Grand Officers presided over assemblies.‖ · Their emblems were exactly similar to those of Free Masonry,¶ and the candidate advanced from one degree to another, till he received all the lessons of wisdom and virtue which the priests could impart.** But beside these cir· cumstances, there are two facts transmitted to us by ancient authors, which have an astonishing similarity to the ceremonies of the third degree of Free Masonry. So striking is the resemblance, that every brother of the order who is acquainted with them, cannot question, for a moment, the

* Hesychius in *Hydran.*
† Clemens. Alexand. Strom. lib. 1, p. 325. lib. 7, p. 845.
‡ Porphyr. ap. Stob. Eclog. Phys. p. 142.
§ Arrian in Epictet. lib. 3, cap. 21, p. 440.
‖ Robertson's Greece, p. 127.
¶ Euseb. Prepar. Evangel. lib. 3, cap. 12, p. 117.
** Pe·av. ad Themist. p. 414, Anacharsis tom. 3, p. 582.

opinion which we have been attempting to support.*

*The Sentiments of Cotemporaries, respecting the
Eleusinian Mysteries and Free Masonry.*

Having thus mentioned some features of resemblance between the mysteries of Eleusis and
those of Free Masonry, let us now attend to the
sentiments of cotemporaries respecting these secret associations, and we shall find, that they have
been treated with the same illiberality and inso-
lence. There were some men, who, from self-suffi-
ciency, or unsocial dispositions, refused to be admitted into these orders; and there were others,
whose irregular conduct excluded them from initiation. Men of this description represented the
celebration of Eleusinian mysteries, as scenes of
riot and debauchery, and reproached the members
of the association, that they were not more virtuous and more holy than themselves;† but it is
the opinion of cotemporary writers, that these
rumors were wholly conjectural, and originated in
the silence of the initiated, and the ignorance of
the vulgar. They even maintain that the mysteries of Eleusis produced sanctity of manners, attention to the social duties, and a desire to be as

* The Brethren of the Order may consult, for this purpose,
the article Eleusinia, in the 6th vol. of the last edition of the
Encyclopedia Britannica, and Robertson's History of Ancient Greece, p. 127

† Robertson's Greece, p. 127. Porphyr. de Abstinentia lib.
4, p. 353. Julian Orat. 5, p. 173.

distinguished by virtue as by silence.* The illustrious Socrates could never be prevailed upon to
partake of these mysteries,† and Diogenes, having
received a similar solicitation, replied, that Patæcion,
a notorious robber, obtained initiation, and that
Epaminondas and Agesilaus never desired it.‡
But did not these know, that in all human societies,
the virtuous and the noble must, sometimes, associate with the worthless and the mean? Did they
not know that there often kneel in the same temple,
the righteous and the profane; and that the saint
and the sinner frequently officiate at the same altar?

Thus did the philosophers of antiquity calumniate
and despise the mysteries of Eleusis; and in the
same manner have some pretended philosophers of
our own day, defamed the character, and questioned
the motives of Free Masons.

*Similarity in the Origin of Free Masonry, and of the
Mysteries of Ceres.*

The similarity of treatment which the mysteries of Ceres and Free Masonry have received, is
no small proof of the similarity of their origin,
and their object. To this conclusion, however,
it may be objected, that though the points of resemblance between these secret societies are nu-

---

* Encyclopedia Britannica, article Euleusinia.
† Lucian in Demonact. t. 2, p. 380.
‡ Plut. de aud. Poet. t. 2, p. 21.   Diog. Laert. lib. 6, § 39.

merous, yet there were circumstances in the celebration of the Eleusinian mysteries, which have
no counterpart in the ceremonies of Free Masonry.
The sacrifices, purifications, hymns and dances,
which were necessary in the festival of Ceres, have,
indeed, no place in the society of Free Masons.
But these points of dissimilarity, instead of weaken-
ing, rather strengthen our opinion. It cannot be
expected that in the reign of Polytheism, just sentiments of the Deity should be entertained; and
much less, that the adherents of Christianity should
bend their knees to the gods of the heathens.
The ancients worshiped those beings which conferred on them the most signal benefits, with sacrifices,
purifications, and other tokens of their humility and
gratitude.   But, when revelation had disclosed
to man more amiable sentiments concerning the
Divine Being, the society of Free Masons banished
from their mysteries those useless rites, with
which the ancient brothers of the order attempted
to appease and requite their deities, and modeled
their ceremonies upon this foundation, that there is
but one God, who must be worshiped in spirit and
in truth.

Spread of the Mysteries of Ceres.

The mysteries of Ceres were not confined to the
city of Eleusis; they were introduced into Athens
about 1356 years before Christ,* and with a few

* Playfair's Chronology.

slight variations were observed in Phrygia, Cyprus, Crete and Sicily.*

They had reached even to the capital of France;† and it is highly probable that, in a short time after, they were introduced into Britain and other northern kingdoms. In the reign of the Emperor Adrian,‡ they were carried into Rome, and were celebrated in that metropolis, with the same rites and ceremonies which were performed in the humble village of Eleusis. They had contracted impurities, however, from the length of their duration, and the corruption of their abettors; and the forms of initiation were still symbolical of the original and noble objects of the institution, yet the licentious Romans mistook the shadow for the substance; and while they underwent the rites of the Eleusinian mysteries, they were strangers to the object for which they were framed.

About the beginning of the 5th century, Theodosius the Great prohibited, and almost totally extinguished the Pagan Theology in the Roman empire,§ and the mysteries of Eleusis suffered in the general devastation.‖ It is probable, however, that these mysteries were secretly celebrated, in spite of the severe edicts of Theodosius; and that

* Lucii Apuleii Metamorph. lib. 11, pp. 197, 198.
† Praise of Paris, or a Sketch of the French Capitol, 1803, by S. West, F. R. S.
‡ A. D. 117.   Encyclop. Brit. vol. 6, p. 555.   Potter's Antiquities, vol. 1, p. 389.
§ Gibbon's History of the Decline and Fall of the Roman Empire, 8vo. vol. 5, p. 120.
‖ Zosim. Hist. lib. 4.

they were partly continued during the dark ages,
though stripped of their original purity and splen
dor: we are certain, at least, that many rites of the
pagan religion were performed under the dissembled
name of convivial meetings, long after the publication of the Emperor's edict;* and Psellus† informs
us, that the mysteries of Ceres subsisted in Athens
till the eighth century of the Christian era, and
were never totally suppressed.

Having thus considered the origin and decline
of the mysteries of Eleusis, and discovered in
them numerous and prominent features of resem
blance to those of Free Masonry, we may reasonably
infer, that the Egyptian mysteries which gave rise
to the former, had a still nearer affinity to the latter; and from this conclusion, the opinions which
were formerly stated concerning the antiquity of the
order, and the origin of Egyptian knowledge, will
receive very considerable confirmation.

*The Dionysia: their origin and connection with the
Mysteries of Ceres.*

Let us now direct our attention to the Dionysia,
or mysteries of Bacchus, which were intimately
connected with those of Ceres, and perhaps still
more with the mysteries of Free Masonry. Herodotus informs us that the solemnities in honor of

* Gibbon, vol. 5, p. 110.
† In his Treatise on the gods which the Greeks worship-
ed, quoted by Mr. Clinch in the Anthologia Hibernica, for
January, 1794, p. 36.

Dionysius, or Bacchus, were originally instituted in Egypt, and were transported from that country into Greece by one Melampus.* But, not only did the mysteries of Ceres and Bacchus flow from the same source: the one was in some measure interwoven with the other, and it is almost certain, from what we are now to mention, that those who were initiated into the former, were entitled to be present at the celebration of the latter. The sixth day of the Eleusinian festival was the most brilliant of the whole. It received the apellation of Bacchus, because it was chiefly, if not exclusively devoted to the worship of that god. His statue, attended by the initiated, and the ministers of the temple, was conducted from Athens to Eleusis with much pomp and solemnity,† and after it had been introduced into the temple of Ceres, it was brought back to Athens with similar ceremonies. The connection betweeen the Eleusinian and Dionysian mysteries is manifest also, from the common opinion that Ceres was the mother of Bacchus ;‡ and Plutarch assures us that the Egyptian Isis was the same with Ceres that Osiris was the same with Bacchus, and that the Dionysia of Greece was only another name for the Pamylia of Egypt.§ As Bacchus was the

* Lib. 2.
† Anacharsis, tom. 3, p. 531. Plut. in Phoc. tom. i. p. 754. Meurs. in Eleus. Myst. cap. 27.
‡ Potter, Vol. i. p. 393.
§ De Iside et Osiride. Idee du Gouvernement Ancier et Modern de l'Egypte, p. 26, Paris, 1743.

inventor of theatres, as well as of dramatical rep
resentations, that particular class of Masons, who
were employed in the erection of these extensive
buildings, were called the Dionysian artificers,*
and were initiated into the mysteries of their
founder, and consequently into those of Eleusis.†
But from the tendency of the human mind to em·
brace the ceremonial while it neglects the sub-
stantial part of an institution, the Dionysian festival, in the degenerate ages of Greece, was more
remarkable for inebriation and licentiousness than
for the cultivation of virtue and science ; and he
who at first was celebrated as the inventor of arts,
was afterwards worshiped as the god of wine.
Those who were desirous of indulging secretly in
licentious mirth, and unhallowed festivity, cloaked
their proceedings under the pretence of worship-
ing Bacchus, and brought disgrace upon those
mysteries which were instituted for the promotion
of virtue, and the improvement of art.

Institution of the Bacchanalia.

About two hundred years before Christ, an illit·
erate and licentious priest came from Greece to
Tuscany, and instituted the Bacchanalia, or feast
of the Bacchanals.‡ From Tuscany they were
imported to Rome; but the promoters of these
midnight orgies, having proceeded to the furthest

* Aulus Gellius, lib. xx. c. 4.
† Vide Potter, vol. i. p. 41.
‡ Tit. Liv. lib. 39, cap. 8

extremity of dissipation and disloyalty, they were abolished throughout all Italy, by a decree of the senate.* It has been foolishly supposed that the Bacchanalia were similar to the Dionysian myste ries, merely because they were both dedicated to Bacchus. The Liberalia of Rome was the festival corresponding to the Dionysia of Greece ;† and it is probable that this feast was observed, through out the Roman Empire, till the abrogation of the Pagan theology, in the reign of Theodosius.

The Spread and Influence of the Dionysian Mysteries.

Hitherto we have considered the Dionysian mysteries under an unpropitious aspect; let us now trace them in their progress from Europe to Asia, where they retained their primitive lustre, and effectually contributed to the rapid advance ment of the fine arts. About a thousand years before Christ,‡ the inhabitants of Attica, complain ing of the narrowness of their territory and the unfruitfulness of its soil, went in quest of more extensive and fertile settlements. They sailed to Asia Minor, drove out the inhabitants, seized upon the most eligible situations, and united them under the name of Ionia, because the greatest number of the refugees were natives of that Grecian province.§ As the Greeks, prior to the

* Liv. lib. 39, cap. 18.
† Vid. Universal History, vol. 13, p. 262.
‡ Playfair says in 1044, Gillies in 1055, and Bartnelemy in 1076, B. C.
§ Herodotus. lib. i. cap. 142. Gillies' Hist. of Greece, 8vo., vol. 1, p. 102.
22*

Ionic migration, had made considerable progress
in the arts and sciences;[*] they carried these
along with them into their new territories, and introduced into Ionia the mysteries of Minerva and
Dionysius,[†] before they were corrupted by the licentiousness of the Athenians. In a short time,
the Asiatic Colonies surpassed the mother country
in prosperity and science. Sculpture in marble
and the Doric and Ionian Orders, were the result
of their ingenuity.[‡]

They returned even into Greece, and communicated to their ancestors the inventions of their
own country, and instructed them in that style
of architecture which has been the admiration of
succeeding ages. For these improvements, the
world is indebted to the *Dionysian Artificers*, an
association of scientific men, who possessed the
exclusive privilege of erecting temples, theatres,
and other public buildings in Asia Minor.[§] They
supplied Ionia, and the surrounding countries as
far as Hellespont, with theatrical apparatus, by
contract, and erected the magnificent temple at
Teos, to Bacchus, the founder of their order.[||]
These artists were very numerous in Asia, and ex-

[*] According to the author of Anarcharsis' Travels, the
Arts took their rise in Greece, about 1547, B. C.
[†] Chandler's Travels in Asia Minor, p. 100, 4to. 1775.
The Panathenea and the Dionysian mysteries were institu-
ted about 300 years before the Ionic migration.
[‡] Gillies' Hist. Ant. Greece, vol. 2, p. 162.
[§] Strabo, lib. 4. Chishull Antiquitates Asiaticæ, p. 107.
Robison's Proofs of Conspiracy, p. 20.
[||] Ionian Antiquities, published by the Society of Dile-
tanti, p. 4. Strabo. lib. 4. Chishull Antiq. Asiat. p. 139.

isted under the same appellation in Syria, Persia, and India.* About three hundred years before the birth of Christ, a considerable number of them were incorporated by command of the Kings of Perga- mus, who assigned to them Teos, as a settlement, it being the city of their tutelary god.† The members of this association, which was intimately connected with the Dionysian mysteries, were distinguished from the uninitiated inhabitants of Teos, by the science which they possessed, and by appropriate words and signs by which they could recognize their Brethren of the Order.‡ Like Free Masons, they were divided into Lodges, which were distinguished by different appellations.§ They occasionally held convivial meetings, in houses erected and conse- crated for this purpose; and each separate associa- tion was under the direction of a master and presi- dent, or wardens.‖

They held a general meeting once a year, which was solemnized with great pomp and festivity, and at which the Brethren partook of a splendid enter- tainment, provided by the master, after they had finished the sacrifices to their gods, and especially to their patron, Bacchus.¶ They used particular utensils in their ceremonial observances, some of

* Strabo. p. 471. Ionian Antiquities, p. 4.
† Chandler's Travels, p. 100. Chishull Antiq. Asiat., p 138. Ionian Antiq. p. 4.
‡ Robison's Proofs of a Conspiracy, p. 20.
§ Chishull, p. 139.
‖ See the two decrees of these artists, preserved in Chi hull, pp. 138–149.
¶ Chandler's Travels, p. 103.

which were exactly similar to those which are employed by the Fraternity of Free Masons,* and the more opulent artists were bound to provide for the exigencies of their poorer Brethren.† The very monuments which were reared by these Masons to the memory of their masters and wardens, remain to the present day in the Turkish burying grounds at Siverhissar and Eraki.‡ The inscriptions upon them express, in strong terms, the gratitude of the Fraternity, for their disinterested exertions in behalf of the order, for their generosity and benevolence to its individual members, for their private virtues as well as for their public conduct. From some circumstances which are stated in these inscriptions, but particularly from the name of one of the lodges, it is highly probable that Attalus, King of Pergamus, was a member of the Dionysian Fraternity. Such is the nature of that association of architects, who erected those splendid edifices in Ionia, whose ruins even afford us instruction, while they excite our surprise. If it be possible to prove the identity of any two societies, from the coincidence of their external forms, we are authorized to conclude, that the Fraternity of the Ionian architects and the Fraternity of Free

* See the decree of the Attalists in Chishull, particularly the passages at the bottom of pp. 141, 142.

† Chishull, p. 140.

‡ Chandler's Travels, p. 100. These monuments were erected about 150 years before Christ. The inscriptions upon them were published by Edmund Chishull, in 1728, from copies taken by Consul Sherard in 1709, and examined in 1716. Ionian Antiq., p. 3.

Masons, are exactly the same; and as the former practised the mysteries of Bacchus and Ceres, several of which we have shown to be similar to the mysteries of Masonry, we may safely affirm that in their internal, as well as external procedure, the Society of Free Masons resembles the Dionysiacs of Asia Minor.[*]

The Opinions that Free Masonry existed at the build ing of Solomon's Temple, not absurd.

The opinion, therefore, of Free Masons, that their order existed and flourished at the building of Solomon's temple, is by no means so pregnant with absurdity as some men would wish us to believe. We have already shown, from authentic sources of information, that the mysteries of Ceres and Bacchus were instituted about four hundred years before the reign of Solomon;[†] and there are strong reasons for believing that even the association of the Dionysian Architects existed before the building of the temple. It was not, indeed, till about three hundred years before the birth of Christ, that they were incorporated at Teos, under the King of Pergamus; but it is universally allowed that they arose long before their settlement

* Dr. Robison, who will not be suspected of partiality to Free Masons, ascribes their origin to the Dionysian artists It is impossible, indeed, for any candid inquirer to call in question their identity.

† According to Playfair's Chronology, the temple of Solomon was begun in 1016, and finished in 1008, B. C. The Eleusinian mysteries were introduced into Athens in 1356, a considerable time after their institution.

in Ionia, and what is more to our present purpose, that they existed in the very land of Judea.* It is observed by Dr. Robison,† that this association came from Persia into Syria; and, since we are informed, by Josephus,‡ that that species of architecture was used at the erection of the temple, we are authorized to infer, not only that the Dionysians existed before the reign of Solomon, but that they assisted this Monarch in building that magnificent fabric, which he reared to the God of Israel. Nothing, indeed, can be more simple and consistent than the creed of the Fraternity concerning the state of their order at this period. The vicinity of Jerusalem to Egypt, the connection of Solomon with the royal family of that Kingdom,§ the progress of the Egyptians in architectural science, their attachment to mysteries and hieroglyphic symbols, and the probability of their being employed by the King of Israel, are additional considerations, which corroborate the sentiments of Free Masons, and absolve them from those charges of credulity and pride with which they have been loaded.

To these opinions it may be objected, that if the Fraternity of Free Masons flourished during the reign of Solomon, it would have existed in Judea in after ages, and attracted the notice of sacred and profane historians. Whether or not

* Robison's Proofs of a Conspiracy, p. 20.
† Proofs of a Conspiracy, pp. 20, 21.
‡ Jewish Antiquities, book 8, chap. 5.
§ Josephus' Jewish Antiquities, book 8, chap. 2.

this objection is well founded, we shall not pretend to determine; but if it can be shown that
there did exist, after the building of the temple,
an association of men resembling Free Masons,
in the nature, ceremonies, and object of their institution, the force of the objection will not only be
taken away, but additional strength will be communicated to the opinion which we have been supporting. The association here alluded to is that of
the Essenes, whose origin and sentiments have occasioned much discussion among ecclesiastical historians: they are all of one mind, however, respecting
the constitution and observances of this religious
order. When a candidate was proposed for admission, the strictest scrutiny was made into his character.* If his life had hitherto been exemplary,
and if he appeared capable of curbing his passions
and regulating his conduct according to the virtuous, though austere maxims of their order, he was
presented, at the expiration of his novitiate, with a
white garment, as an emblem of the regularity of his
conduct and the purity of his heart.† A solemn
oath was then administered to him, that he would
never divulge the mysteries of the order, that he
would make no innovations on the doctrines of the
society, and that he would continue in that honorable
course of piety and virtue which he had begun to

* Pictet. Theologie Chretienne, tom. 3, pt. 3, p. 109. Basnage's History of the Jews, book 2, chap. 12, § 24.

† Pictet. Theolog. Chret., tom. 3, pt. 3, pp. 107, 108, 109.
Basnage's History of the Jews, book 2, chap. 12, § 24.

pursue.* Like Free Masons, they instru ted the young members in the knowledge which they derived from their ancestors.†

They admitted no women into their order.‡ They had particular signs for recognizi g each other, which have a strong resemblance to those of Free Masons.§ They had colleges or places of retirement,‖ where they had resorted to practice their rites and settle the affairs of the society; and, after the performance of these duties, they assembled in a large hall, where an entertainment was provided for them by the president, or master of the cottage, who allotted a certain quantity of provisions to every individual.¶ They abolished all distinctions of rank; and if preference was ever given, it was given to piety, liberality, and virtue.** Treasurers were appointed in every town to supply the wants of indigent strangers. The Essenes pretended to higher degrees of piety and knowledge than the uninitiated vulgar, and though their pretensions were high, they were never questioned by their enemies. Austerity of

* Pictet. Theolog. Chret., tom. 3, pt. 3, p. 107. Basnage's History of the Jews, b. 2, chap. 12, § 24.
† Philo de Vita Contemplativa, apud opera, p. 691. Basange, b. 2, ch. 13, § 8.
‡ Basnage, b. 2, chap. 12, § 26. Id. Id. § 22.
§ Philo's Treatise de Vita Contemp., p. 691.
‖ Basnage, b. 3, c. 12, § 14. Vide opera Philonis, p. 679.
¶ Basnage, b. 3, c. 12, § 21.
** Id. Id. 20, 22. Philonis Opera, p. 678.
For a more particular account of the Essenes, the reader may consult Dr. Prideaux's Connexions, vol. 3, pp. 453, 475.
EDITOR.

manners was one of the chief characteristics of the Essenian Fraternities. They frequently assembled, however, in convivial parties, and relaxed for a while the severity of those duties which they were accustomed to perform. This remarkable coincidence between the chief features of the Masonic and Essenian Fraternities, can be accounted for, only by referring them to the same origin. Were the circumstances of resemblance either few or fanciful, the similarity might have been merely casual. But, when the nature, the object, and the external forms of two institutions, are precisely the same, the arguments for their identity are something more than presumptive. Concerning the origin of the Essenes, there is a great diversity of opinions with both sacred and profane historians. They all agree, however, in representing them as an ancient association, originating from particular fraternities which formerly existed in the land of Judea And although they were patronised by Herod, and respected by all men for the correctness of their conduct, and the innocence of their order ;* yet they suffered severe persecutions from the Romans till their order was abolished, about the middle of the 5th century,† a period extremely fatal to the venerable institutions of Egypt, of Greece, and of Rome.

* Philo's Treatise apud Opera, p. 678.
† Basnage, b. 2, chap. 12, §§ 25, 26.

23

The Institution of Pythagoras.

Connected with Essenian and Masonic Fraternities, was the institution of Pythagoras at Crotona. After this philosopher, in the course of his
travels through Egypt, Syria, and Ionia, had been
initiated into the mysteries of those enlightened
kingdoms, he imported into Europe the sciences of
Asia, and offered to the inhabitants of his native
soil the important benefits which he himself had
received.* The offers of the sage having been
rejected by his countrymen of Samos,† he settled
at Crotona in Italy, where more respect was paid
to his person, and more attention to his precepts.‡
Pythagoras, inspired by the animating prospects of
success among his people, selected a number of
his disciples, who seemed best adapted for for-
warding the purposes he had in view.§ He
formed these into a fraternity, or separate order of
men, whom he instructed in the sciences of the
East, and to whom he imparted the mysteries and
rites of the Egyptian, Syrian, and Ionian associations.‖ Before any one was received into the
number of his disciples, a minute and diligent inquiry was made into his temper and character.¶
If the issue of this inquiry was favorable to the

* Pythagoras returned from Egypt about 560 B. C.
† Iamblichus de vita Pythagoræ, part 1, cap. 5, p. 37.
‡ Id. Id. cap. 6, pp. 42, 43.
§ Gillies' History of Ancient Greece, vol. 2, p. 27.
‖ Aulus Gellius, book 1, cap. 9. Gillies, vol. 2, p. 27
¶ Iamblichus de vita Pythagoræ, cap. 17, p. 76. Gillies,
vol. 2, p. 27.

candidate, he bound himself by a solemn engagement, to conceal from the uninitiated the mysteries which he might receive, and the sciences in
which he might be instructed.* The doctrines
of charity, of universal benevolence, and especially of affection to the brethren of the Order,
were warmly recommended to the young disciples;† and such was the influence which they
had upon their minds, that discord seemed to have
been banished from Italy,‡ and the golden age to
have again returned. Strangers of every country,
of every religion, and of every rank in life, were
received, if properly qualified, into the Pythagorean association.§ Like Free Masons, they had
particular words and signs, by which they might
distinguish each other and correspond at a distance.‖ They wore white garments as an emblem of their innocence.¶ They had a particular
regard for the East.** They advanced from one
degree of knowledge to another.†† They were
forbidden to commit to writing their mysteries,
which were preserved solely by tradition.‡‡ The

* Iamblichus, cap. 23, p. 104.
† Id. cap. 8, p. 53; cap. 33, p. 193; cap. 6, p. 43; cap. 23,
p. 102. Basnage's History of the Jews, b. 2, cap. 13, § 21.
Anthologia Hibernica for March, 1794, p. 181.
‡ Iamblichus, cap. 7, p. 46.
§ Gillies, vol. 2, p. 28. Iamblichus, cap. 33, p. 202.
‖ Gillies, vol. 2, p. 27. Anthologia Hibernica for March,
1794, p. 181.
¶ Basnage, b. 2, chap. 13, § 21. Anthol. Hibern. March,
1794, p. 183.
** Basnage, b. 2, chap. 13, § 21.
†† Iamblichus, cap. 17, p. 72.
‡‡ Iamblichus, cap. 17, p. 72.

Pythagorean symbols and secrets were borrowed
from the Egyptians, the Orphic and Eleusinian
rites, the Magi, the Iberians, and the Celts.*
They consisted chiefly of the arts and sciences
united with theology and ethics, and were communicated to the initiated in cyphers and symbols.†
To those who were destitute of a cute discernment,
these hieroglyphic representations seemed pregnant
with absurdity, while others of more penetration,
discovered in them hidden treasures, calculated to
inform the understanding, and purify the heart.‡
An association of this nature, founded upon such
principles, and fitted for such ends, did not continue
long in obscurity.   In a short time it extended over
the kingdoms of Italy and Sicily, and was diffused
even through Ancient Greece, and the Islands of
the Ægean Sea.§

But like other secret societies, it was vilified by
weak and wicked men, and the innocent Pythagoreans were often necessitated to sustain the vengeance of the disappointed and enraged; for even
the lodges wherein they were assembled, were set on
fire. ‖   But no sufferings or hardships, not even
death in its agonizing form, caused them to violate
their engagements; nor did banishment to distant

---

* Warburton's Divine Legation of Moses, book 3, § 3, vol.
2, pp. 132, 133. Iamblichus, cap. 8, p. 139. Gillies, vol. 2.
p. 27.
† Iamblichus, cap. 8, p. 139. Gillies *ut supra.*
‡ Iamblichus, cap. 23, p. 104; cap. 32, pp. 191, 192.
§ Gillies, vol. 2, p. 28. Iamblichus, cap. 35, p. 207.
‖ Iamblichus, p. 208 *et seq.*

countries diminish their sympathy, or cool their love
for each other.

The similarity of Free Masonry and the Institu tion of Pythagoras, the Eleusinia, &c.

From these observations, it is manifest, that the
Pythagorean and Masonic institutions were similar in their external forms, as well as in the objects which they had in view; and it will not be
denied, that both have experienced from cotemporaries unmerited reproach. Is it not fair, then,
to conclude, that Masonry is a continuation of the
Pythagorean association, and that the principles
which constituted the basis of the Pythagorean
school, were gathered by Pythagoras himself from
the remains of the Eleusinian, Dionysian and
Ionian Fraternities, in Egypt, in Syria, and in
the land of Judea? There is one objection to the
view which we have taken of this subject, which,
although it has been slightly noticed, it may be
necessary more completely to remove. Although
it will be acknowledged, by every unbiased reader,
that Free Masonry has a wonderful resemblance
to the Elusinian and Dionysian mysteries, the
fraternity of Ionian architects, and the Essenian
and Pythagorean associations; yet some may be
disposed to question the identity of these institutions, because they had different names, and be
cause some usages were observed by one, which
were neglected by another. But these circumstances of dissimilarity arise from those necessa ry
23*

changes which are superinduced upon every institution, by a spirit of innovation, by the caprice of
individuals, and by the various revolutions in
civilized society. Every alteration or improvement
in philosophical systems, or ceremonial institutions
generally produces a corresponding variation in
their name, deduced from the nature of the improvement, or from the name of the innovator.

When the mysteries of the Essenes were imported by Pythagoras into Italy, without undergoing
much variations, they were then denominated the
mysteries of Pythagoras; and in our own day,
they are called the secrets of Free Masonry, because many of their symbols are derived from the
art of building, and because they are believed to
have been invented by an association of architects,
who were anxious to preserve among themselves
the knowledge which they had acquired.* The
difference in the ceremonial observances of these
institutions, may be accounted for nearly upon the
same principles. From the ignorance, or superior
sagacity of those who presided over the ancient
fraternities, some ceremonies would be insisted
on more than others, some of less moment would
be exalted into consequence, while others of greater importance would be depressed into obscurity.
In process of time, therefore, some trifling changes
would be effected upon these ceremonies, some

* Symbols derived from the art of building, were also employed by the Pythagoreans, for conveying instruction to
those who were initiated into their Fraternity. Vid. Proclus
in Eucl. lib. 11, def. 2, &c.

rites abolished and some introduced. The chief difference, however, between the ancient and modern mysteries, is in those points which concern religion. But this arises from the great changes which have been produced in religious knowledge. It cannot be supposed that the rites of the Egyptians, Jewish, and Grecian religions, should be observed by those who profess only the religion of Christ, or that we should pour out libations to Ceres and Bacchus who acknowledge no heavenly superior but the true and living God.

It may be proper here to take notice of an objection urged by M. Barruel, against the opinion that the mysteries of Free Masonry are similar to the mysteries of Egypt and Greece.* From the unfairness with which this writer has stated the sentiments of his opponents on this subject, from his confidence in his own, and from the disingenuity with which he has supported them, many inattentive readers may have been led to adopt his notions, and to form as despicable an idea of the understanding of Masons as he would wish them to form of their characters. He takes it for granted that all who embrace the opinion which we have endeavored to support, must necessarily believe, that a unity of religious sentiments and moral precepts, was maintained in all the ancient mysteries, and that the initiated entertained just notions of the unity of God, while the vulgar were addicted to the grossest polytheism. Upon this gratuitous supposition—which we wholly dis-

* Memoirs of Jacobinism, vol. 2, pp. 355–360.

avow, because it has no connection with our hypo
thesis—does M. Barruel found all his declamations
against the connections of our Order with the Pythagorean and Eleusinian institutions; and upon
this sophism rest all those reproachful epithets which
he so lavishly bestows upon us, while representing
us the children of sophistry, deism and pantheism.*

But this writer should recollect, that the son is
not accountable for the degeneracy of his parents;
and if the ancient mysteries were the nurseries of
such dangerous opinions as this writer, in opposition
to authentic history, lays to their charge, it is to the
glory of their posterity, that they have shaken off
the yoke, and embraced that heavenly light which
their ancestors affected to despise.

*The progress of Free Masonry, from the reign of
Theodosius to the present day.*

Having finished what may properly be denominated the Ancient History of Free Masonry, we are
now to have its progress from the abolition of hea
then rites, in the reign of Theodosius, to the present day; and though the friends and enemies of
the Order seem to coincide in opinion upon this
part of this history, the materials are as scanty as
before, and the incidents equally unconnected.
In those ages of ignorance and disorder which
succeeded the destruction of the Roman empire,
the minds of men were too debased by superstition

---

* Vid Barruel, vol. 2, p. 357. I do not find, in any system
of Chronology, that Christianity existed in the time of Pythagoras, or at the establishment of the Eleusinian mysteries

nd too contracted by bigotry, to enter into associations for promoting mental improvement and mutual
benevolence.   The spirit which then raged was not
a spirit of inquiry.

The motives which then influenced the conduct
of men, were not those benevolent and correct principles of action which once distinguished their ancestors, and which still distinguish their posterity.
Sequestered habits, and unsocial dispositions characterized the inhabitants of Europe in this season
of mental degeneracy.   Science was synonymous
with heresy in the view of the church of Rome, and
every scientific and secret association was overawed
and persecuted by the rulers of Europe.

But, though the political and intellectual condition of society was unfavorable to the progress of
Free Masonry, and though the secret associations of
the ancients were dissolved in the fifth century by
the command of the Roman Emperor; yet there are
many reasons for believing that the ancient mysteries were observed in private, long after their publication, by those enemies of Christianity who were
still attached to the religion of their fathers.   Some
authors* even inform us that this was actually the
case, and that the Grecian rites existed in the eighth
century, and were never completely abolished.†
These considerations enable us to connect the heathen mysteries with that trading association of arch

* Gibbon, 8vo. vol. 5, p. 110.
† Vid. Anthologia Hibernica for Jan. 1794, p. 36 and pp.
253, 254, *supra*.

itects, which appeared, during the dark ages, under the special authority of the See of Rome.

The insatiable desire for external finery and gaudy ceremonies, which was displayed by the Catholic priests in the exercise of their religion, introduced a corresponding desire for splendid monas teries and magnificent cathedrals. But as the de mand for these buildings was urgent, and continually increasing, it was with great difficulty that artificers could be procured, even for the erection of such pious works.

In order to encourage the profession of architecture, the bishops of Rome, and the other poten tates of Europe, conferred on the fraternity of Free Masons the most important privileges, and allowed them to be governed by laws, customs, and ceremonies peculiar to themselves. The association was composed of men of all nations:—of Italian, Greek, French, German, and Flemish artists, who were denominated Free Masons, and who, ranging from one country to another, erected those elegant churches and cathedrals, which, though they once gratified the pride and sheltered the rites of a corrupted priesthood, now excite the notice of antiquarians, and administer to the grandeur of king doms. The government of this association was remarkably regular. Its members lived in a camp of huts, reared beside the building in which they were employed. A surveyor, or master, presided over, and directed the whole. Every tenth man was called a warden, and overlooked those who were under his charge ; and such artificers as were not members of this Fraternity, were prohibited from engaging in those buildings which Free Masons alone had a title to rear.*

It may seem strange, and perhaps inconsistent with what we have already said, that the fraternity of Free Masons should have been sanctioned, and even protected by the bishops of Rome ; but the church of Rome, instead of approving of the principles of Free Masonry, only employed them as instruments for gratifying their vanity and satiating their ambition : for, afterward, when Masons were more numerous, and when the demand for religious structures was less urgent than before, the bishops of Rome deprived the fraternity of those very privileges which had been conferred upon them without solicitation, and persecuted with unrelenting rage the very men whom they had voluntarily taken into favor, and who had contributed to the grandeur of their ecclesiastical establishments. Wherever the Catholic religion was taught, the meetings of Free Masons were sanctioned and patronized.

Free Masonry introduced into Scotland.

The principles of the Order were imported into Scotland,† where they continued for many years in

* Wren's Parentalia, or a History of the family of Wren, pp. 306, 307.   Henry's History of Great Britain, 8vo. vol. 8, p. 273, b. 4, chap. 5, § 1.   Robison's Proofs of a Conspiracy, p. 21.

† A. D. 1140.   Vid. Statistical Account of Scotland, vol. 11, Parish of Kilwinning ; or Edinburgh Magazine for April, 1802, p. 243.

their primitive simplicity, long after they had been
extinguished in the continental kingdoms. In this
manner, Scotland became the centre from which
those principles again issued, to illuminate, not only
the nations on the continent, but every civilized portion of the habitable world. What those causes
were which continued the societies of Free Masons
longer in Britain than in other countries, it may
not, perhaps, be easy to determine ; but as the fact
is unquestionably true, it must have arisen either
from some favorable circumstance in the political
state of Britain, which did not exist in the other
governments of Europe, or from the superior policy
by which the British Masons eluded the suspicion
of their enemies, and the superior prudence with
which they maintained the primitive simplicity and
respectability of their Order.*

The Origin of Chivalry.

About the time of the Knights Templar, chivalry had arrived at its highest perfection. It had
its existence, indeed, prior to this period ; but, as
it continued to influence the minds of men long
after the destruction of that unhappy order, it was
thought proper to defer its consideration till the
present stage of our history. When chivalry

* The mysteries of Free Masonry were preserved and
transmitted by the Orders of Knighthood, viz: the Knights
of Malta, the Knights Templar, &c.; for a full account of
which, the reader is referred to the Templars' Chart by the
author of this book, second edition.

made its appearance, the moral and political condition of Europe was in every respect deplorable.
The religion of Jesus existed only in name: a de-
grading superstition had usurped its place, and
threatened ruin to the reason and the dignity of
man: the political rights of the lower orders were
sacrificed to the interests of the great: war was
carried on with a degree of savage cruelty equal
led only by the sanguinary contentions of the
beasts of prey: no clemency was shown to the
vanquished, no humanity to the captive: the female sex were sunk below the natural level: they
were doomed to the most laborious occupations,
and were deserted and despised by that very sex
on whose protection and sympathy they have so
natural a claim. To remedy these disorders, a
few intelligent and pious men formed an associa
tion, whose members swore to defend the Christian
religion, to practice its morals, to protect widows,
orphans, and the weaker sex; and to decide judi-
cially, and not by arms, the disputes which might
arise about their goods or effects. It was from this
association, undoubtedly, that chivalry arose;* and
not, as some think, from the public investiture with
arms, which was customary among the ancient Germans. But whatever was its origin, chivalry produced a considerable change in the manners and
sentiments of the great. It could not, indeed,

* Bontainvilliers on the Ancient Parliaments of France,
Letter 5, quoted in Brydson's Summary View of Heraldry,
pp. 24, 25, 26.

24

eradicate that ignorance and depravity which engendered those awful evils which we have already
enumerated. It has softened, however, the ferocity
of war. It has restored the fair sex to that honorable rank which they now possess, and which at all
times they are entitled to hold. It has inspired
those sentiments of generosity, sympathy, and
friendship, which have already contributed very
much to the civilization of the world.

Chivalry a branch of Free Masonry.

Such was the origin of chivalry, and such the
blessings it imparted. That it was a branch of
Free Masonry, may be inferred from a variety of
considerations, from the consent of those who
have made the deepest researches into the one,
and who were intimately acquainted with the spirit,
rites, and ceremonies of the other. They were
both ceremonial institutions. Important precepts
were communicated to the members of each, for
the regulation of their conduct as men, and as
brethren of the order.* The ceremonies of chivalry, like those of Free Masonry, though unin-
telligible to the vulgar, were always symbolical
of some important truths.† The object of both
institutions were the same, and the members bound
themselves by an oath to promote it with ardor
and zeal.‡ In chivalry there were also different

---

* Brydscn's Summary View of Heraldry, p. 31.
† Id. p. 95.   ‡ Id. p. 32.

degrees of honor, through which the youths were obliged to pass before they were invested with the dignity of Knighthood ;* and the Knights, like Free Masons, were formed into fraternities or orders, distinguished by different appellations.†

From these circumstances of resemblance, we do not mean to infer that chivalry was Free Masonry under another name ; we mean only to show that the two institutions were intimately connected ; that the former took its origin from the latter, and borrowed from it, not only some of its ceremonial observances, but the leading features, and the general outline of its constitution. The one was adapted to the habits of intelligent artists, and could flourish only in times of civilization and peace ; the other was accommodated to the dispositions of a martial age, and could exist only in seasons of ignorance and war. With these observations, indeed, the history of both fraternities entirely corresponds. In the enlightened ages of Greece and Rome when chivalry was unknown, Free Masonry flourished under the sanction of government, and the patronage of intelligent men. But during the reign of Gothic ignorance and barbarity which followed the destruction of imperial Rome, Free Masonry languished in obscurity, while chivalry succeeded in its place, and proposed to accomplish the same object by differ

* Id. pp. 36, 37.
† Id. pp. 38, 40.

ent means, which, though ,more rough and violent,
were better suited to the manners of the age.
And when science and literature revived in Europe
and scattered those clouds of ignorance and bar-
darism with which she had þeen overshadowed,
chivalry decayed along with the manners which
gave it birth, while Free Masonry arose with increasing splendor, and advanced with the same
pace as civilization and refinement. The connection between chivalry and Free Masonry, is
excellently exemplified in the fraternity of the
Knights Templars. It is well known that this
association was an order of Chivalry, that the
Templars performed its ceremonies, and were
influenced by its precepts, and that the same
association was initiated into the mysteries, was
regulated by the maxims, and practised the rites,
of Free Masonry.* But, though they then existed
in a double capacity, it must be evident to all who
study the history of the Templars, that their masonic character chiefly predominated ; and that
they deduced the name of their institution, and
their external observances, from the usages of chivalry, in order to conceal from the Roman Pontiff
the primary object of their order, and to hold their
secret meetings free from suspicion and alarm.

Before leaving this subject, it may be interesting
to some readers, and necessary for the satisfaction
of others, to show in what manner the Knights

* See note on page 276, *supra*.

Templars became depositaries of the Masonic mysteries. We have already seen, that almost all the secret associations of the ancients, either flourished or originated in Syria and the adjacent countries. It was here that the Dionysian artists and the Essenes arose. From this country also came several members of that trading association of masons, which appeared in Europe during the dark ages;[*] and we are assured that, notwithstanding the unfavorable condition of that province, there exists at this day on Mount Libanus, one of these Syriac fraternities.[†] As the order of the Templars, therefore, was originally formed in Syria, and existed there for a considerable time, it would be no improbable supposition that they received their masonic knowledge from the Lodges in that quarter. But we are fortunately, in this case, not left to conjecture, for we are expressly informed by a foreign author,[‡] who was well acquainted with the history and customs of Syria, that the Knights Templars were actually members of the Syriac fraternities.

Progress of Free Masonry in Britain.

Having thus compared Free Masonry with those secret associations which arose during the dark ages, let us now direct our attention to its progress in Britain, after it was extinguished in the other

---

[*] Anthologia Hibernica for April 1794, p. 280.
[†] Id. Id. p. 279.
[‡] Alder de Drusis Montis Libani, Rom. 1786.
24*

kingdoms of Europe. We have already seen that a trading fraternity of Free Masons existed in Europe during the middle ages; that many special favors were conferred upon them by the Roman See; that they had the exclusive privilege of erecting those magnificent buildings, which the pride of the Church of Rome, and the misguided zeal of its members, had prompted them to rear; and that several masons travelled into Scotland, about the beginning of the twelfth century, and imported into that country the principles and ceremonies of their order. And we illustrated several causes which preserved this association in Britain, after its total dissolution on the continent.

That Free Masonry was introduced into Scotland by those architects who built the abbey of Kilwinning, is manifest, not only from those authentic documents by which the existence of the Kilwinning lodge has been traced back as far as the end of the fifteenth century, but by other collateral arguments, which amount almost to a demonstration. In every country where the temporal and spiritual jurisdiction of the Pope was acknowledged, there was a continual demand, particularly during the twelfth century, for religious structures, and consequently for operative masons, proportioned to the piety of the inhabitants, and the opulence of their ecclesiastical establishments; and there was no kingdom in Europe where the zeal of the inhabitants for popery was more ardent, where the kings and nobles were more liberal to the clergy, and where, of consequence, the church was more richly endowed, than in Scotland.* The demand, therefore, for elegant cathedrals and ingenious artists must have been proportionally greater than in other countries, and that demand could be supplied only from the trading associations on the continent. When we consider, in addition to these facts, that this association monopolized the building of religious structures in Christendom, we are authorized to conclude, that those numerous and elegant ruins which still adorn the villages of Scotland, were erected by foreign Masons, who introduced into this island the customs of their order.† It was probably about this time also, that Free Masonry was introduced into England ; but whether the English received it from the Scotch Masons at Kilwinning, or from other brethren who had arrived from the continent, there is no method of determining. The fraternity in England, however, maintain that St. Alban, the Proto-Martyr, was the first who brought Masonry to Britain ;‡ that the brethren received a charter from King Athelstane, and that his brother Edwin

* The church possessed above one half of the property in the kingdom. Robertson's History of Scotland, vol. 1, pp 137, 65, 269.
† It is a curious fact, that in one of those towns where there is an elegant abbey, which was built in the twelfth century, Mr. A. Lawrie of Edinburgh has often heard that it was erected by a company of industrious men, who spoke in a foreign language, and lived separately from the town's people : and stories are still told about their petty quarrels with the inhabitants.
‡ About the end of the third century.

summoned all the brethren to meet at York, which formed the first Grand Lodge of England.* But these are merely assertions, not only incapable of proof from authentic history, but inconsistent, also with several historical events which rest upon indubitable evidence.† If the antiquity of Free Masonry in Britain can be defended only by the forgery of silly and uninteresting stories, it does not deserve to be defended at all.

After the establishment of the Kilwinning an. York Lodges, the principles of Free Masonry were rapidly diffused throughout both Kingdoms, and several lodges were erected in different parts of the island. As all these derived their authority and existence from the two mother lodges, they were likewise under their jurisdiction and control; and when any differences arose which were connected wih the art of building, they were referred to the general meetings of the fraternity, which were always held at Kilwinning and York. In this manner did Free Masonry flourish for a while in Britain, when it was completely abolished in every part of the world.

But even here it was doomed to suffer a long and serious decline, and to experience those alter nate successions of advancement and decay which mark the history of every human institution; and

* A. D. 926. Preston's Illustrations of Masonry, p. 148 Smith's Use and Abuse of Free Masonry, p. 51. Free Mason's Calendar, 1778.

† See Dr. Plot's Natural History of Staffordshire, chap. 8 pp. 316–318.

though during centuries after the importation of
Free Masonry into Britain, the brethren of the
order held their public assemblies, and were sometimes prohibited from meeting by the interference
of the legislature, it can scarcely be said ' to have
attracted general attention till the beginning of the
seventeenth century. The causes of this remarkable retardation which the progress of Masonry
experienced, it is by no means difficult to discover.
In consequence of the important privileges which
the order received from the church of Rome, many
chose the profession of an architect, which, though
at all times an honorable employment, was par·
ticularly in the highest request during the mid
dle ages. On this account, the body of operative
masons increased to such a degree, and the rage,
as well as the necessity of religious edifices, was
so much diminished, that a more than sufficient
number of hands could, at any time, be procured for supplying the demands of the Church
and of pious individuals. And as there was now
no scarcity of architects, the very reason which
prompted the Church to protect the fraternity, no
longer existed; they therefore withdrew from them
that patronage and those favors which they had
spontaneously proffered, and denied them even
the liberty of holding their secret assemblies,
the unalienable privilege of every free-born com·
munity. But these were not the only causes
which produced such a striking change in the conduct of the church to the masonic order. We have

already mentioned, that the spirit of Free Masonry was hostile to the principles of the church of
Rome.

The intention of the one was to enlighten the
mind; the object and policy of the other to retain
it in ignorance. When Free Masonry flourished,
the power of the Church must have decayed. The
jealousy of the latter, therefore, was aroused;
and, as the civil power in England and Scotland
was almost always in the hands of ecclesiastics,
the church and the state were both combined
against the principles and practice of Free Masonry. Along with these causes, the domestic and
bloody wars which convulsed the two kingdoms from
the thirteenth to the seventeenth century, conspired,
in a great degree, to produce that decline of the
Fraternity for which we have been attempting to
account.

But, notwithstanding these unfavorable circumstances, Free Masonry seems to have flourished
and attracted the attention of the public, in the
reign of Henry VI., who, when a minor, ascended
the throne of England in 1422. In the third year
of his reign, the parliament passed a severe act
against the fraternity, at the instigation of Henry
Beaufort Bishop of Winchester, who was then
intrusted with the education of the young King.
They enacted that the masons should no longer
hold their chapters and annual assemblies; that
those who summoned such chapters and assemblies, should be considered as felons; and that

those who resorted to them, should be fined and imprisoned.* But it would appear that this act was never put in execution; for in the year 1429, about five years after it was framed, a respectable lodge was held at Canterbury, under the patronage of the Archbishop himself.† When King Henry was able to take into his own hands the government of his kingdom, and to form an opinion of his own respecting the use and tendency of the Masonic fraternity, in order to allow for the vigorous conduct of his Parliament, he not only permitted the order to hold their meetings without molestation, but honored the lodges with his presence as a brother. Before he was initiated, however, into the mysteries of the order, he seems to have examined, with scrupulous care, the nature of the institution, and to have perused the charges and regulations of the fraternity as collected from their ancient records.

These facts are contained in a record written in the reign of his successor, Edward IV., and confirmed by a manuscript in King Henry's own hand-writing, which is familiar to every person who has studied the history of our order.‡

* Henry VI. cap. 1, A. D. 1425. See Ruffhead's Statutes. Dr. Plot's Natural History of Staffordshire, chap. 8, p. 318.
† Manuscript Register of William Molart, prior of Canterbury, p. 28. In this Register are mentioned the names of the masters, wardens, and other members of the lodge.
‡ We have hitherto been careful to bring forward no facts upon the sole evidence of the records, or the opinions of Free Masons: such evidence, indeed, can never satisfy the minds of the uninitiated public. But when these records contain facts, the fabrication of which could be of no service to

While Free Masonry was flourishing in England under the auspices of Henry VI., it was at the same time patronized in the sister Kingdom by King James I. By the authority of this monarch, every Grand Master who was chosen by the brethren, either from nobility or clergy, and approved of by the Crown, was entitled to an annual revenue of four pounds scots, from each master mason, and likewise to a fee at the initiation of every new member. He was empowered to adjust any differences which might arise among the brethren, and to regulate those affairs connected with the fraternity, which it was improper to bring under the cognizance of the courts of law. The Grand Master, also, appointed deputies, or wardens, who resided in the chief towns of Scotland, and managed the concerns of the order, when it was inconvenient to appeal to the Grand Master himself.

In the reign of James II., Free Masonry was by no means neglected. The office of Grand Master was granted by the crown to William St. Clair, Earl of Orkney and Caithness, Baron of Roslin, and founder of the much admired chapel of Roslin. On account of the attention which this nobleman

the fraternity, they may, in this case, be entitled to credit; or, when facts which do reflect honor upon the order, are confirmed by evidence from another quarter, the authority of the record entitles them to a still greater degree of credit. With respect to the facts mentioned in the text we have not merely the authority of the record and manuscript alluded to, but we have proof that there was no collusion in the case; for the record is mentioned in the book of Constitutions by Dr Anderson, who had neither seen nor heard of the manuscript

paid to the interests of the order, and the rapid propagation of the royal art under his administration,
King James II. made the office of Grand Master
hereditary to his heirs and successors in the Ba-
rony of Roslin, in which family it continued till
the institution of the Grand Lodge of Scotland.
The Barons of Roslin, as heriditary Grand Masters
of Scotland, held their principal annual meetings
at Kilwinning, the birth place of Scottish Masonry;
while the Lodge of that village granted constitutions, and charters of erection, to those brethren of
the order who were anxious that regular Lodges
should be formed in different parts of the Kingdom.
These Lodges all held their charters under the
jurisdiction of the Lodge at Kilwinning, and, in
token of their respect and submission, joined to
their own name that of their mother Lodge, from
whom they derived their existence as a corpora-
tion.*

During the succeeding reigns of the Scottish
monarchs, Free Masonry still flourished, though
very little information can be procured respecting
the peculiar state of the fraternity. In the privy
seal book of Scotland, however, there is a letter
dated at Holyroodhouse, 25th September 1590, and
granted by King James VI. " to Patrick Copland
of Udaught, for using and exercising the office of
Wardanrie over the art and craft of masonrie, over
all the boundis of Aberdeen, Banff, and Kincardine, to hold wardan and justice courts within the

* Such as Canongate Kilwinning, &c.
25

said boundis, and there to minister justice."[*]
This letter proves beyond dispute that the Kings
of Scotland nominated the office bearers of the
order; that these provincial masters, or wardens,
as they were then called, administered justice in
every dispute which concerned the "art and craft
of masonrie;" that lodges were established in all
parts of Scotland, even in those remote, and, at
that time, uncivilized counties of Aberdeen, Banff
and Kincardine: and it completely overturns the
unfounded assertion of Dr. Robison, who maintains,[†] that the celebrated antiquary, Elias Ashmole, who was initiated in 1646, is the only distinct and unequivocal instance of a person being
admitted into the fraternity, who was not an architect by profession. The minutes of St. Mary's
chapel, which is the oldest lodge in Edinburgh, extend as far back as the year 1598.
It appears, from these minutes, that Thomas
Boswell, Esq., of Auchinleck, was made a warden
of the lodge in 1600; and that the honorable
Robert Moray, Quarter-Master-General to the
army in Scotland, was created a Master Mason
in 1641. These facts are deserving of notice, as
they show, in opposition to Dr. Robison, that persons were early admitted into the order, who were
not architects by profession.

When James VI. ascended the throne of Eng-
and, he seems to have neglected his right of nomi-

* Privy Seal Book of Scotland, p. 61, F. 47.
† Proofs of a Conspiracy, p. 21.

uating the office bearers of the craft.   In Hay's
Manuscript, in the Advocates' Library, there are two
charters, granted by the Scottish Masons, appointing
the Sinclairs of Roslin their hereditary Grand
Masters.   The first of them is without a date, but is
signed by several masons, who appointed William
St. Clair of Roslin, his heirs and successors, to be
their "patrons and judges."   The other is in some
measure a ratification of the first, and is dated 1630,
in which they appoint Sir William St. Clair of Roslin, his heirs and successors, to be their "patrons,
protectors and overseers, in all time coming."
In the first of these deeds, which seems to have
been written a little after the union of the Crowns,
it is stated, that the want of a protector, for some
years, had engendered many corruptions among the
masons, and had considerably retarded the progress of the craft; and that the appointment of
William Sinclair, Esq., was with the advice and
consent of William Shaw, Master of Work to His
Majesty.   After presiding over the order for many
years, William St. Clair went to Ireland, where
he continued a considerable time, and, in consequence of his departure, the second charter was
granted to his son, Sir William St. Clair, investing
him with the same powers which his father enjoyed.   It deserves also to be remarked, that in both
these deeds, the appointment of William Sinclair,
Earl of Orkney and Caithness, to the office of Grand
Master, by James II. of Scotland, is spoken of as a
fact well known and universally admitted.   These

observations will set in a clear point of view what
must have hitherto appeared a great inconsistency
in the history of Scottish Masonry. In the deed
by which William Sinclair, Esq., of Roslin, resign·
ed the office of hereditary Grand Master, in 1736,
it is stated that his ancestors, William and Sir
William St. Clair, of Roslin, were constituted pa·
trons of the fraternity by the Scottish Masons them
selves; while it is well known, that the grant of
hereditary Grand Master was originally made by
James II. of Scotland, to their ancestor, William
Sinclair, Earl of Orkney and Caithness. But,
when we consider that James VI., by not exercising his power, virtually transferred to the craft the
right of electing their office-bearers, the inconsis·
tency vanishes; for Mr. Sinclair and his predeces-
sors, as far back as the date of their charters, held
their office by the appointment of the fraternity
itself. Lest any of Mr. Sinclair's posterity, however, might, after his resignation, lay claim to the
office of Grand Master, upon the pretence that this
office was bequeathed to them by the grant of
James II. to the Earl of Caithness and his heirs,
he renounces not only the right to the office which
he derived from the brethren, but any right, also,
which, as a descendant of the Earl of Caithness, he
might claim from the grants of the Scottish Mon·
archs.

Notwithstanding those civil commotions which
disturbed Britain in the seventeenth century, Free
Masonry flourished in Scotland under the auspices

of the Sinclairs of Roslin.   No particular event, however, which is worthy of notice, occurred during that time, or even during the remainder of the century.   The annual assemblies of the fraternity were still held at Kilwinning, and many charters and constitutions were granted by the lodge of that village, for the erection of lodges in different parts of the kingdom.

In the year 1736, William St. Clair, Esq., of Roslin, who was then Grand Master of Scotland, was under the necessity of disposing of his estate, and as he had no children of his own, he was anxious that the office of Grand Master should not be vacant at his death.   Having, therefore, assembled the Edinburgh and neighboring lodges, he represented to them the utility that would accrue to the order, by having a gentleman or nobleman of their own choice, as Grand Master of Masonry in Scotland; and at the same time intimated his intention to resign into the hands of the brethren, every title to that office which he at present possessed, or which his successors might claim from the grants of the Scottish Kings, and the kindness of the fraternity.   In consequence of this representation, circular letters were dispatched to all the lodges of Scotland, inviting them to appear either by themselves or proxies, on next St. Andrew's day, to concur and assist in the election of a Grand Master.   When that day arrived, about thirty-two lodges appeared by themselves or proxies, and after receiving the deed of resignation from Wm

25*

Sinclair, Esq., proceeded to the election of another Grand Master; when, on account of the zeal which William Sinclair, Esq., of Roslin, had always shown for the honor and prosperity of the order, he was unanimously elected to that high office, and proclaimed Grand Master Mason of all Scotland. Thus was the Grand Lodge of Scotland instituted, the future history of which will be resumed in its proper place.

We have already brought down the history of Masonry in England to the end, nearly, of the fifteenth century. During the whole of the sixteenth, and the beginning of the seventeenth century, no events occurred which can be inserted in a general history of the order. The lodges continued to meet, but seem neither to have attracted the notice nor excited the displeasure of the legislature.

During the civil wars, however, between the King and the Parliament, the fraternity appears to have been better known; and many were initiated into its mysteries who were equally distinguished by their literary talents and their rank in life. Elias Ashmole informs us, that he and Col. Mainwaring were admitted into the order at Warrington, in October, 1646.* This gentleman was the celebrated antiquarian who founded the Ashmolean Museum at Oxford. His attachment to the fraternity is evident from his diligent inquiries into its origin and history, and his long and frequent attendance upon its meetings.† Charles II

* Ashmole's Diary, p. 15.   † Ashmole's Diary, p. 66.

too, was a member of the fraternity, and frequently honored the lodges with his presence.*

From this fact, chiefly, Dr. Robison asserts, that Free Masonry was employed by the Royalists for promoting the cause of their Sovereign, and that the ritual of the master's degree seems to have been formed, or twisted from its original institution, in order to sound the political principles of the candidate.† The strained and fanciful analogy by wh'ch this notion is supported, is perhaps one of the most striking instances that could be adduced to show to what puerile arguments the most learned will resort, when engaged in the defence of a bad cause.

An opinion of an opposite nature, though equally extravagant, has been maintained by Pivati,‡ and the author of "Free Masonry Examined." These writers assert that Free Masonry originated in the times of the English Commonwealth ; that Oliver Cromwell was its inventor ; that the level was the symbol of republican equality ; and that the other signs and ceremonies were merely arbitrary, and formed for concealing their political designs. That Free Masonry existed before the time of Oliver Cromwell, is as capable of demonstration, as that Cromwell himself ever existed. It is really entertaining to observe what inconsist-

* Proofs of a Conspiracy, p. 22.
† Proofs of a Conspiracy, p. 21.
‡ Pivati Art. Liberi Muratori auvero Francs Macons Venezia, quoted by Mr Clinch.

ent and opposite opinions are formed upon the
same subject. According to one writer, Free Masonry was invented and employed by the adherents
of the King; according to another, it was devised
by the friends of the Parliament: in the opinion
of some, it originated among the Jesuits, who used
it for the promotion of their spiritual tyranny and
superstition; while others maintain, that it arose
among a number of unprincipled sceptics, who
employed it for destroying the spiritual tyranny
and superstition of the Jesuits!

*Introduction of Free Masonry into the Continental
Kingdoms.*

It was about this time, according to Dr. Robison, that Free Masonry was introduced among the
continental kingdoms.

After James II. of England had abdicated the
throne, and taken refuge in France with several
of his adherants, it is probable that they would
communicate additional spirit to the French lodges;
but that the English refugees were the first who
exported Masonry from Britain, or that they employed it for re-establishing the Stuart family on
the English throne, it is impossible to prove. Notwithstanding the difficulty, however, of determining the precise period when the principles of Free
Masonry were imported into France, it is manifest,
from the universal consent of the continental lodges, that it was of British origin; and it is more

than probable, that the French received it from Scotland about the middle of the sixteenth century, during the minority of Queen Mary. It is well known, that there was at this time a freer intercourse between Scotland and France than at any other period. Mary, Queen of Scots, was then married to the heir apparent of France ; and Mary of Guise, sister to the French King, was at the same time Regent of Scotland. In consequence of this intimate connection between the two kingdoms, French troops were sent to the assistance of the Scots, who having resided many years in the kingdom, and being habituated to the manners and customs of their allies, would naturally carry along with them into their native country those customs which afford them pleasure ; and none, we know, could be more congenial to the taste and dispositions of Frenchmen, than the *ceremonial* observances of Free Masonry. But it is not upon these considerations merely, that our opinion depends : it receives ample confirmation from a fact, of which Dr. Robison seems to have been totally ignorant. In the year 1645, a particular jurisdiction for masons called *Maconnerie*, or Masonry, was established in France. ' All differences which related to the art of building, were decided by particular judges, who were called Overseers of the art of Masonry ; and several counsellors were appointed for pleading the causes, which were referred to their decision. This institution has such a striking resemblance to the warden courts which exist-

ed in Scotland in the sixteenth century, that it
must have derived its origin from these. In both
of them, those causes only were decided which related to Masonry, and overseers were chosen in
both for bringing these causes to a decision. But
as similar tribunals were held in no other part of
the world, and as the warden courts were first established in Scotland, it is almost certain that the
French borrowed from the Scots the idea of their
Masonic tribunal, as well as Free Masonry itself
at that particular period when there was such a
free communication between the two kingdoms.
That the French received Free Masonry from
Scotland, may be presumed also from the singular
pre-eminence which was always given by foreigners
to Scottish masonry, and from the degree of *Cheva-
lier Macon Ecossois*, which, as a mark of respect to
Scotland, the French had added to the three symbolical degrees of Masonry, about the beginning of
the eighteenth century. Had Free Masonry not
been introduced into France till after the Revolution in 1688, as Dr. Robison affirms, it is wonderful how such a fact should have been forgotten;
for it was unknown, about thirty or forty years
afterwards, at what period the French received it
from Britain; and if the exiled family had employed Free Masonry for overturning the Hanoverian
succession, it was still more strange that such a
circumstance should be unknown in a country where
concealment was certainly unnecessary. When
any new custom is introduced into a nation, the

time of its introduction may be remembered for seventy or eighty years by one individual, without being committed to writing: and though it be not of sufficient importance, tradition will preserve it from oblivion for a much greater length of time. If Free Masonry, therefore, never existed in France till after the revolution in 1688, is it not absurd to suppose that the period when such a singular institution was established, should be utterly forgotten, at the distance of thirty or forty years from its establishment, though during that time it was never persecuted by the French government?

But at whatever period, and from whatever source, Free Masonry was introduced into France, it assumed there a very remarkable form. The attachment of that people to innovation and external finery, produced the most unwarrantable alterations upon the principles and ceremonies of the order. A number of new degrees were created; the office bearers of the craft were arrayed in the most splendid and costly attire; and the lodges were transformed into lecturing rooms, where the wiser brethren supported the most extravagant opinions, discussed the most abstruse questions in theology and political economy, and broached opinions which were certainly hostile to true religion and sound government. In the other countries of the continent, similar innovations, in a greater or less degree, prevailed; while the British lodges preserved the principles of the craft in their primi-

tive simplicity and excellence. Such dangerous
innovations have not the smallest connection with
the principles of Free Masonry. They are unnatu
ral excrescences, formed by a warm imagination,
and fostered by the interference of designing men.
Those who reprehend Free Masonry, therefore,
for the changes which it underwent in the hands
of foreigners, may throw equal blame upon religion,
because it has been a cloak for licentiousness
and hypocrisy; or upon science, because it has
been converted into an instrument of iniquity.
The changes of which we have been treating,
arose altogether from the political condition of the
countries were they were made. In France, and
the other kingdoms of Europe, where popery was
the ecclesiastical establishment, or where abso-
lute power was in the hands of their monarchs,
the most slavish restraints were imposed upon
the conduct and conversation of the people. None
durst utter his own sentiments, or converse upon
such metaphysical subjects as militated against
the theology and politics of the times. Under
such restraints, speculating men, in particular,
were highly dissatisfied; those powers which
Heaven had bestowed, and on the exercise of
which their happiness depended, were fettered by
human laws, and that liberty of speech restrained
which tyranny had no right to control. For these
reasons, the lodges were frequented by men of
philosophical habits, who eagerly embraced an opportunity of declaring their sentiments, and dis

cussing the favorite objects of their study, without dreading the threats of government, or the tortures of the Inquisition. In this view the lodges may be compared to little republics, enjoying the rational liberties of human nature, in the midst of an extensive empire, enslaved by despotism and superstition. In the course of time, however, that liberty was abused and doctrines were propagated in the French and German lodges, which it is the duty and policy of every government to discover and suppress. But these corruptions had no necessary connection with Free Masonry: they arose wholly from the political condition of the continental kingdoms. In Britain, where the order subsisted much longer than in any other country, its history is stained by no glaring corruption, or offensive innovations: more attention was paid to the intrinsic value of the order than to its external observances; and the British lodges had a greater resemblance to charitable meetings than to pompous and splendid assemblies. Blessed with a free constitution, and allowed every innocent liberty of our nature, we can indulge our sentiments with the greatest freedom, we can mark even the errors of administration without any to make us afraid. In such circumstances, Britons are under no temptation to introduce into the lodges religious and political discussions The liberty of the press enables them to give the widest circulation to their opinions, however new or extravagant; and they are

26

liable to no punishment, by publicly attacking the established religion of their country. The British lodges, therefore, have retained their primitive purity; they have been employed in no sinister cause: they have harbored in their bosoms neither traitors, nor atheists, nor French philosophers

Extentsion of Masonry in England from the beginning of the Eighteenth Century.

While the French were busily engaged in the decoration of their lodges, and in the invention of new degrees and trifling ceremonies, the masons in England were more wisely employed in extending the boundaries of the royal art. About the beginning of the eighteenth century, during the reign of Queen Anne, Free Masonry seems to have rapidly declined in the south of England. Four lodges only existed in the South, and few hopes could be entertained of a revival, while the seat of the Grand Lodge was at such a distance as the city of York. In such circumstances, the four lodges met in 1717; and, in order to give vigor to their declining cause, and advance the interest of the Fraternity in the South, they elected themselves into a Grand Lodge, and chose Anthony Sayer, Esq., for their first Grand Master.

Thus was instituted the Grand Lodge of England which has now attained to such a pitch of prosperi-

ty and splendor. The motive which suggested
this institution was certainly laudable and useful;
but every person must be aware, that the four
lodges were guilty of a considerable impropriety
in omitting to request the countenance of the
Grand Lodge of York. Notwithstanding this neg-
ligence, the greatest harmony subsisted between
the two Grand Lodges till 1734; and under the
auspices of both, the order flourished in every part
of the kingdom, but particularly in the South of
England, where it had formerly been in such a
languishing condition. In the year 1734, however, the Grand Lodge of England, having granted constitutions to lodges within the district of
York without the consent of their Grand Lodge,
incurred to such a degree the displeasure of the
York masons, that the friendly intercourse which
had formerly subsisted between them was com
pletely broken off, and the prosperity of the one was
always viewed by the other with a suspicious eye
In 1739, also, some trifling innovations upon the
ancient customs of the order having been impru-
dently sanctioned by the Grand Lodge of England, several of the old London Masons were
highly offended, and after seceding from the
Grand Lodge, and pretending to act under the
York constitution, they gave themselves the appellation of *Ancient Masons*, while they attached
to those connected with the Grand Lodge the odi-
ous appellation of *Moderns*, who, in their opinion,
never existed till the year 1717 The Ancient

Masons after their secession, continued to hold
their meetings, without acknowledging a superior
till the year 1772, when they chose for their Grand
Master the Duke of Athol, who was then Grand
Master elect for Scotland. Since that period, both
the Grand Lodges of England have attained to a
high degree of prosperity; but such has been their
mutual antipathy that the members of the one
have had no correspondence or communion with
those of the other until a very recent date. The
Irish and Scotish masons, however, who seemed
rather to have favored the Ancients, held commun
ion with both the Grand Lodges, and were allow
ed to be present at all their meetings. It is much
to be regretted that such respectable bodies as the
two Grand Lodges of England, should have retarded the progress of Masonry by their mutual jealousies and dissentions. Schisms in societies generally
arise from misconduct on both sides, which was
certainly the case in the schism under consideration.

The Moderns undoubtedly departed from their
usual caution and propriety of conduct, by author
izing the slightest innovations upon the ceremonies
of an ancient institution. But the Ancients were
guilty of a greater impropriety by being the active
promoters of the schisms, and still more by holding
up the Moderns to the ridicule of the public. These
errors, however, have been mutually acknowledged
and buried in oblivion, and the breach repaired
which so long separated the two lodges, and which

the Scotish and Irish masons always regarded with pity and indignation.

Rapid Spread of Free Masonry.

After the institution of the Grand Lodge of England in 1717, Free Masonry assumed a bolder and a more independent aspect. It was no longer confined to the British Isles, or to the capital of France, but was destined to irradiate every portion of the globe; and while the Grand Lodges of Scotland and England contemplated with pleasure the propagation of the royal art, their diligence was fully rewarded by the gratitude and liberality of the foreign lodges for the gift they received.

In the year 1729, Free Masonry was introduced into the East Indies, and, in a short time after, a provincial Grand Master was appointed to superintend the lodges in that quarter. In 1730, the Grand Lodge of Ireland was instituted, lodges were erected in different parts of America, and a provincial deputation was granted to Monsieur Thuanus for the circle of Lower Saxony. A patent was sent from England in 1731, to erect a lodge at the Hague, in which Francis Stephen, Duke of Lorrain, and afterwards Emperor of Germany, was initiated into the order; and provincial Grand Masters were appointed for Russia, and Andalusia in Spain. In 1736, lodges were erected at Cape Coast in Africa, and at Geneva; and provincial deputations were granted for Upper Sax-

26*

ony and the American Islands. In 1738, a lodge was instituted at Brunswick, under the patronage of the Grand Lodge of Scotland, in which the late King of Prussia was initiated when Prince Royal. His Majesty was so pleased with the maxims and ceremonies of the order, that he ever afterwards was its most zealous partizan, and requested even that a lodge should be established in the capital of his own dominions. In this lodge many of the German Princes were initiated, who afterwards filled the office of Grand Master, with much honor to themselves and advantage to the fraternity.

Persecutions of Free Masons.

But while Free Masonry flourished in these parts of the world, and in many other places which it would be tedious to enumerate, it was doomed to undergo a variety of persecutions from the unfounded jealousies of a few despotic rulers, and the deep rooted superstition of a few Catholic priests. These persecutions took their rise in Holland, in the year 1735. The States General were alarmed at the rapid increase of Free Masons, who held their meetings in every town under their government; and as they could not believe that architecture and brotherly love were their only object, they resolved to discountenance their proceedings. In consequence of this determination, an edict was issued by government, stating, that though they had discovered nothing in the practices of the fraternity either injurious to the interests of the republic, o contrary to the character of good citizens, yet, in order to prevent any bad consequences which might ensue from such associations, they deemed it prudent to abolish the assemblies of Free Masons. Notwithstanding this prohibition, a respectable lodge having continued to meet privately at Amsterdam, intelligence was communicated to the magistrates, who arrested all the members and brought them to the Court of Justice. Before this tribunal, in presence of all the magistrates of the city, the masters and wardens boldly defended themselves, and declared upon oath that they were loyal subjects, faithful to their religion, and zealous for the interests of their country; that Free Masonry was an institution venerable in itself, and useful to society; and that though they could not reveal the secrets and ceremonies of their order, they would assure them that they were contrary to the laws neither of God nor man, and that they would willingly admit into their order any individual in whom the magistrates could confide, and from whom they might receive such information as would satisfy a reasonable mind. In consequence of these declarations, the brethren were dismissed, and the town secretary was requested to become a member of the fraternity. After initiation, he returned to the Court of Justice, and gave such a favorable account of the principles and practice of the society, that all the magistrates became brethren of the order, and zealous patrons of Free Masonry.

After Free Masonry had thus honorably triumph-
ed over her persecutors in Holland, she had to con-
tend in France with prejudices equally inveterate,
though less impregnable. Although many persons
of distinction defended the fraternity, and expos-
tulated with the court on the impropriety of severe
measures, their assemblies were abolished in 1737,
under the common pretence, that beneath their
inviolable secrets they might cover some dreadful
design, hostile to religion and dangerous to the
kingdom. But when those derelictions of party spirit
and private malice had subsided, the prohibition
of government was gradually forgotten, and the
fraternity in France recovered their former prosperity and splendor. In Germany, too, the tranquility of the order was interrupted by the malice
of some ignorant women. The curiosity of the
female sex is proverbial. A few German ladies,
who possessed a greater share of this commodity
than is necessary for shining in a drawing-room
conversation, were anxious to discover the secrets
of Free Masonry. Having been baffled in all their
attempts upon the fickleness of their husbands,
and the fondness of their admirers, they converted their curiosity into revenge, and attempted to
influence the mind of Maria Theresa, the Empress
Queen against the lodges in Vienna. Their at-
tempt was in some measure successful, as they
persuaded her to issue an order for surprising all
the masons in the city, when assembled in their
lodges. This plan 'however, was frustrated by the

Intervention of the Emperor, Joseph I., who, being himself a mason, declared his readiness to answer for their conduct, and showed the ladies and their friends, that the charges which they had brought against the order were false and defamatory.

When the flame of persecution is once kindled, its devastations are seldom confined to the country where it originated. The example of one nation is urged as an excuse for the conduct of another; and, like the storm on the sandy desert, its effects are ruinous in proportion to its progress. In Holland and France, the hostility of the legislature against Free Masonry was in a short time disarmed. But when the flame reached the ecclesiastical states of Italy, it broke out in ungovernable rage—its effects were more cruel, and its direction more lengthened. In the year 1738, a formidable bull was thundered from the conclave, not only against Free Masons themselves, but against all those who promoted or favored their cause, who gave them the smallest countenance or advice, or who were in any respect connected with a set of men who, in the opinion of his Holiness, were enemies to the tranquility of the state, and hostile to the spiritual interests of souls. Notwithstanding the severity of this bull, which threatens excommunication to every offender, no particular charge, either of a moral or political nature, is brought against a single individual of the order. It is merely stated that the fraternity had spread far and wide, and were daily increasing; that they admitted men of every religion into their society; and that they bound their members by oath to preserve with inviolable secrecy the mysteries of their order. These circumstances, indeed, were sufficient grounds for exciting the church of Rome to oppose a system so contrary to their superstitious and contracted views, in religion and government.

This bull was followed by an edict, dated 14th January, 1739, containing sentiments equally bigoted, and enactments equally severe. The servitude of the gallies, the tortures of the rack, and a fine of a thousand crowns in gold, were threatened to persons of every description who were daring enough to breathe the infectious air of a masonic assembly.

About a month after this edict was issued, a decree was emitted by his Holiness, condemning a French book, entitled "An Apology for the Society of Free Masons," and ordering it to be burnt by the ministers of justice, in one of the most frequented streets of Rome.

In consequence of these enactments at Rome, the catholic clergymen of Holland attempted, in the year 1740, to enforce obedience to the commands of their superiors. It was customary, among the divines of that country, to examine the religious qualifications of those who requested a certificate to receive the holy sacrament. Taking advantage of their spiritual power, they concluded their examination of the candidates by asking if they were Free Masons. If they were, the certificates

were refused, and they were expelled forever from
the communion table. After the priests had exert
ed their authority in the expulsion of several re
spectable characters, the subject excited general
attention; and when many pamphlets had been
published in defence of both parties, the States
General interfered, and prohibited the clergy from
asking questions that were unconnected with the
religious character of the individual.

Association of the Mopses.

Several Free Masons of distinction in Germany,
though steady friends to the church of Rome, dis-
approved highly of its proceedings against the fraternity, and were anxious to preserve the order
from that ruin which it was fast approaching. In
order to effect this, they instituted a new association, formed upon the same principles, and proposing
to itself the same object, as Free Masonry. The
members were denominated Mopses, from the German word *mops*, denoting a young mastiff, which
was deemed a proper emblem of the mutual fidelity
and attachment of the brethren. But that they
might preserve the mysteries of Free Masonry from
those members of the new association who were not
Masons, they rejected from their ritual all the masonic ceremonies, words, and signs; and that they
might escape the vengeance of the Roman church,
they softened all those parts of the institution which
had a tendency to give offence to narrow and superstitious minds.

Instead, therefore, of binding the members by an oath, they took their word of honor, that they would never reveal the mysteries and ceremonies of the order.

It is well known to every person acquainted with the history of Masonry, that the exclusion of ladies has been a fertile source of calumny against the brethren. It was supposed that actions were performed in the lodges inconsistent with the delicacy of the female sex, and, as in the case of the Templars, that the most unnatural crimes were perpetrated and authorized. In order to avoid this ground of defamation, the Mopses admitted women into their lodges, who were allowed to hold any office, except that of Grand Mopse. The association of the Mopses was patronized by some of the most illustrious characters in Germany; the lodges consisted of the most respectable members of the community, and several of the Princes of the Empire were Grand Masters of their order. The admission of protestants or heretics into the masonic lodges in catholic countries, gave great offence to the church of Rome, and was one of the causes which prompted the severity of their proceedings. Aware of this circumstance, the Mopses resolved to initiate none into their mysteries but the steady friends of the catholic communion. This, however, was merely a pretence to deceive his Holiness; for they admitted into their order, without the smallest scruple, men of every religion and every country.

As the bulls of the Pope had no authority in

Switzerland, Free Masonry flourished in that republic till the year 1745, when a most unaccountable edict was issued by the council of Berne, prohibiting, under the severest penalties, the assemblies of Free Masons. No reason is assigned by the council for their conduct; no charges are advanced against any of the brethren. The council of Berne are terrified by secret association; and on this account, forsooth, they must persecute and destroy. More intolerant in their bigotry, and more cruel in their conduct than the church of Rome, they are not satisfied with abolishing all the lodges in the republic. Every Free Mason in Switzerland must accuse himself before the magistrates of the district. He must renounce his obligations to secrecy, and swear, in the presence of the great God of heaven, to trample upon those engagements which, before the same Being, he has sworn to revere. Such an instance of tyranny over the minds and consciences of men, is a remarkable fact in the history of a republic where the reformed religion has been protected from its infancy, and where Free Masons have always conducted themselves with exemplary propriety.* The severe treatment, therefore, which they experienced, must have originat-

* Free Masonry seems to have been directly imported into Switzerland from Great Britain; as a deputation was granted by the Grand Lodge of England, for erecting a Lodge at Lausanne, in the canton of Berne, in the year 1739. It could not, therefore, in so short a time, be corrupted by those offensive innovations which were superinduced upon it in France.

27

ed in some private quarrel between the members of the council and the fraternity. It could be prompted by no patriotic motive, by no regard for the welfare of the state, or the safety of individuals. But notwithstanding these persecutions. Free Masonry was afterwards revived in Switzerland, and practiced without molestation, though with less eagerness and success than in the other states of Europe.

During these various persecutions, of which we have only given a general account, many individuals of the fraternity underwent the severest treatment; and in their relief, that practical benevolence was strongly exemplified which Free Masons are taught to exhibit to the distressed brethren of their order. In 1739, after Pope Eugenius had issued his bull against Free Masonry, one Crudeli, a Free Mason, was imprisoned at Florence by the Inquisition, and suffered the most unmerited cruelties for maintaining the innocence of the asssociation. When the Grand Lodge of England was informed of his miserable situation, they recollected that a foreigner, however low his rank and however distant his abode, had a claim upon their sympathy: they transmitted to him twenty pounds for procuring the necessaries of life, and exerted every nerve for effecting his liberation. A brother, confined at St. Sebastians in Spain, experienced from the English Masons the same attention and generosity. At Lisbon, in the year 1742, James Mouton, a French artist, and John Coustos, a native of Berne, in Switzerland, were imprisoned by the bloody Inquisition. They were accused of belonging to a society by which sacrilege and sodomy were allowed, and were requested to dis -cover to their persecutors the true design of Free Masonry After defending the institution as useful and innocent, they were extended on the rack, in expectation that a confession would be extorted by its torments. Force, however, had no control over a mind conscious of integrity. Coustos, having maintained his innocence, after having been thrice stretched on this instrument of agony, was at last sentenced to walk in the procession of the *Auto-de-Fè*, and to serve in the gallies for four years. At the instance of the English Masons, however, George II. authorized the British minister at Lisbon to demand, in his Majesty's name, from the King of Portugal, the liberation of Coustos; which was granted in 1744, after a dreadful confinement of two years and a half.

Instances of the benefits of Free Masonry.

From such scenes of inhuman barbarity, it is pleasing to turn to examples of real benevolence and generosity. As the consideration of these is always gratifying to a human mind, they certainly deserve to be recorded in a History of Free Masonry. In the year 1748, Monsieur Preverot, a gentleman in the navy, and brother of the celebrated M. Preverot, doctor of medicine, in the faculty at Paris, was unfortunately shipwrecked on an

island whose viceroy was a Free Mason. Along
with his ship, M. Preverot had lost all his money
and effects. In this destitute condition, he presented
himself to the viceroy, and related his misfortune
in a manner which completely proved that he was
no impostor. The viceroy made the Masonic
signs, which being instantly returned by the
Frenchman, they recognized and embraced each
other as brethren of the same order. M. Preverot
was conducted to the house of the viceroy, who
furnished him with all the comforts of life, till a
ship bound for France touched at the island. Before his departure in this vessel, the viceroy
loaded him with presents, and gave him as much
money as was necessary for carrying him into his
native country.

In the battle of Dettingen, in 1743, one of the
King's guards having his horse killed under him,
was so entangled among its limbs that he was unable to extricate himself. While he was in this
situation, an English dragoon galloped up to him,
and, with his uplifted sabre, was about to deprive
him of life. The English soldier having with
much difficulty made the signs of Masonry, the
dragoon recognized him as a brother, and not only
saved his life, but freed him from his dangerous
situation. He was made a prisoner by the English
dragoon, who was well aware that the ties of Masonry cannot dissolve those of patriotism.

In the year 1749, Free Masonry was introduced
into Bohemia, and eagerly embraced by all the

dis inguished characters in the city of Prague.
They call themselves Scotish Masons, and are remarkably inquisitive into the characters of those
whom they admit into the order. On this account,
they perform with punctuality those duties which
they owe to their brethren of the order, as is strik-
ingly exemplified in the following story:—A Scotish gentleman, in the Prussian service, was taken
prisoner at the Battle of Lutzen, and was conveyed
to Prague, along with four hundred of his companions in arms. As soon as it was known that
he was a Mason, he was released from confinement,
he was invited to the tables of the most distinguished citizens, and requested to consider himself as a
Free Mason, and not as a prisoner of war. About
three months after the engagement, an exchange of
prisoners took place, and the Scotish officer was
presented by the fraternity with a purse of sixty
ducats to defray the expenses of his journey.*

Persecutions of Masonry in Britain.

The persecutions which Free Masonry encoun-
tered were hitherto confined to the continent. The
tide of religious frenzy, however, now rolled to the
shores of Britain. In the year 1745, the Associate
Synod, consisting of a few bigoted dissenters, attempted to disturb the peace of the fraternity.

* Several striking and curious instances of the extensive
benevolence of Free Masons, may be seen in Smith's Use
and Abuse of Free Masonry, pp. 374, 377, 378, &c.

In the beginning of this year, an overture was laid before the Synod of Sterling, stating, that many improper things were performed at the initiation of Masons, and requesting that the Synod would consider whether or not the members of that order were entitled to partake in the ordinances of religion. The Synod remitted this overture to all the kirk-sessions under their inspection, allowing them to act as they thought proper. In 1755, however, they appointed all their kirk-sessions to examine every person who was suspected to be a Free Mason, and to demand an explicit answer to any question which they might ask concerning the administration of the Mason oath. In the course of these examinations, the kirk-sessions discovered (for they seem hitherto to have been ignorant of it) that men who were not architects were admitted into the order. On this account the Synod, in the year 1757, thought it necessary to adopt stricter measures. They drew up a list of foolish questions, which they appointed every kirk-session to put to those under their charge. These questions related to what they thought were the ceremonies of Free Masonry; and those who refused to answer them, were debared from religious ordinances. The unrighteous oppressions created by these acts, outstrip, in some respects, the tyranny and cruelty inflicted on the fraternity by the church of Rome, and the severe edicts of the council of Berne. And ought not the criminality—may we not say the villany—of such proceedings, to be held up to the ridicule and detestation of the public ?*

Free Masonry flourishes in defiance of Persecution.

Notwithstanding these persecutions, Free Masonry flourished, and was in the highest estimation in Great Britain, France, Germany, and several other kingdoms of Europe. In 1743, it was exported from Scotland to Denmark ; and the lodge which was then instituted is now the Grand Lodge of that kingdom. The same prosperity has attended the first lodge in Sweden, which was erected at Stockholm in 1754, under a patent from Scotland. In 1765, a splendid apartment was erected at Marseilles for the accommodation of the brethren. It was adorned with the finest paintings, representing the most interesting scenes which occur in the history of the Old and New Testaments, and calculated to remind the spectator of his various duties as a man, a subject, and a Christian. The representation of Joseph and his brethren, of the Samaritan and the Jew, of Lot and the angels, must have reminded every brother of the beauty of charity and forgiveness, which are the first principles of Masonry, as they are the first duties of man. The picture of Peter and the Apostles paying tribute to Cæsar, must have recalled to every individual his obligations as a citizen to revere and support the

* It is remarkable that the Grand Lodge of Scotland did not deign to take the smallest notice of these proceedings.

constituted authorities. And the representation of
Job in his misfortunes lifting up his hands to
Heaven, must have forced upon the minds of the
most inconsiderate this important reflection : that
fortitude and resignation to the will of God are the
duties of all in distress, and that the Divine bless
ing will ultimately attend those who bear without
murmuring the chastisements of their Father, and
preserve, amidst the severest trials, their patience
and virtue unimpaired.* These observations, ap
parently trifling, are important in one respect, as
they show that the French lodges had not at that
time fostered in their bosom the votaries of scepti
cism and disloyalty. The other lodges in France
were at this time numerous and magnificent. The
Grand Lodge contained about twenty offices, which
were all filled by noblemen of the highest rank.
They had provincial Grand Masters similar to those
of Scotland, and the insignia and jewels of all the
office-bearers were as rich and splendid as the lodges
where they assembled.

In the year 1767, a lodge under an English
constitution was established in Berlin, under the
appellation of *Le Royale York*, in honor of the
Duke of York, who was initiated into the fraternity
by that lodge while he was traveling on the continent. In 1768, the Free Masons of Germany were
authorized to hold their assemblies by a charter
granted by the King of Prussia, the Elector of

* For a further account of this building, see Smith's Use
and Abuse of Free Masonry, p. 165.

Saxany, and the Queen of Hungary and Bohemia, and afterwards ratified by the Emperor of Germany himself. By another charter from England in 1789, a lodge was erected at Brunswick, which, in 1770, became the Grand Lodge of that part of Germany. Its Grand Master was Prince Ferdinand of Brunswick, who, a short time after, received a provincial deputation from England, for superintending the lodges in Lower Saxony. In the year 1773, a compact was entered into between the Grand Lodge of England, under Lord Petre, and the Grand Lodge at Berlin, under the Prince of Hesse Darmstadt, which had a few years before been duly erected into a Grand Lodge, at a meeting of the masters and wardens of twelve regular lodges. In this compact, it was stipulated that the Grand Lodge of Berlin should be acknowledged as the Grand Lodge of the whole Empire of Germany, including the dominions of his Prussian Majesty; that it should exercise no Masonic power out of the Empire of Germany, or within the district under the authority of the Grand Lodge of Brunswick; that the Electorate of Hanover should be free to both the Grand Lodges in Germany; and that the contracting parties should unite their efforts to counteract all innovations in Masonry, and particularly the proceedings of a set of masons in Berlin, who, under the denomination of *Stricte Observantz*, had annihilated their former constitutions, erected themselves into a Grand Lodge, and sanctioned very improper innovations

upon the principles and ceremonies of the frater
nity. This compact was highly approved* of by
the King of Prussia, who immediately erected the
Grand Lodge of Berlin into a corporate body.
In 1777, the King of Prussia was Protector of all
the Masons in Germany. Ferdinand, Duke of
Brunswick and Lunenburgh, was Grand Master of
all the United Lodges in Germany; and the other
offices were filled by the most able and illustrious
princes of the empire. Under the auspices of
such distinguished personages and the jurisdiction of the Grand Lodges of Berlin and Brunswick,
Free Masonry has flourished to the present day in
that extensive empire.

In Germany, Denmark and Sweden, Charity
Schools were erected by the lodges for educating
the children of Free Masons whose poverty debar-
red them from this advantage. In the one which
was formed at Brunswick, they were instructed
even in classical learning and various branches of
mathematics, and were regularly examined by the
Duke of Brunswick, who rewarded the most deserving with suitable donations. At Eisenach,
several seminaries of this kind were established.
The teachers were endowed with fixed salaries;
and in a short time after their institution, they had
sent into the world 700 children, instructed in the
principles of science and the doctrines of Christianity. In 1771, an establishment of a similar kind
was formed at Cassel, in which the children were
maintained and educated till they could provide

for themselves. In 1773, the United Lodges of Drèsden, Leipsic and Gorlitz, erected at Fredorickstadt a seminary of learning for children of every denomination, in the Electorate of Saxony. The masonic subscriptions were so numerous, that the funds of the institution were sufficient for its maintenance; and in the space of five years, above 1100 children received a liberal education. In the same year, an extensive workhouse was erected at Prague, in which the children were not only initiated into the first principles of learning, but into those branches of the useful and fine arts which might qualify them for commercial and agricultural situations. It deserves to be remarked, that the founders of these institutions, amid their anxiety for the public prosperity, never neglected the spiritual interests of their children. They saw that early piety is the foundation of all that is useful and honorable in life; and that without this, speculative knowledge and practical skill are of little avail. How inconsistent are such facts with those fabulous accounts of the German lodges which have been published in England by a few party men.

While these things were going on in Germany, the brethren in Portugal were exposed to the persecution of its bigoted rulers. Major Francois d'Alincourt, a Frenchman, and Don Oyres de Ornellas Pracao, a Portuguese nobleman, were, in 1766, imprisoned by the governor of Maderia for their attachment to the order. Being afterwards carried to Lisbon, they were confined for fourteen months, till they were released by the general inter-cession of the brethren in that city. In the follow-ing year, several Free Masons were confined at Na-ples, but were soon liberated by the intercession of foreign princes, and the eloquence of an Italian advocate.

Notwithstanding the persecutions which the fra-ternity experienced in Holland, Free Masonry was flourishing in that republic in 1779. At that time, a compact was entered into between the Grand Lodge of Holland, held at the Hague, and that of England. In this compact, it was stipulated that the Grand Lodge of Holland should be permited to erect lodges within her territories, both at home and abroad, and to appoint provincial Grand Masters over each dis-trict. In consequence of this accession of power to the Grand Lodge of Holland, Free Masonry flourish-ed under its auspices in the Dutch settlements in India, Africa and South America.

Rise of the Illuminati in Germany.

Let us now direct our attention to a new secret association, which about this time arose in Ger-many, and which was imagined to have taken its rise from Free Masonry, and to have planned a diabolical conspiracy against every religious and political establishment in Europe. In 1775, the order of the Illuminati was founded by Doctor Adam Weishaupt, Professor of Canon Law in the University of Ingolstadt.

In this association speculative opinions were inculcated, which were certainly inconsistent with the principles of sound religion and social order. But that Illuminism originated from Free Masonry, that it brought about the French Revolution, or ever planned any dangerous conspiracy, are circumstances for which the shadow of a proof has not as yet been adduced.   Dr. Robison, indeed, expressly affirms, that Illuminism " took its rise among the Free Masons, but was totally different from Free Masonry ;" and, by a deceitful anachronism, he presents Weishaupt as an active member in the German Lodges, before he acquaints his readers that he was the founder of the Illuminati, for no other reason than to make them believe that Weishaupt was a Free Mason before he plan ned his new association.*   Now the case was very different indeed.   Barruel himself asserts, " that it is a fact demonstrated beyond a doubt, that Wei shaupt became a Mason in 1777 only ; and that two years before this, when he established Illuminism, he was totally unacquainted with the mysteries of Free Masonry."†

Here, then, is an important fact, which strikes at the root of all Dr. Robison's reasoning against Free Masonry.   Barruel maintains that Weishaupt was not a mason till two years after the organiza· ιion of his new institution ; and Dr. Robison allows

* Proofs of a Conspiracy, Introduction, pp. 15, 101.
† Memoirs of Jacobinism, part 3, Preliminary Observations, p. xv. and p. 12.

that Illuminism was totally different from Free Masonry. The two institutions, therefore, were totally unconnected; for the members of the one were never admitted into the lodges of the other without being regularly initiated into the myste ries of both. Upon these simple facts we would arrest the attention of every reader, and those in particular who have been swindled out of their senses by the united exertions of a priest and a philosopher.

After Weishaupt had organized his institution, he exerted every nerve to disseminate its principles. For this purpose he became a Free Mason in 1777 ; and; by means of emissaries, he attempted to circulate his opinions among the French and German lodges. In these attempts, indeed, he was sometimes successful. But it should be recollected, by those who on this account calumniate Free Masonry, that the same objection may be urged against Christianity, because impostors have sometimes gained proselytes, and perverted the wavering minds of the multitude. These doctrines, however, were not merely circulated by Weishaupt in a few of the lodges, and taught at the assemblies of the Illuminati: they were published to the world in the most fascinating form by the French Encyclopedists, and inculcated in all the eloquence with which some of the most celebrated philosophers on the continent could adorn them. It can only be said of Weishaupt, therefore, that he was not just such a determined

infidel as Voltaire and his associates.   Such is a
short, and, it is hoped, an impartial view of the ori
gin and progress of the Illuminati.

After the French Revolution, which, as Mouniei
has well shown, arose from other causes than those
to which Barruel and Robison ascribe it; the plans
of these parties were not carried on in Germany
so systematically as before; and, notwithstanding
the fabrications with which the Jesuitical Barruel
has calumniated the lodges in that country, Free
Masonry prevails to this day, respected by the most
virtuous and scientific members of the community
and patronized by the most distinguished princes of
the Empire.

In Germany, the qualifications for a Free Mason
are great and numerous.   No person is initiated
into the order without the consent of every mem
ber of the lodge; and it frequently happens, that
a German is excluded by a single dissenting voice
On this account, the lodges of that country are
filled with persons of the first rank and respecta
bility, and everything is conducted with the great
est decorum and solemnity.   As Masonry is there
held in the highest estimation, an Englishman
will obtain an easier introduction to the chief no
bility and literati of Germany in a Mason lodge, than
in any other place; and will never repent of having
been initiated into the order of his native country *

* Dr. Render's Tour through Germany, Introduction to
vol. 1, pp. 30, 33. Dr. Render maintains, that Free Masonry
has greatly improved the manners and dispositions of the
Germans. See vol. ii. p. 200, note.

After the publication of the works of Barruel
and Robison, the progress of Free Masonry in
Britain was retarded by an act of Parliament in
1799, for the suppression of seditious societies, in
which the fraternity were virtually prohibited from
erecting new lodges in the Kingdom. But this
act was not prompted by the calumnies of these
writers. It became necessary from the political
condition of the Kingdom ; and the exceptions which
it contained in favor of Free Masons, are a complete proof that government never credited the re-
ports of these alarmists, but placed the most implicit
confidence in the loyalty and prudence of British
Masons. Dr. Robison, indeed, asserts that the
emissaries of corrupted Free Masonry and Illuminism were lurking in the British empire, and plotting
its destruction.

But such monsters of iniquity have never yet
been discovered within the circuit of our island:
they have never polluted the British lodges. Tell
us then no more, that our lodges are the recepta-
cles of sacrilegious and revolutionary miscreants.
I see them frequented by men of unaffected piety,
and undaunted patriotism. Tell us no more, that
our brethren of the order are less holy and virtuous than the uninitiated vulgar. I see them in
the church and in the Senate, defending, by their
talents, the doctrines of our religion, exemplifying
in their conduct the precepts it enjoins, kind to
their friends, forgiving to their enemies, and benevolent to all. Tell us no more, that they are

traitors, or indifferent to the welfare of their coun
try. I see them in the hour of danger, rallying
around the throne of our King, and proffering, for
his safety, their hearts and their arms. I see
them in the form of heroes at the head of our
fleets and our armies ; and the day will arrive
when a Free Mason shall sway the sceptre of
these Kingdoms, and fill with honor and with
dignity the British throne.

History of the Grand Lodge of Scotland.

I have already brought down the history of
Scotish Masonry to the institution of the Grand
Lodge in 1736, and given a short account of the
different circumstances which occasioned and accompanied that important event. I shall now, in
as concise a manner as is consistent with my present design, continue the history of the doings of
this body down to the late period of 1803. No
more will be attempted, than to notice so many of
their acts as will show to my brethren in America
the pure principles, the excellent order, and the
truly Masonic practice, which have uniformly
characterized the Grand Lodge of Scotland—the
.odge to whom the fraternity in America owe
much of their origin, order, and success, and for
whose future prosperity all true Masons will devoutly pray.

In 1736, the Grand Lodge of Scotland was instituted, in consequence of which, almost all the
28*

Scotish Lodges applied for and received new charters, and by a ready and voluntary renuncia·tion of their former rights, evinced the steadiness of their attachment to the Grand Lodge, and their unfeigned acknowledgments of its jurisdiction and power.

This year the Grand Lodge ordered that a fee should be exacted of every person who had been initiated into the order since its organization, or who might afterwards be initiated, and that this fee should make a part of .the charity fund for the relief of the indigent and distressed brethren, and other benevolent purposes. The same year, the opulent inhabitants of Edinburgh and its environs having resolved to erect an infirmary, or hospital, for the reception of poor patients, the Grand Lodge proposed to pay, out of their own funds, a certain number of operative masons to assist in building the infirmary, provided that the managers of that institution would allot a particular apartment in the hospital, for the reception of a few Infirm Masons who should be recommended by the Grand Master.

The Grand Lodge decreed, also, that the annual election should no longer be celebrated on the 24th of June, the birth day of St. John the Baptist, as had been the usage from time immemorial, and that in future, for many weighty reasons, it should be held on the 30th of November, the birth day of St. Andrew.

On the 2d of August, 1738, the foundation stone

of the New Royal Infirmary of Edinburgh, patron-ized by the Grand Lodge, was laid in due and ample form.

On the 30th of November, 1738, it was reported to the Grand Lodge, by George Drummond, Esq., that the directors of the Royal Infirmary, out of gratitude to the Society of Free Masons for their countenance and aid in building that edifice, had unanimously agreed that preference should always be given to distressed and infirm Free Masons in one of the galleries of the Hospital.

From the institution of the Grand Lodge, the principles of the craft had been so rapidly propagated through every part of the kingdom, that it was found necessary this year to appoint provincial Grand Masters over particular districts, who were employed to hold general meetings, and to take cognizance of everything relating to Masonry within the bounds of their district.

In the year 1739, the son of an operative mason in Edinburgh, having been left at his father's death in the most friendless and indigent condition, was recommended to the patronage of the Grand Lodge. With a readiness which enhanced the value of the action, they agreed to take him under their own charge, to bind him to an operative mason for eight years, for the freedom of St. Mary's chapel, and during that time to furnish him with clothes and other necessaries. It was agreed, also, if any similar applications were made, the same action should be performed every three years.

During the year 1740, it was proposed and unanimously agreed that a correspondence should be
opened between the Grand Lodges of Scotland and
England, and that the assistance of the latter, in
building the Royal Infirmary, should be particularly requested.

In the year 1747, the Grand Lodge empowered
Alexander Drummond, Esq., provincial Grand Master of the west of Scotland, who had taken up his
residence at Alexandretta in Turkey, and erected
several mason lodges in that country, to constitute
lodges in any part of Europe or Asia bordering on
the Mediterranean Sea, to superintend the same, or
any others already erected in those parts of the
world, and to transmit an account of his proceed
ings to the Grand Lodge, as soon as he found it con
venient.

During the year 1749, the funds of the Grand
Lodge were much diminished, by numerous donations to indigent brethren.

In the year 1752, a message was brought to the
Grand Lodge, informing them that the foundation
stone of the Royal Exchange was to be laid on the
13th of September, and that a splendid procession
of the Grand Lodge, attended by the other lodges
in and about Edinburgh, would take place on that
occasion. Accordingly a plan of the procession was
seasonably transmitted to the brethren by the Grand
Master, which was highly approved of and unanimously adopted ; and on the day appointed, the
ceremony was witnessed in due and ample form.

In the year 1753, the Grand Lodge of Scotland was petitioned by the Scotish Lodge in Copenhagen, requesting a charter of confirmation, and also the liberty of electing a Grand Master, with full power to erect new lodges in any part of the kingdom. This petition was not answered in the fullest extent; but it was resolved to grant a patent of constitution and erection in the usual form, and a provincial commission to a qualified person, empowering him to erect new lodges in the kingdoms of Denmark and Norway, and to superintend those which were already erected, provided that this provincial Grand Master should be always subject to the Grand Lodge of Scotland, and that the lodges which he constituted should recognize and acknowledge her as their paramount superior.

After the election of the office-bearers, in the year 1751, the brethren, to the number of four hundred, walked in procession from Mary's Chapel to the High School, accompanied with bands of music, and directed by the light of torches. This is the first instance of a procession by torch light that occurs in the records of the Grand Lodge.

In the year 1755, it was represented to the Grand Lodge, that the interests of Masonry would be greatly promoted by the division of Scotland into districts, and the appointment of provincial Grand Masters to each district. This suggestion being taken into consideration, it was resolved to nominate a number of respectable gentlemen who were qualified for the discharge of that important office.

In compliance with the request of the Lodge of Canongate and Leith, the Grand Lodge this year appointed Mr. John M'Clure, Grand Chaplain, to consecrate a new room which was fitted up for masonic meetings. This ceremony was performed in the presence of the Grand Master, and other office-bearers of the Grand Lodge.

In the year 1756, a provincial commission was granted to Colonel John Young, who had been for many years Deputy Grand Master for Scotland, over all the lodges in America and the West Indies. A patent of erection was also granted for a lodge at Boston, in New England.

In the year 1757, a charter of constitution was granted to the lodge of Fredericksburgh, Virginia,

In the year 1758, the committee of charity resolved to expend ten guineas in the purchase of clothes and other necessaries, for the French prisoners confined in the Castle of Edinburgh, giving preference to those who were brethren of the order, without neglecting the necessities of such as were uninitiated. This year Mr. John M'Clure was installed Chaplain to the Grand Lodge, and was advanced to the proper rank and precedency in the Grand Lodge.

1759. This year several brethren who were Scots masons, having instituted a lodge at Charleston, South Carolina, transmitted five guineas to the Grand Lodge of Scotland, for the use of their poor. Grateful for this unexpected instance of benevolence, the Grand Lodge ordered a charter to be instantly made out, and transmitted to them by the first opportunity.

In the year 1761, two French prisoners in Edinburgh Castle who were Free Masons, were allowed four guineas from the Grand Lodge.

On the 21st of October 1763, the Grand Lodge, agreeably to request from the Lord Provost, Magistrates, and Town Council of Edinburgh, met and proceeded to lay the corner stone of the North Bridge. The same year a Military Lodge was erected in Holland, under the name of the Union Lodge. The Grand Lodge of Scotland granted the constitution, at the request of the chief officers in General Marjoribanks' regiment, in the service of the States General of the United Provinces.

1764. In the course of this year, two guineas were transmitted to the charity fund by St. John's Lodge in Virginia. Thus we see, in more instances than one, that the wide Atlantic, even, cannot separate the hearts of the Brethren.

During the year 1767, the practice of granting diplomas was introduced into the Grand Lodge.

In the course of the year 1771, the foundation stone of the Cowgate Episcopal Chapel was laid, with the usual deposits, by His Excellency, Lieut. Gen. Oughton, Grand-Master-Mason of Scotland, attended by several gentlemen of distinction.

Nov. 30th, 1772, the Grand Lodge of Scotland

received a communication from the Grand Lodge of England, requesting that a mutual correspondence might be maintained between them, which request was cordially complied with on the part of the Grand Lodge of Scotland.

1775. Some difference having arisen in the course of this year between the two Grand Lodges of England, those who denominated themselves the Ancients, submitted the case to the Grand Lodge of Scotland, who, from motives of delicacy, declined to intermeddle in the affair.

On the 24th of June, 1776, the foundation stone of the High-School was laid, with great solemnity, by Sir William Forbes, Bart. Grand-Master of Scotland, in presence of the Lord Provost and Magistrates, the Principal and Professors of the University, the Rector, Masters and Scholars of the High-School, and the Masters, Officers and Brethren of all the lodges of Free Masons in the city and neighborhood, besides an innumerable crowd of spectators. No ceremony in the city for many years, had yielded such heartfelt satisfaction to the inhabitants. The importance of the objects, the dignity of the procession, the numerous train of brethren, and above all, the charming exhibition of above 350 fine boys, afforded a most animating spectacle.

On the 24th of January, 1778, William Sinclair, Esq., of Roslin, died at the age of 78. In consequence of the loss of this amiable man and zealous Mason, the Grand Master ordered a funeral lodge to be held on the 14th of February. Above four hundred of the Brethren, dressed in deep mourning, having assembled on that occasion, Sir William Forbes, Bart., as Grand Master, delivered the funeral oration.

1778. It is remarkable, that at this time the Duke of Athol was Grand Master both in Scotland and England.

1781. Many new lodges were instituted this year, and much money was distributed among the poor.

In the year 1783, a charter for a lodge at St. Petersburgh, under the name of the Imperial Scotish Lodge of St. Petersburgh, was granted to a petition of several Scotish masons, who had been commissioned by the Empress of all the Russias, to settle in her capital.

During the year 1784, the Grand Lodge granted a confirmation of the Pythagorean Lodge at Antigua.

On the first of August, 1785, the foundation stone of the South Bridge was laid, with great solemnity, by the Right Honorable Lord Haddo, Grand-Master-Mason of Scotland.

During this same year, a charter of confirmation was granted to the Union Lodge, in the Island of St. Christophers ; and a correspondence was opened between the Grand Lodges of Scotland and Berlin ; also, immediate relief was granted to a distressed Turk, who, upon examination, was found to be a brother of the order.

29

In the course of the year 1786, a charter was granted to a French Lodge at Aix in Provence, under the title of *La Douce Harmonie*.

1787. This year a charter was granted to a number of brethren, to hold a lodge at Rouen, in France, under the title of *Ardente Amitie*, and another for the city of Marseilles, under the name of the *Faithful Friend*. Lewis Clavel, Master of the Scotish Lodge at Rouen, in Normandy, was appointed Provincial Grand Master over all the lodges in France which held of the Grand Lodge of Scotland.

In the year 1788, it was agreed that all gentle men in the clerical line, should pay no fees for being initiated into the Fraternity.

In 1799, a new lodge, under the title of the Mount Olive Lodge, was instituted at St. Christophers under a patent from Scotland.

During the year 1791, a provincial deputation was granted for the Leeward Carribee Islands.

1795. This year the Grand Lodge of Scotland addressed his Royal Majesty, on the subject of his escaping from the hands of an assassin, congratulating him, and expressing their sense of the Divine goodness in delivering him from the murderous designs of the most wicked of men.

In the course of the year 1796, a correspondence was opened with the Grand Lodge of Ireland.

In the year 1799, the Parliament of England passed several acts *for the more effectual suppression of societies established for seditious and treasonable purposes;* and although provisions were made in these acts favorable to all those societies which could prove themselves truly Masonic, yet they operated to the embarrassment of many lodges under the jurisdiction of the Grand Lodge of Scotland; and although the Grand Lodge was conscious that those acts were the result of unfounded jealousies and in a degree oppressive, yet they immediately acquiesced in all the proscriptions of Parliament, and exerted themselves to carry those acts into full effect with the greatest possible expedition: thus at once evincing their loyalty, and their readiness to submit to the most rigid scrutiny which government deemed necessary to institute.

1800. A charter was this year granted to the officers of the 51st regiment, stationed in the Island of Ceylon, to hold a lodge under the denomination of the Orange Lodge.

On the 14th of May, 1801, the foundation stone of the Wet Docks at Leith, was laid by the Grand Master, in due and ample form, in the presence of about 1200 brethren, and a splendid concourse of citizens.

1802. This year a circular letter was received from the Grand Lodge of America. The spirit of illumination which it breathed, and the supernumerary degrees, amounting to about fifty, which it authorized, were sufficient reasons for drawing down the contempt of Scotish masons, whose honor it is to have preserved Free Masonry **for**

many centuries in its original and simple form;
and whose pride it shall ever be, to transmit to the
latest posterity the principles and ceremonies of
their order unpolluted and unimpaired.

On the evening of the 30th November, 1803, the
brethren were assembled to celebrate the festival
of St. Andrew, when they were honored with the
company of His Excellency the Earl of Moira,
Commander-in-Chief of his Majesty's forces in Scotland, and Acting Grand Master of the Grand Lodge
of England. From the presence of this nobleman,
the friends of the Grand Lodge of England antici·
pated an union between that respectable body and
the Grand Lodge of Scotland.

Union between the Grand Lodges of Scotland and England.

In the general history of Free Masonry, we have
already given an account of the schism which took
place in the Grand Lodge of England, by the
secession of a number of men, who, calling themselves Ancient Masons, invidiously bestowed upon
the Grand Lodge the appellation of Moderns.
These Ancient Masons, who certainly merit blame
as the activie promoters of the schism, remained,
without acknowledging a superior, or being acknow·
ledged an independent body, from the year 1739
to the year 1772, when they chose for their Grand
Master, in connection with the Grand Lodge of
York, his grace the Duke of Athol, who was then
Grand Master elect for Scotland, and from that

time they were acknowledged as a component part of the Grand Lodge of York.

From this circumstance, more than from any predilection on the part of the Grand Lodge of Scotland for the Ancient Masons, a friendly intercourse has always subsisted between the two Grand Lodges; but as the Scotish Masons, from their union with ihe Ancients,—that is the York Masons and those of London who seceded from the Grand Lodge of England—imbibed the same prejudices against the Grand Lodge of England, under the Prince of Wales and Lord Moira—arising merely from some trifling innovations in ceremonial observances which the Grand Lodge of England had inconsiderately authorised—they never cherished that mutual friendship, which, by the principles of Free Masonry, they were bound to preserve.   Such was the relative condition of the Grand Lodge of Scotland, and that of England under the Prince of Wales, when the Earl of Moira appeared before the Grand Lodge of Scotland.

At this meeting an opportunity was offered for the discussion of this subject, and the Earl of Moira, in an impressive and eloquent speech, related at considerable length the conduct of the Grand Lodge of England to the Ancient Masons. He stated that the hearts and arms of the Grand Lodge had ever been open for the reception of their seceding brethren, who had obstinately refused to acknowledge their faults, and return to the bosom of their mother lodge ; and that though the Grand Lodge of England differed in a few tri-fling observances from that of Scotland, they had ever entertained for Scotish Masons that affection and regard which it is the object of Free Masonry to cherish, and the duty of Free Masons to feel His Lordship's speech was received by the breth· ren with loud and reiterated applause—the most unequivocal mark of their approbation of its senti ments.

From this period we may date the origin of an union between the Grand Lodge of Scotland and that of England, which, we hope, will soon be completely effected. From such a junction under the auspices of his Royal Highness, the prince of Wales, aided by the distinguished talents and re-spectability of the Earl of Moira, and the abilities, and conciliating manners of the Earl of Dalhousie. Free Masonry, we hope, will receive additional respectability and vigor, and preserve in these kingdoms its primitive purity and simplicity. And while its influence is diffused from the British empire to every corner of the world, we trust that it will continue to be, as it has been, the bane of despotism and oppression, the enemy of superstition and fanaticism, the promoter of civilization and good order, the friend of uncorrupted science, if true benevolence, and unaffected piety.

APPENDIX

TO THE SIXTEENTH EDITION OF THE

TRUE MASONIC CHART,

OR,

HIEROGLYPHIC MONITOR.

~~~~~~~~~~~~~~~

To the Masonic Fraternity :—

IN presenting the sixteenth edition of the TRUE MA-
SONIC CHART, OR HIEROGLYPHIC MONITOR to the Masonic
World, the author would, with it, return his heartfelt
thanks to the craft, for the very liberal patronage they
have bestowed upon him in times past—and offer to
them a new and greatly improved work, which is not
only calculated, in his judgment, in these trying times
in the institution, to preserve the ancient landmarks
and perpetuate the Work and Lectures as he received
them, nearly forty years ago, from very old, bright and
experienced Masons of that day; but also to prevent
the shameful innovations which are constantly being
made by a set of designing men, with a view of revolu-
tionizing the Institution, in order to get it under their
control.

The Author has spent over forty years in the service
of the Order as a Lecturer. During all this time, he
has labored diligently to preserve carefully everything

connected with the "*Work*" as he received it. From
the commencement to the present, he has constantly
been laboring to make it known; and he therefore
thinks that, as far as "*correctness*" is concerned in the
work of the Order, his opinion is entitled to some respect. That the extent of his efforts may be fully understood, he gives to the reader the following Diary, for
which he asks an attentive perusal:—

The system of "*Work and Lectures*" as taught by
the Author of the True Masonic Chart, was adopted
about the year 1800—and by the New England States
in 1810, so far as they had the opportunity of acquir-
ing it.

Until the year 1797, no Grand Chapter of Royal
Arch Masons was organized in America. Previously
to this period, a competent number of Companions of
that degree, possessed of sufficient abilities, under the
sanction of a Master's Warrant, proceeded to exercise
the rights and privileges of Royal Arch Chapters, whenever they thought it expedient and proper. This unre-
strained mode of proceeding was subject to many in-
conveniences, and productive of many irregularities in
the mode of work. Sensible of the existence of these
things, a convention of Delegates, from several Chapters
in the Northern States, assembled at Masons' Hall in
Boston, on the 24th of October, 1797, to deliberate upon
the propriety and expediency of forming and establishing a Grand Chapter of Royal Arch Masons, for the
government and regulation of the several Chapters
within the said States

On the fourth Wednesday in January, 1798, the De-legates met at Hartford, in Connecticut, and after seve-ral days' deliberation upon the subject, they formed and adopted a Constitution for the Government of Royal Arch Chapters; and having elected and installed their Grand Officers, the Grand Chapter became completely organized.

The long-desired and necessary authority for correct-ing abuses and regulating the concerns of Royal Arch Masonry, being thus happily established, the Order soon became flourishing and respectable. The second meet-ing of the General Grand Chapter took place on the 9th of January, 1806, at Middletown, Conn., (septen-nial.) The casualties of war having prevented the septennial meeting, which was to have been holden in 1812, after the return of peace, the General Grand Chapter was convened in New-York city, on the 6th of June, 1816.

The Grand Royal Arch Chapter of Massachusetts was formed in						1798
"	"	"	Rhode Island	"	"	1798
"	"	"	Connecticut	"	"	1798
"	"	"	New-York	"	"	1798
"	"	"	Vermont	"	"	1806
"	"	"	South Carolina	"	"	1812
"	"	"	Ohio	"	"	1816
"	"	"	Kentucky	"	"	1816
"	"	"	New Hampshire	"	"	1819

The remaining Grand Chapters came in after this time.

After the Grand Lodges of the several States had de-clared themselves free and independent, and the Gene-ral Grand Chapter was formed and organized in 1798, it was deemed advisable to adopt a regular and uniform mode of Lecturing and Work for the whole; and in order to accomplish this great desideratum, the expert workmen from various parts of the country met together. The work was completed and adopted fully by the year 1810. It was at this period, the Author commenced Lecturing in the New England States, with all those bright and well-informed Masons, who had been so assiduous in selecting and arranging the above system, which was by them adopted as the most correct. Taking the "Ancient York Rite" for a standard, they selected from the "Scottish Rite" those things which approximated to the former, and out of the two systems they formed a very perfect and complete set of Lectures; which are beautiful in themselves, and have been preserved entire to the present hour. After spending some years in the New England States, in the year 1815, the Author visited New-York city, where he received the ineffable degrees, and was regularly constituted and appointed by the Council a Sov. Gr. In. Gen'l of the 33rd and last degree—received as a member of said Council, and invested with full power to confer the said degrees.

Early in the year 1816, having been sanctioned as a Grand Lecturer by the officers of the General Grand Chapter of the United States of America, and by other Grand Bodies, with a view of establishing this uniform mode of Work and Lectures, he repaired to the city of New-York in the month of June, and attended the meeting of the General Grand Chapter then in session. Receiving all necessary authority and instructions from that body, he proceeded on his tour, and visited several Lodges and Chapters in New Jersey, and from thence to Philadelphia; but owing to the fact that Pennsylvania had not acknowledged the jurisdiction of the General Grand Chapter, and declining still to do so; also their mode of Work and Lecturing being entirely different from that adopted by the General Grand Chapter, he passed on to Delaware, where he lectured in several of the Lodges and Chapters, and was warmly received by the brethren of that State. He then visited Baltimore, the residence of P. P. Eckels, Esq., one of the officers of the General Grand Chapter. He there became acquainted with Ill. Comp. Hezekiah Niles, a bright Mason, who had made great progress in the Ancient Mysteries.

The Author received from Companions Niles and Eckels, a Warrant to confer the Royal and Select Masters' Degrees, they being explanatory of the Royal Arch, and to establish Councils in all places where there was a Royal Arch Chapter, if they so desired. By authority of this Warrant, he established Councils in most of the places he visited in the Western and Southern States.

The places in which they became most proficient in the system he taught, were Pittsburg, Wheeling, Marietta, Zanesville, Chillicothe, Cincinnati, Maysville, Lexington, Frankfort and Louisville; at these places he spent several months.

While at Cincinnati, Frankfort and Lexington, he

was joined by Companions T. S. Webb and J. Snow, officers of the General Grand Chapter, who were making a western tour of pleasure, and for the purpose of installing several Royal Arch Chapters.

While at Cincinnati and Louisville, the Author was visited by Companions from Indiana and Missouri, who obtained and carried home with them, a correct knowledge of the Master Masons, Royal Arch, and Royal and Select Masters' Degrees. The knowledge imparted in the two latter degrees was so important a history of the Royal Arch, that those degrees were universally adopted by the Chapters.

The Author would mention one Companion, William G. Hunt, Esq., who resided at that time in Lexington, Ky., as one very expert, and who acquired a perfect knowledge of all the degrees up to and including the Royal and Select Masters', with the view of imparting the knowledge to his Companions, wherever he might sojourn.

The Author was introduced to the Hon. Henry Clay, at that time a zealous Mason, and member of the Lodge in Lexington.

Finishing his travels in the West, he pressed on to Natchez and New Orleans; at which latter place, he, in the year 1817, was received and acknowledged by the Council as Sov. Grand Inspector General of the 33rd degree—was presented with a full and perfect set of all the degrees, their histories, accompanied with the drawings, emblems, seals, &c., and was fully empowered to preside as Grand Commander of the Northern Jurisdiction in his turn, with many flattering expressions of their hospitality and benevolence.

Returning from New Orleans to Baltimore, he tarried for a short time with his Companions, Eckels and Niles, and by their desire visited the Eastern Shore of Maryland, Delaware and New Jersey.

In June, 1817, he returned to the New England States, and entered into an engagement with the Most Excellent John Hart Lynde, Esq., an officer of the General Grand Chapter, to visit the several Lodges and Chapters of Connecticut. In the autumn of the same year he went to Virginia, stopping at Alexandria, to visit the Lodge of which George Washington was a member, where were kept the apron and jewel which he used to wear when visiting the Lodge, with several other relics of the Father of his country and the patron of Masonry. His great attachment to the Institution was shown by the tenor of a note addressed to the W. M. of the Lodge, declining an invitation to attend some Masonic celebration on account of ill health.

The Author visited several of the Lodges and Chapters in Virginia, and spent several weeks at Richmond, where they acquired a very correct knowledge of his mode of Work and Lectures. Being under an engagement with Comp Lynde, of Connecticut, he left Virginia early in the spring of 1818, and proceeded to New Haven, Conn.,—where he was appointed Grand Lecturer of the Grand Lodge and Grand Chapter of that State, and spent two years in visiting the Lodges and Chapters, and perfecting them in the correct mode of Lecturing and Work.

It was at this time, while having some leisure, and having by experience felt the want of a uniformity of Lecturing and Work, and of keeping those parts belonging to one degree of Masonry from being mixed up with others, that he commenced arranging the Emblems and Illustrations agreeably to his mode of Lecturing and Work—and of designing many new illustrations which were first brought out in a small volume, called the "True Masonic Chart, or Hieroglyphic Monitor," first published in 1819. The publication of the Masonic Chart was something new in the annals of Masonry, there never having been any emblems published before, more than those which were on what is called the "*Master's Carpet.*"

The introduction of so many new emblems, and the arranging of them in a systematic manner, was found to be quite an acquisition to the craft, and the Work met with a universal reception, and rapidly passed through several editions. Many of the Grand Lodges adopted it as their text-book, and the members of nearly all the subordinate Lodges used it as their guide.

In the year 1820, the Author of the Masonic Chart brought out the Templar's Chart, with similar emblems and illustrations, being assisted in the arrangement of the Work by an officer of the General Grand Encampment of the U. S. A. This Work met with equally flattering success as the Masonic Chart.

The General Grand Encampment of the United States of America, was formed and established on the 21st of June, 1816, at New-York city, and was composed of the following Grand Encampments:—

Massachusetts, Rhode Island, New-York, Louisiana and Pennsylvania.

The Grand Encampment of Pennsylvania was first formed, on the 12th day of May, 1797, and was composed of four Encampments.

The Grand Encampment of Massachusetts and Rhode Island was formed on the 6th day of May, 1805, and was composed of five Encampments, viz :

Encampment of K. T., - - Boston.
    do.   do.   - - Newburyport.
Council of K. R. C.,   - - Portland.
St. John's Encampment, - - Providence.
Encampment of K. T., - - Newport.

The Grand Encampment of the State of New-York was formed June 18th, 1814, and was composed of the following Encampments:

Old Encampment,   - - New-York City.
Jerusalem Encampment, - -   do.
Columbian   do.   - -   do.
Temple   do.   - - Albany
Montgomery   do.   - - Stillwater.

The Lectures and Work of the Encampment were under the same efficient supervision and arrangement, as the degrees of the Blue Lodges and Royal Arch Chapters. There are now Grand Encampments in '- most every State in the Union.

The Author, at this time, became acquainted with Comp. James Cushman, with whom he lectured, and perfected him in all the Lectures up to and including the orders of Knighthood, and gave him a certificate as being well skilled in all those degrees for the purpose of his Lecturing in the Southern States. His family residing at the time in New Jersey, he visited nearly all the Lodges in that State; also lectured in Delaware, Maryland, and all the Lodges of Virginia, in which labor he spent several years, occasionally visiting North Carolina, South Carolina and Georgia.

About the same time, Comp. John Barker also obtained the Lectures, and became very expert and well qualified to teach the mode of Lecturing and Work in all the degrees, up to the Order of the Knights of Malta; and being presented with a certificate of his qualifications, he went to South Carolina for the purpose of diffusing a correct knowledge of Masonry in the several Lodges and Chapters there. He spent several years in the south, lecturing in the Lodges, Chapters, and Encampments, visiting Georgia, Alabama, Mississippi and Tennessee. In the latter place he found some very bright Masons, who had obtained the Lectures from Companion W. G. Hunt, who had moved there from Kentucky, and diffused the knowledge he so correctly possessed.

The same system of Lecturing and Work as taught by the Author, was adopted by the Grand Lodge of New-York, he having had an opportunity of hearing the Lectures as given by their Grand Lecturers, Companions Wadsworth and Enos, in the presence of the Most Excellent Companions T. S. Webb and J. Snow.

At a subsequent period, Companion Barney, who obtained the Lectures in Vermont, perfected himself by lecturing with the Author, and was appointed Grand Lecturer of the Lodges of Ohio; he also lectured very

extensively in the Western States. Thus the mode of
Lecturing and Work as taught by the Author, became
nearly universal throughout the United States, save the
Lodges in Philadelphia and parts of the State of Pennsylvania.

From 1820 to 1833, the Author made his residenc
at New Haven, Conn., for the publication of his Masonic and Templar's Charts, and occasionally lecturing
with the Lodges, Chapters, Councils and Encampments
of that State, and with Companions and Sir Knights of
other States, as they called on him for instruction.

In 1824, the Author received from the Sovereign
Grand Council of the 33rd degree, sitting in the valley
of Charleston, S. C., by the hands of Illustrious Companion John Barker, who was deputized for the purpose—Letters PATENT and WARRANT, with expressions of " *Health, Stability, Power,*" constituting the Author a Sovereign Grand Inspector General of the 33rd
and last degree of Masonry, and authorizing and empowering him for *life*, to ESTABLISH, CONGREGATE, SU-
PERINTEND and INSPECT Lodges, Chapters, Colleges
Consistories, and Councils of the Royal and Military
Orders of Ancient and Modern Free Masonry over the
surface of the two hemispheres.

The Author, deeming that all the beauties of Ancient
Masonry were contained in the nine first degrees, suffered the powers with which he was invested, to remain
dormant until the present emergency in the affairs of
Masonry. These emergencies have induced him to
take the command of the Northern Jurisdiction.

During the Anti-Masonic excitement, Masonry in

most of the New England States was at a low ebb, save in a few places. The Institution was regularly kept up at New Haven and vicinity, and many other places in Connecticut. In the Southern States the excitement had but little effect, as the Institution continued to prosper, and a regular call for the Masonic and Templar's Charts was received and supplied by the Author.

In 1834, the Author removed to the city of New-York, and entering into mercantile pursuits, was much engaged in his avocation for several years, in which time he was seldom employed in Masonic labors.

In 1845, the Author published improved editions of his Masonic and Templar's Charts, which continued to be the standard works of those degrees of which they treat.

The Masonic Chart having passed through fifteen editions, the Author flatters himself that his Brethren and Companions will still continue the use of a work, so universally acknowledged to be the most correct and best adapted to guide the Craftsmen in their labors.

For the purpose of improving the work and guarding against some designing individuals, who are making great efforts to change the present system of our Ancient Institution, by making alterations, and removing landmarks, he has introduced new and improved designs of the emblems and illustrations of the Chart, with several entirely new illustrations, which the Brethren will at once acknowledge to be appropriate, and well calculated to guard against some of these attempted innovations.